Lethbridge Community College Library

SO-AUJ-489

# Supreme at Last

## The Evolution of the Supreme Court of Canada

Peter McCormick

James Lorimer & Company Ltd., Publishers
Toronto, 2000

© 2000 Peter McCormick

All rights reserved. No part of this book may be reproduced or transmitted in any form or by any means, electronic or mechanical, including photocopying, or by any information storage or retrieval system, without permission in writing from the publisher.

James Lorimer & Company Ltd. acknowledges the support of the Ontario Arts Council. We acknowledge the support of the Government of Canada through the Book Publishing Industry Development Program (BPIDP) for our publishing activities. We acknowledge the support of the Canada Council for the Arts for our publishing program.

Cover design: Kevin O'Reilly

**Cataloguing in Publication Data**

McCormick, Peter
    Supreme at last: the evolution of the Supreme Court of Canada

Includes index.
ISBN 1-55028-693-5 (bound) ISBN 1-55028-692-7 (pbk)

1. Canada. Supreme Court – History. I. Title.

KE8244.M32 2000      347.71'035'09      C00-930190-9
KF345.M32 2000

James Lorimer & Company Ltd., Publishers
35 Britain Street
Toronto, Ontario
M5A 1R7

Printed and bound in Canada.

# Contents

*For my parents*

# List of Tables

# Acknowledgements

This book is the culmination of fifteen years as a "court-watcher," and it brings together the two major components of my work over that period — first, an interest in the overall patterns of judicial caseload (volume, types of cases, reversal rates, winners and losers); and second, a curiosity about the process of making and explaining judicial decisions (dissents and concurrences, voting blocs, judicial leadership, citation patterns). This preoccupation with courts and judges is somewhat curious in light of the fact that I emerged from graduate school as a political theorist (social contract, anyone?), and the change in direction is largely the product of the enthusiastic blandishments of my friend and colleague Ian Greene, now at York University. I am also grateful to Alvin Esau of the Manitoba Legal Research Institute, and Mr. Owen Snider, of the Alberta Law Foundation, who provided funding for various parts of my research.

A number of students have helped with the data collection, including Suzanne Maisey, Charlene Jahnert, Stephen Smith, David Barva, Tammy Praskach and Debra Woodske. I also appreciate the feedback from my constitutional law classes over the last few years, who patiently listened while I worked through various formulations of these ideas, and whose questions and comments obliterated some but helped to refine others.

I owe a large debt to Stephanie Fysh; she reined in some of my more flamboyant prose and her gentle hints — typically yellow stick-it notes with comments like "Do we really need this?" — helped to shorten some of the chapters. My thanks also go to Diane Young, my editor at Lorimer, who had to be persuaded that a book really needed to be this long, but whose ego-bruising insistence on significant revisions has made it much better than it would otherwise have been.

Above all, I would like to thank my wife Lorraine, who not only put up with several months of excuses as to why I couldn't cut the lawn or defrost the freezer, but also sat and listened patiently while I read through at least two versions of every chapter. She suggested which explanations were clear enough and which were not, which sections were "working" and which weren't; and there are some ideas (such as the chapter title format, and the historical context at the start of each chapter) which were hers. This paragraph represents just the first down-payment on my gratitude and appreciation.

# The Rebirth of the Supreme Court

It is a rare week today that does not see a major news story dealing with the Supreme Court of Canada. In October 1999, the Supreme Court dealt with the case of a Mi'qmaq's fishing for eels and touched off a dispute between Aboriginal communities and their neighbours that teetered on the brink of violence for several weeks until the Supreme Court spoke again to calm the situation. In January 2000, the Supreme Court heard solemn arguments on whether the Charter right to freedom of expression overrode the sections of the Criminal Code that prohibited the possession of "kiddie porn." In between, the Court looked at the rights of defendants in sexual assault cases (the controversial "rape shield" case), and at the education rights of francophone parents in Prince Edward Island who objected to their children's lengthy bus rides. On all of these occasions, elected politicians and their bureaucrats waited anxiously to see if legislation would survive or if new policies would be ordered. And this represents just a normal few months in the life of the modern Supreme Court of Canada.

But it was not always so. For much of its existence, the Supreme Court was very much a minor player on the national political scene — a "quiet court in a quiet country," as it was sometimes described. Its personnel was frequently undistinguished, its caseload was dominated by minor cases of little enduring significance, and its decisions were subject to appeal to a higher court (actually a quasi-court) in London, England. Today, conferences are held on the subject of whether Canada has become a "judocracy" (ruled by judges) rather than a democracy (ruled by the people), and it makes sense to ask who has more power, the prime minister of Canada or the chief justice of the Supreme Court.[1] It is hard now to imagine that the Supreme Court could be just a bystander in most of the important political debates of the day, but fifty years ago it was even harder to imagine that the Court could speak with such authority and such broad support on such a wide range of issues as it does today.

The Supreme Court's evolution from bit player to leading actor is one of the most important developments in Canadian politics in the past few decades. One way to think of this change is as a kind of second birth of the institution. In the most obvious sense, the Supreme Court of Canada was born in 1875, eight years after the Dominion of Canada was established. It was created by The Supreme Court Act, which received royal assent on April 8 and was brought into force on September 17. The six judges (increased to seven in 1927)[2] took office on October 8 and sat for the first time on Monday, January 17, 1876 — although there were no appeals ready to be heard until they met again in June. In the modern understanding of national high courts, it seems odd that the existence and powers of the Court are not included within the constitution, but at the time, it was not thought inappropriate that the Court be established by Parliament by means of a constitutional section authorizing "a General Court of Appeal for Canada." The most obvious date from which to begin a history of the Court, then, is 1875, and most books begin precisely there. From one point of view, the Supreme Court of Canada is an institution that has existed for over a century and that will celebrate its 125th birthday sometime in the fall of the year 2000.

But in another sense, the Supreme Court was born in 1949. Major amendments to The Supreme Court Act were introduced in Parliament in the late summer of 1949 and came into force on December 23. The most important element of these changes was the end of appeals to the Judicial Committee of the Privy Council; the Supreme Court became a court from whose decisions there was no further appeal. The Court was also increased in size — to the nine that we now find so natural, with one-third from the bar of the province of Quebec — and the new judges took office on December 23, hearing their first case early in 1950. The institution itself is still not entrenched in the constitution, although there are some features of the Court that cannot be changed without a constitutional amendment.

In this sense, then, the age of the Supreme Court is not a century and a quarter but only half a century. My purpose in this book is to examine what has happened to the institution since this rebirth. At the end of 1999 this truly supreme Supreme Court marked its fiftieth year as a highest national court of appeal. It is therefore appropriate to take note of the occasion by reviewing what has happened over that time period. Of the several plausible candidates for the date on which we should mark the starting point of this massive transition, I see the best candidate as December 23, 1949.

But the timing is just an excuse. The real reason for this book is that there is a story to be told, and it is a more intriguing story than most people realize. Fifty years ago, the Supreme Court of Canada was a minor blip on the Canadian political scene, a small and undistinguished body that limited itself to giving short, technical (and, to laypeople, virtually unreadable) decisions. The 1950s and 1960s saw flickering moments of promise but little in the way of substantial change; the 1970s — the Laskin years — transformed the Court on almost every front; and the 1980s and 1990s (finally) saw the Supreme Court fill its long anticipated position near the centre of the stage of Canadian public life, largely because of its role in interpreting the Canadian Charter of Rights and Freedoms. This is an important story, because the Supreme Court is now, in this, the "Age of the Charter," so clearly and undeniably important.

The nature of the Supreme Court caseload has changed — the kinds of law it spends most of its time dealing with, the types of litigants who appear before it, its evolving readiness to "intervene" (the term is Burton Atkins's) in the decisions of the lower courts. The way in which the Supreme Court processes its caseload has also changed, with the tighter time frames, larger panels, and less fragmented decisions. The Supreme Court's explanations of itself (and, arguably, the people to whom it sees itself as doing the explaining) have changed; it now produces longer decisions and more thorough explanations of backgrounds, social contexts, and public issues, and it makes more use of academic and social scientific material. And the way in which the Supreme Court treats judicial authority has changed; we have seen the progressive disappearance of English case law, a brief (but I think, ultimately, only a passing) flirtation with American authority, and an increasing focus on the Court's own prior decisions, especially its very recent ones. The point, of course, is not simply to recite detailed statistics, but rather to explain why these changes matter and then to use the statistics to show how things have changed.

This is still just one half of the story. To some extent, the Supreme Court is an evolving institution that just happens at any specific moment to be comprised of nine different individuals; to this extent, it is worth focusing on the institution and leaving the individuals to one side. But the Court is also the interaction of these nine individuals, an interaction that changes as individuals leave and are replaced by new ones; this is the other half of the story. Some judges lead, some follow, and some go their own way. Some of them combine to create the voting blocs that direct the general doctrinal direction of the Court, others form smaller groups (sometimes a voice of the past, sometimes a voice of the future, and sometimes neither) that try on occasion to detach the outlying members of the major faction, and still others follow their own, independent trail in dissent or separate concurrence. Some judges leave a legacy of doctrine and analysis on which the Court still draws decades later; others vanish from the acknowledged jurisprudential background. Some of them have luminous reputations that reach beyond the bench into the academy; others remain minor figures or even disappointments. These variations constitute a parallel history of the Supreme Court, largely neglected in the literature, which I have previously pursued in fragments through the medium of journal articles and that I now consolidate.

As a result of all these changes, it is necessary to think of the Supreme Court as an institution that has consciously reinvented itself, that has visibly and demonstrably changed its relationship to and its understanding of the law and of its own tradition, as well as its relationship to the other institutions of Canadian public life and to the Canadian public itself. This is the real story of the last fifty years, and the fifty-year point is a good time at which to be telling it.

In the concluding chapter, I will explain why I think this is more than just a story about Canada and about the past. Our Supreme Court is far from the only such institution to have been invented or reinvented in the closing years of the millennium. We are looking at a global phenomenon that is transforming the way we think about democracy — grand stuff indeed. I will put our Supreme Court in the context of this double shift and point out what I see as significant structural flaws that we cannot long ignore without risk.

What did the Court look like then, what does it look like now? When and how did those changes come about? And why should we, as Canadian citizens, care? These, in general, are the questions that I tackle, but I do so in an unusual way. This is not a book that would please a professional historian — I have not consulted memoirs, narrowly tracked chronological developments, or gained access to some hitherto unexamined set of personal letters. Nor is this a book that would satisfy a law professor — I am not primarily concerned with the evolution of legal doctrine within specific fields or with the detailed wording of a decision as it bears on some very specific question. I do talk to some extent about individual cases but only insofar as they open a window on some broader phenomenon. This is a book written by an outsider, a social scientist rather than a lawyer, working from statistical databases on the Supreme Court rather than from firsthand experience. What I am trying to capture here is the story of an evolving institution whose members have filled hundreds of pages of the law reports telling us what they thought they were doing and why they were doing it, of an institution that is now a more significant element of our democratic practices than it has ever been before and that promises to be more so in the future.

# Under the Shadow: The Judicial Committee and the Supreme Court

The 1875 Supreme Court Act established a Supreme Court of Canada, but the term was misleading. In fact, it was not truly supreme, because its decisions were still subject to appeal to another judicial body, the Judicial Committee of the Privy Council of the United Kingdom.

Even that statement contains a triple simplification. For one thing, the body called "the Judicial Committee" was not formally constituted as a court — initially, its members did not even need to be lawyers — although over time, it evolved into something virtually indistinguishable from a court. For a second, in addition to the normal appeal process, it was also possible, with the consent of both parties, for an appeal from a decision of a provincial court of appeal to be carried directly to the Judicial Committee, bypassing the Supreme Court altogether — but the finding in that decision still constituted binding precedent for the Supreme Court. For a third, the situation was for a time uncertain, and both the initial plan of the Liberal government in 1875 and the general public impression of the effect of the legislation were that all appeals to London had been abolished.[1] This impression was reinforced when the first application for leave to appeal (the *Church Pew* case[2]) was refused. Within five years, however, the number of applications for leave was up, the Judicial Committee was hearing Canadian cases, and sometimes (although not inordinately often) it was reversing the Supreme Court. The shadow of the Judicial Committee began to grow.

The Judicial Committee was not part of the regular English court system, and it was not initially staffed by judges. Essentially, it was an outgrowth of the British imperial experience, a mechanism for handling legal appeals from "territories that were held by the Crown which were not considered part of the English realm, and which were therefore not subject to the regular courts or the governance of Parliament."[3] In English practice, the colonies had nothing to do with Parliament but were under the direct authority of the monarch. This made it inappropriate for appeals from them to flow into the ordinary English courts and more logical for these appeals to come to the king himself — or, more correctly, to the council of his personal advisors. This practice seems to date back to the sixteenth century. By the end of the seventeenth century, the king had established an appellate committee within the Privy Council, although its proceedings were by modern standards not very formal and not very judicial — to be expected from a body that was at least as political as it was judicial. In 1833, those who were not lawyers were finally excluded and a more stable membership was created. The members of the Judicial Committee, from which the panel for any particular appeal was drawn, included a number of people who were or had been members of the English appellate courts or the House of Lords, up to four people appointed specifically to the committee, a number of people who had served in the Supreme Courts of India, and, finally, the lord chancellor of the government of the day.[4] The largest element of the Committee's caseload came from the Indian subcontinent and the remainder from the English-speaking dominions (Canada, Australia, and New Zealand, in that order).

In 1895, the British government made provision for senior justices from Australia, South Africa, and Canada to serve on the Judicial Committee. James Snell and Frederick Vaughan[5] note that the Canadian chief justice was always appointed, although not necessarily immediately, and that Lyman Duff was the only puisne (i.e., non-chief) justice of the Supreme Court ever designated. "It is not clear how significant the reform was," however, given the fact that Supreme Court judges could only attend when the Supreme Court was not in session. The other countries made even less use of the opportunity.

At first glance, this looks like a straightforward mechanism of imperial control, although with the important qualification that the Judicial Committee was (at least after the 1833 reforms) less and less a political body and more and more a judicial one. "We are really judges," said Lord Haldane[6] (one of the handful of dominant figures in the history of the committee, who handed down a number of important decisions in Canadian constitutional cases), and over time, the style of the committee's decisions resembled more and more closely the legal decisions of (for example) the House of Lords. In fact, there was no truth "in any suggestion that the Privy Council's power of review was used to further imperial policy" and "no tangible connection, either personal, constitutional or political between the Judicial Committee and the Colonial Office [existed]."[7] The imperial power of disallowance was by far the preferred device of imperial control.

The committee's major function was to ensure that the colonial legislatures did not pass measures that were "repugnant" to imperial statutes. This mandate took rather a different turn for those countries in which the constitution was itself an imperial statute (such as Canada's British North America Act). In such circumstances, the Committee "comes to stand in the relationship of a Super-Supreme Court, administering not an imperial but a national constitution"[8] — in principle not unlike the long-standing role of the United States Supreme Court (USSC), except that the committee sat in and its personnel was almost entirely drawn from another country. Indeed, it has been suggested that the Judicial Committee was the inspiration for the judicial review function of the USSC itself.[9] Logically, if a genuinely neutral adjudicating body is desired, then the Judicial Committee had a great deal to recommend itself. Its Achilles' heel is the argument that the judges should be familiar with the cultural, historal, and political contexts of the dispute, and on this score the Judicial Committee must necessarily have scored very low. There is also the argument that English judges, familiar with a unitary system based on the supremacy of the national Parliament, were poorly positioned to understand the niceties of federal constitutions, although this is contrary to the accusation that it was provincial power, not national power, that the Judicial Committee favoured.

The normal size of a panel seems to have been five, although they could be larger. One curious feature was the practice of issuing only a single decision, unlike other appellate bodies (such as the House of Lords) who routinely issue plural decisions. This is usually explained as an accident of historical evolution: the Privy Council consisted of the king's personal advisors, and advice is more conveniently rendered to the king in the form of a single reasoned judgment. More recently, the committee has abandoned this practice, and dissents are "not infrequent" and are published.[10] The committee was for seventy-five years the final court of appeal for Canada, but it was not created specifically for Canada nor was it disbanded or discontinued when Canadian appeals ended.

The volume of Canadian cases considered by the Judicial Committee was not inordinately large. Over the seventy-five years between Confederation and the patriation of judicial authority, the committee heard a total of 667 Canadian appeals, 253 (or well under 4 per year) from the Supreme Court itself and 414 *per saltum* appeals that bypassed the Supreme Court and came directly to London from the provincial courts of appeal. Nor does it appear that the Supreme Court was reversed particularly often,[11] although sometimes the tone and the text of the Judicial Committee's decisions could be slighting; on one occasion, the Supreme Court declined to give any reasons for a decision because they knew the case was on the way to London and, complained the Court, the Judicial Committee never read the reasons anyway.[12]

Did the Judicial Committee have an impact on the Supreme Court and on Canada? Without a doubt. It is generally agreed that the Fathers of Confederation drafted a centralist document with limited provincial powers. The Judicial Committee took quite a different approach, interpreting very narrowly the federal powers implied by such clauses as "peace, order and good government" and "trade and commerce" and dealing very generously with the provincial jurisdiction over "property and civil rights within the province." On paper, the British North America Act (now The Constitution Act 1867) does not create a system with a particularly strong claim to be federal; by the time the Judicial Committee was finished with it, the BNA Act was clearly federal in practice.[13]

At the time, many Canadians expressed extreme frustration with the way in which decisions in London were circumscribing federal powers. More recently, the debate as to whether the Judicial Committee impact was pernicious has been revisited, for example, by Alan Cairns[14] and Frederick Vaughan.[15] The main point of contention was whether political decentralization had been created by the Judicial Committee's decisions or whether the decentralizing forces within Canada were so great that those decisions did little more than recognize the inevitable. But certainly these developments happened on the Judicial Committee's watch, and the decisions bear its collective signature. And at least on very early indications[16] (before Judicial Committee precedents rolled them back), the Supreme Court of Canada initially seemed prepared to follow through on the letter of a rather centralist document. Especially during the interwar period, many Canadians were ready to blame the Judicial Committee without waiting for the final balance of argument and evidence.

The impetus for the end of appeals was greatly accelerated when major elements of the Bennett government's "New Deal" legislation were struck down as unconstitutional by the Judicial Committee during the depths of the Great Depression. To many Canadian scholars and academics, this was the last straw, a paralysis of national effort that could only be broken by a Canadian court responding to Canadian values. This argument is somewhat disingenuous. One reason the legislation fell before the Judicial Committee was that R.B. Bennett had been soundly defeated in the 1935 federal election and the new Liberal government was neither aggressive in pursuing the appeals nor aggrieved by the outcome. The argument that only a hidebound foreign court could be so unrealistic is refuted by the example of the United States, where a stubbornly resistant Supreme Court similarly turned back the comparable American legislation until the Court was "stared down" by President Franklin Delano Roosevelt in an unprecedented struggle of political will.

At any rate, the experience of the Great Depression triggered a growing pressure for the end of appeals to the Judicial Committee. Ian Bushnell has suggested that one rather oblique element of this was a playing up of the calibre of Supreme Court Chief Justice Lyman Duff as the greatest jurist in the history of the Court, the implicit message being that such a Supreme Court was up to the challenges of supremacy.[17] F.R. Scott even published a witty poem in a law journal (hardly the usual venue for poetry) lambasting the Judicial Committee's decision, although you need to know the arcane jargon of Canadian constitutional law to appreciate it.[18] The Liberal government decided that the time was right to proceed, but a previous attempt to end some (but not all) appeals to the Judicial Committee had been found (by the Judicial Committee, of course) to be unconstitutional in the 1926 case of *R. v. Nadan.*[19] It was probably true that the British Statute of Westminster had improved the prospects for a Canadian initiative, but in such matters it is better to check first than to be surprised later. The government therefore submitted a draft bill to the Supreme Court in a reference case and then referred the matter to the Judicial Committee for a final ruling. After the interruption of World War II, the Judicial Committee — sitting with a seven-judge panel rather than the usual five-judge panel, apparently in recognition of the occasion — ruled that the proposed bill was within federal competence.[20] The legislation was duly enacted, receiving royal assent on December 10, 1949, and coming into force on December 23.

One final complication remained. The bill was not retroactive, so it applied only to actions commenced after that date; this meant that for cases that were already in the system the right of appeal remained. The right of appeal was exercised a number of times, including (somewhat inconsistently) in some appeals by the federal government itself. The last Canadian appeal, *Ponoka-Calmar Oils v. Wakefield,*[21] was decided in 1959, although the last appeal that raised a significant constitutional issue was probably *Winner,* in 1954, which dealt with the dividing line between intra-provincial (and therefore provincially regulated) transportation and inter-provincial (and therefore federally regulated) transportation.

The era of the Judicial Committee was over. The Supreme Court of Canada was finally supreme.

# The Rinfret Court: October 1949 to June 1954 "The Initiator"

On the day that appeals to the Judicial Committee ended, the chief justice and longest-serving member of the Supreme Court was Thibaudeau Rinfret. He had been appointed to the Supreme Court by William Lyon Mackenzie King on September 16, 1924, at the relatively young age of 45. The age factor was not insignificant: at the time, the justices' average age was just over 65, and one member in particular (John Idington) was 86 years old, in poor health, and increasingly incapacitated. The government had been embarrassed in 1923 when it passed Rinfret over to appoint a judge (Albert Malouin) who was seriously ill and who served an undistinguished eight months before resigning. Rinfret had served for two years on the Quebec Superior Court, earning a reputation for energy, ability, and hard work.[1]

Rinfret became the ninth chief justice of Canada on January 8, 1944, replacing Sir Lyman Poore Duff. Duff was the most highly regarded member of the Supreme Court in its first seventy-five years,[2] and his thirty-seven years on the Court made him the longest-serving one as well. The fact that Duff's retirement date had been twice postponed by special action of Parliament gives some indication of the shoes Rinfret had to fill. Seniority was the major factor in Rinfret's selection (as it has usually been in naming a new chief justice), but it was also advantageous that he was French Canadian at a time when Prime Minister Mackenzie King was anxious to soothe ethnic tensions in the midst of a war more strongly supported in English Canada than in French Canada.[3] Rinfret had also been one of the more active members of the Duff Court, not always the case for the Quebec justices, although on the down side, there were some reservations about his health. If there is now some convention of an alternation between Quebec and non-Quebec chief justices, it dates only from Rinfret's appointment; of the first eight chief justices, only two (Henri-Elzéar Taschereau and Charles Fitzpatrick, the fourth and fifth chief justices) were from Quebec.

The Rinfret Court presided over a Canada in which the Liberal Party was the national government, the mantle of leadership passing from William Lyon Mackenzie King to Louis St. Laurent almost exactly one year before the ending of appeals. The postwar economic boom was just beginning; at the time, it would have registered as little more than a pleasant surprise that a major war had not been followed by the usual major recession. The baby boom that has dominated Canadian politics for decades was just beginning and would have amounted at the time to little more than a surge in primary school enrolments. In international politics, the major development was the emergence of the Cold War, as both the United States and the Soviet Union became nuclear superpowers, and the major event was the Korean War.

## The Personnel of the Rinfret Court

**Patrick Kerwin**, the second senior member of the Court, was appointed by the Bennett government on July 20, 1935; he was 45 years of age and had served for three years on the Ontario Supreme Court.[4] He had been the law partner of Bennett's minister of justice, Hugh Guthrie, and served for a time as treasurer of the Conservative Party.[5] This appointment was from the ranks of lower court judges with limited experience and modest reputation, demonstrating a recurrent problem with finding good judges for the Supreme Court. In keeping with the representational priorities of the time, he was Catholic, as was the man (Hughes) whom he replaced. As I will demonstrate later, there are good reasons for thinking of him as the decision-leader of the Rinfret Court, although not to the extent of some of his successors on later Courts.

If there is an aristocracy of the Supreme Court, it carries the name of Taschereau. Jean-Thomas Taschereau was one of the first six Supreme Court judges appointed in 1875, and when he stepped down for reasons of poor health three years later, he was replaced by his nephew Henri-Elzéar, who became the fourth chief justice in 1902. Forty years later, J.-T. Taschereau's grandson, **Robert Taschereau**, was appointed, on February 9, 1940, at the unusually young age of the 43; since then, Duff (at 42) has been the only younger appointee.[6] Robert Taschereau's father, Louis-Alexandre, was premier of Quebec until he was defeated by Maurice Duplessis; Robert himself was elected three times to the Quebec legislature (in 1930, 1931, and 1935) but never served in the provincial cabinet. At the time that he was appointed to the Supreme Court, Robert Taschereau had no prior judicial experience. He and Gerald Fauteux voted together more often than any other pairing on the Court.

**Ivan Cleveland Rand**, from New Brunswick, was appointed to the Supreme Court on April 22, 1943, replacing Oswald Crocket (the Supreme Court seat conventionally assigned to the Maritimes did not rotate to Nova Scotia, as many had expected, but remained with New Brunswick). Rand, 59 years old, had practised law in both Alberta and New Brunswick before becoming counsel for Canadian National Railways in Montreal. He was also one of the few Supreme Court judges up to that time to have studied law in the United States, having graduated from Harvard Law School. He was a Liberal and had briefly served as attorney-general of New Brunswick, but his reputation transcended party lines and his appointment had been seriously considered by the Bennett government in 1932.[7] If Duff was considered by his contemporaries to be the greatest judge on the Supreme Court up until that time, Rand was a candidate for the shortlist. He lacked judicial experience, but he brought to the bench a wide range of experience in corporate, labour, and administrative law.[8] On the Court, however, he was something of a loner, writing his own dissents or separate concurrences rather than leading the Court or some recognizable faction within it.

**Roy Kellock** was appointed on October 3, 1944, at the age of 50. He had practised law in Ontario for twenty years with some distinction and had been a judge on the Ontario Court of Appeal for two years prior to his appointment to the Supreme Court. He was second only to Kerwin in writing decisions for the Court, although this was a competition rather than a partnership and the poor relations between him and Kerwin were thought to be a reason for his retirement.

**James W. Estey** was appointed on October 6, 1944, at the age of 55. He had an extensive political career, serving in the Liberal government of Saskatchewan (as education minister and attorney-general) for ten years until it was defeated by the CCF shortly before his appointment to the Supreme Court. He had no previous judicial experience. His appointment demonstrated "the King government's criteria for selection: no preference for judicial experience, considerable weight to service to the Liberal party, some minimum level of ability, and influential friends."[9] The Esteys (J.W.

and Willard Z.) are the only father–son combination to have served on the Court so far.

**Charles Locke** was appointed on June 3, 1947, at age 50. He was the last member of the Supreme Court to receive his basic legal training in law offices rather than in a university law school, first practicing law in Winnipeg before going to Vancouver. His appointment was unusual because he had been active in the Progressive Conservative Party and was without direct political connections within the appointing King government. He was, to put it mildly, not the government's first choice; this was symptomatic of the difficulty of attracting first-rank candidates to the Court, partly because of the requirement that justices relocate to Ottawa and partly because of the relatively low salaries.

The ending of appeals also meant an increase in the size of the Court from seven justices to nine. One of these two new justices was to be from Quebec, increasing Quebec's statutorily guaranteed representation from two to three, and the expectation (soon hardened into convention) was that the other new justice would be from Ontario. **John Cartwright** was appointed on December 22, 1949, at the age of 54. He had no judicial experience but was a highly respected lawyer from Toronto.

**Gerald Fauteux** was appointed on December 22, 1949, at the age of 49, making him the first Supreme Court justice born in the twentieth century.[10] He had served with some distinction as a crown prosecutor before becoming a judge of the Quebec Superior Court in 1947. His brother was the speaker of the House of Commons and, subsequently, lieutenant governor of Quebec, and both his grandfather (Honoré Mercier) and his uncle (Sir Jean-Lomer Gouin) had been premiers of Quebec — which suggests that Liberal Party connections remained an implicit criterion. Fauteux had a considerable experience in criminal law — not the normal legal specialization of Supreme Court judges, because it has not until very recently been a large share of the Supreme Court caseload.

The Rinfret Court was composed of nine white males from the two "charter groups" of French Canadians and English Canadians. Only four of the nine had prior judicial experience (and only one had prior appellate experience) before coming to the Court,[11] and only one (Rand) could have been considered outstanding in terms of intellect and talent. Their ages ranged from Fauteux's 49 to Rinfret's 70 and averaged just under 60; their length of Supreme Court experience ranged from Fauteux and Cartwright, with zero, to Rinfret, with twenty-five years, and (at the end of 1949) it averaged just under nine years. After the filling of the two new seats, there were no further appointments for the duration of Rinfret's chief justiceship, making this what American scholars call a "natural court."

## The Caseload of the Rinfret Court

Between October 1949 and June 1954, the Rinfret Court delivered a total of 319 reported decisions, an average of 64 per year.[12] The key word here, of course, is "reported," because until the 1970s, not all Supreme Court decisions were reported; it may be that the actual total was somewhat higher. On the other hand, it is not likely to have been very much higher, according to Snell and Vaughan, the total number of cases (reported and unreported) for the five previous years was only 295.[13]

Most of these cases (180 out of 319, or 56%) involve what I am calling "private law": lawsuits between private individuals and/or businesses. With entrancing neatness, there were about half as many cases (94) involving what I am calling "public law" (non-criminal cases involving official government actors) and only half as many as that (45) dealing with criminal law. This was characteristic of the caseload of the Supreme Court; indeed, the proportion of private law cases was even higher and the proportion of criminal law cases even lower in earlier years. Until very recently, the major function of the Court was to resolve disputes between private actors, not between people and government, and especially not between governments and other governments.

The largest single element of the Supreme Court's caseload was economic and business cases (banks, bankruptcies, trusts, leases, debts, and non-criminal property cases), with just over 100 examples, followed by transportation cases, which totalled 75 — 44 dealing with automobiles, 14 with shipping, 8 with railways, 7 with trams and streetcars, and 2 with aircraft.[14] These numbers bear out Lawrence Friedman's general observation that the law of torts (damages arising from accidents) was basically created in the nineteenth century around the railroads and has been reconstructed in the twentieth around the automobile.[15] There were 46 cases involving taxes (mostly corporate taxation) but only 8 dealing with insurance matters. Not very visible were women (there were only 26 cases in which women were parties and only another 11 in which one party was a married couple) and minorities (there were 2 cases involving Aboriginals and 2 raising issues of race). Crime was only a small part of the caseload, and violent crime even smaller, accounting for only 2 or 3 cases each year. Not until the Laskin Court in the 1970s did this pattern change significantly.

Because the Supreme Court is an appeal court rather than a trial court, its work is almost exclusively limited to reconsidering the decisions of other courts, particularly the provincial courts of appeal and (until 1971 when it was replaced by the Federal Court) the federal trial court, which was called the Exchequer Court of Canada. The largest blocks of appeals came from the Ontario Court of Appeal (23%), the Exchequer Court (20%), and the Quebec Court of King's Bench (18.5%), as the Quebec Court of Appeal was then called. On the other hand, the smaller provinces, such as Saskatchewan and Manitoba, contributed only two or three appeals per year to the caseload.

When appeals did come to the Supreme Court, they succeeded almost half the time (48.9%), the readiness to reverse catching even such a reputedly strong court as the Ontario Court of Appeal. The appeals that were most likely to succeed were those that came from the Exchequer Court of Canada; these were allowed 56 percent of the time. The appeals that were least likely to succeed came from the British Columbia Court of Appeal, which was reversed only 41 percent of the time. To be sure, the Supreme Court over any period of time is dealing with such a unique collection of individual cases that it is difficult to suggest, in abstract terms, what an appropriate reversal rate should be; however, this figure of 48.9 percent is somewhat higher than the Supreme Court's own long-term average of just over 42 percent and higher than that of the English Court of Appeal, which allows appeals about 40 percent of the time. On the other hand, it is lower than the United States Supreme Court, which reverses about two-thirds of the time.[16]

The small caseload notwithstanding, most decisions of the Rinfret Court were very brief. They averaged about sixteen pages of text, slightly more for public law cases and slightly less for criminal and private law cases. Then, as now, the normal practice was for the Court not to give its decisions immediately after the oral argument, but to reserve decision until the reasons had been written. These time delays were quite modest — about 2½ months on average for criminal appeals, 4 months for other cases. Backlog does not seem to have been a problem.

## Decision-making by the Rinfret Court

When we talk about "a decision of the Court," most people would expect an outcome accompanied by a single set of reasons. No one would expect this to happen *all* the time — there will inevitably be occasions when one or more of the judges cannot agree, and the larger the panel the more likely that there will be at least partial disagreement — but most people would expect this to happen *most* of the time.

In the case of the Rinfret Court, these expectations would not be met. Less than a quarter of the reported decisions of the Court took the form of a set of reasons delivered by one judge and signed by all the others on the panel. On average, a decision of the Rinfret Court involved three different sets of reasons — and this even though the size of the average panel was smaller than it is today. Typically, half of the judges on any panel felt the need to write, and rather than producing a focused central decision accompanied by brief commentary, they usually all wrote at some length.

But there are two reasons for a judge to write when somebody else is delivering the judgment of the Court. The first is when the judge disagrees with the outcome; this is a *dissent*. The second is when the judge agrees with the outcome but not (or not entirely) with the reasons; this is called a *separate concurrence* (in U.S. terminology, a *special concurrence*). Among the "extra" reasons for judgment provided by the Rinfret Court, separate concurrences were twice as frequent as dissents, meaning that the Court fragmented over reasons more than it did over outcomes. At first glance, this does not seem to matter very much, because the most important thing about a court case (especially if you are involved) is who won, not why they won; I will demonstrate later why the multiplicity of reasons is often problematic.

Even these numbers, however, understate the fragmentation of the written opinions and the frustration of trying to read them. The Court often utilized *seriatim* judgments, particularly on important cases such as constitutional references. In a "pure" *seriatim* decision, every judge writes his own reasons, even if these reasons run almost perfectly parallel to those of one or more of the other judges, and none makes any direct reference to the ideas expressed by other members. There were thirty such decisions by the Rinfret Court,[17] including one[18] from a full panel of nine judges. But there were another forty decisions in which most of the judges wrote, and another eighty-eight cases in which the judges divided among three or more reasons for judgment in such a way that no set of "outcome plus reasons" carried a majority of the panel.

Contemporary opinion finds such practices inappropriate because they constitute "a conspicuous waste of time and an unnecessary cluttering of the reports with separate reasons by individual judges amounting to mere repetition."[19] *Seriatim* decisions are doubly wasteful: firstly, because of the duplication of effort when the judges after the first invest time in reasons that add little or nothing to the initial statement, and secondly, because they prevent the Court from speaking with a clear voice to deliver a focused message, leaving room both for genuine misunderstanding and for deliberate cultivation of the resulting ambiguities.

But the models appropriate for emulation in 1949 were rather more ambiguous.[20] The Judicial Committee had an invariant practice of issuing a single opinion without dissent or separate concurrence, but the English House of Lords routinely issued plural or *seriatim* decisions, even when there was general agreement on both outcome and reasons. Even today, practices vary from one country to another: the French *cour de cassation*[21] issues a single terse opinion, while at the other extreme, the Norwegian Supreme Court is strictly required to deliver multiple opinions.[22] Somewhere in between is the High Court of Australia, which well into the 1990s issued a bewildering mixture of unanimous decisions, multi-authored decisions, and multiple and largely repetitive opinions.

As shown in Table 3.1, all members of the Court contributed to this fragmentation of opinion delivery, but some did so more consistently than others. Rand is the only judge who wrote or signed the decision of the Court in less than half of his panel appearances, and he is also the only member of the Court who wrote an opinion (*seriatim*, decision, separate concurrence, or dissent) in more than two-thirds of his appearances. Kellock comes a close second. At the other extreme, Fauteux is the only judge to have joined the decision of the Court in more than two-thirds of his appearances and to have written in less than one-third. The median figure — the one whose numbers most closely approach the all-Court figures — is Cartwright.

The pervasiveness of the fragmentation is striking: the average member of the Court wrote his own reasons for judgment in fully one-half of all panel appearances, and when the Court divided (which it did most of the time), only two members of the Court — Fauteux

## Table 3.1

### Dissents, Concurrences, and Decisions, by Judge Reported Supreme Court Decisions, 1949–1954

| Judge | Panels | Wrote decision | Contributed to decision | Divided panels | With majority | Conc. | Diss. |
|---|---|---|---|---|---|---|---|
| Rinfret C.J. | 220 | 8.6% | 35.9% | 156 | 46.2% | 32.1% | 21.8% |
| Kerwin | 277 | 23.8% | 59.9% | 206 | 47.1% | 35.9% | 17.0% |
| Taschereau | 264 | 15.9% | 39.4% | 185 | 51.4% | 33.5% | 15.1% |
| Rand | 270 | 15.2% | 67.8% | 205 | 26.8% | 60.0% | 13.2% |
| Kellock | 227 | 21.1% | 66.1% | 168 | 33.9% | 51.8% | 14.3% |
| Estey | 284 | 8.1% | 46.8% | 213 | 39.4% | 48.4% | 12.2% |
| Locke | 267 | 9.7% | 49.1% | 199 | 36.7% | 39.7% | 23.6% |
| Cartwright | 221 | 15.8% | 54.3% | 158 | 36.1% | 43.7% | 20.3% |
| Fauteux | 157 | 12.1% | 26.8% | 115 | 59.1% | 29.6% | 11.3% |
| ALL | 2187 | 14.6% | 50.7% | 1605 | 41.0% | 42.4% | 16.6% |

and Taschereau, both Quebec judges — joined the decision as often as half the time. The average member of the Court dissented one time in every six panel appearances, and no member of the Court dissented less than half this often, or more than half again this often.

## Voting Blocs and Alignments on the Rinfret Court

This raises an important question, one that tends to be obscured whenever we talk about "the Court" reaching a decision and delivering reasons. Most of the time for the Rinfret Court, and much of the time even today, the judges of the Supreme Court did not deliver a single outcome-plus-reasons decision. We therefore need to ask, when the Court fragments, which blocs tend to be the most successful and which judges tend to lead them? The figures in Table 3.1 already suggest part of the answer: there are some judges (such as Fauteux, Taschereau, Kerwin, and Rinfret) who are most frequently part of the "decision of the court" block, there are some judges (such as Locke, Cartwright, and — curiously — Rinfret again) who most frequently dissent, and there are some judges (such as Kerwin and Kellock) who write rather more than their share of the decisions.

One way to put these pieces of the puzzle together is to look at every time that each pair of judges served on a panel together and to calculate the frequency with which they agreed — that is, signed on to the same outcome plus reasons. Since the Rinfret Court between

1949 and 1953 was a "natural court," with zero turnover, there are thirty-six such pairings to calculate, and collectively, they point to a network of allies and opponents as the judges resolved legal issues. To consider the extremes (neither of which ever happens), two judges who signed on together every time would be solid allies, maximizing their opportunity to have an impact on the law — more so if they jointly shared high agreement rates with several of their colleagues — and conversely, two judges who never signed on together would demonstrate a major fault line dividing "wings" of the Court. For the Rinfret Court, the highest two-judge agreement rate is the one that links Taschereau and Fauteux: of the 103 times that these two judges sat on the panel deciding a case, they signed on to the same set of outcome plus reasons 68 times. This compares with the 42.3 percent that is the average of the 36 two-judge agreement rates, and it means that Taschereau and Fauteux were more than half again as likely as any other pair of judges to agree on the disposition of an appeal.

Two things must be conceded. The first is that none of the numbers are particularly high — even Taschereau and Fauteux signed on to different reasons or supported different outcomes fully one-third of the time. This is obviously the flip side of a Court that frequently issues *seriatim* decisions or dissenting and separate concurring reasons. And the second is that the spread between the highest and the lowest numbers is not particularly large. The lowest agreement — the one that presumably identifies the individuals occupying the opposite "ends" of the Court — belongs to Kerwin and Rand, and even these two individuals were in complete agreement in almost one-third (57 of 185) of the occasions on which they sat together. As later chapters will demonstrate, the Supreme Court is capable of much more persistent and polarized divisions than this. What I am describing, then, is not solid blocs into which the Court divides on almost every occasion, but rather "proto-blocs" in terms of which the Court is mildly but not strongly disposed to form — not mountains, but at most medium-size hills.

The most important hill is the one occupied by Rinfret, Taschereau, Kerwin, and Fauteux — the current and three future chief justices, or (to look at it from a different angle) the three Quebec justices and the senior Ontario justice. The six highest two-judge agreement rates link these four individuals. The frequent use of small panels, as well as the overall fragmentation of the Court, makes it strictly unnecessary to search for a fifth member of the bloc, but Estey is the strongest candidate. The spokesman for this group was not Chief Justice Rinfret but Kerwin; the other three signed on to one of his reasons for judgment ninety-five times, while he returned the favour only thirty-five times. To the extent that such a fragmented Court has a "shape," it is formed around this combination of individuals under the general leadership of Kerwin (who wrote sixty-six decisions for the Court) and Taschereau (who wrote forty-two). Fauteux and (somewhat surprisingly) Chief Justice Rinfret himself played more supporting roles, each writing only nineteen decisions — fewer than any other member of the Court.

The impact of Kellock is pronounced, but harder to pin down. On the one hand, he was second only to Kerwin in writing decisions (forty-eight to Kerwin's sixty-six, followed by Taschereau with forty-two). On the other hand, he was not the leader — indeed, not even a part — of any comparable group of judges. Only Fauteux and Locke supported him more often than average, but not much more than average. Kellock's influence appears to have rested on a shifting, rather than Kerwin's relatively constant, coalition of fellow judges. This being the case, it is all the more surprising that he delivered as many decisions as he did — almost half again what we would expect if the Court shared this duty equally.

Rand appears to have been the most marginalized member of the Court, although his low dissent rate suggests that he was following his own path to one side of Court rather than heading in a completely different direction. The average two-judge agreement rate was 42.3 percent, and Rand did not achieve this with even a single colleague. One explanation is simply that Rand wrote so frequently; even when he agreed with the outcome, he typically wrote his own reasons rather than signing on to someone else's. But the flip side is that he was much less able than anyone else to attract (or negotiate) the supporting signatures of his colleagues, if only because he was so much less willing to offer his own signature in return.

But leadership, of course, has two dimensions. One is how often a judge can draw the signatures of his colleagues, what we might call "here and now" leadership. But a second is how often his reasons for judgment contribute to the Court's lasting jurisprudence, or "legacy" leadership. On this yardstick, Rand fares much better, as I will show later in this chapter. We can say now, although we could not without considerable controversy have said so in the 1950s, that Rand was the outstanding member of the Rinfret Court. This can best be explained in terms of a major change in direction, an identifiable moment with a "before" and "after" such that Rand can legitimately be thought of as being ahead of his time rather than simply eccentric. Locating this watershed event will be an important focus of subsequent chapters.

## Citation Practices of the Rinfret Court

It is important to remember that courts (especially Supreme Courts) do not just give *outcomes,* they also give *reasons* supporting these outcomes. It is these reasons that cast their shadows forward over future decisions, more so (of course) for some cases than for others. But it is also important to note that judges typically organize their reasons around citations to authority, especially to the prior decisions of judges in their own and other courts. The preference for judicial citations in the explanatory process distinguishes common law judges from their continental European counterparts, who are more likely to build their arguments around academic textbooks.[23]

Ask them about any specific citation, and judges will tell you that they cite the cases that they need to cite to remain credible to their judicial and legal colleagues; that is to say, we are talking about institutional practice rather than capricious choice. The citation patterns take us to the courts and judges that carry influence, that matter to the judges and to the people to whom they are directing their reasoned explanations and that provide shared reference points on established legal doctrine as well as critical leadership on emerging legal doctrine.

Epigrammatically, dieticians tell us that we are what we eat, cultural nationalists tell us that we are what we read, and I am suggesting that judges are what they cite. More specifically, a court's citations demonstrate a conception of the judicial role — in the mix of its own decisions, those of the courts of other countries, and those of the lower courts; in the shifting balance among current, recent, and more historical cases; and in the way that courts are impersonally cited as collective institutions or outstanding individuals emphasized by being specifically named. These patterns are all the more revealing when they are traced over time.

### *From where did the Supreme Court get its Citations?*

Table 3.6 breaks down all judicial citations by the Supreme Court between 1949 and 1954 in terms of their source. Given the date of the event that justifies this book, the obvious first question is how its new independence affected the Supreme Court's reliance on the prior decisions of the Judicial Committee. As shown in Table 3.2, the

## Table 3.2

### Citations to Judicial Authority by the Rinfret Court Reported Decisions, 1944–1954

| Source | 1949–54 | 1944–48 |
|---|---|---|
| Judicial Committee | 665 (16.1%) | 292 (16.1%) |
| Supreme Court of Canada | 894 (21.7%) | 474 (26.2%) |
| Other English Courts | 1,800 (43.7%) | 650 (35.9%) |
| Other Canadian Courts | 688 (16.7%) | 339 (18.7%) |
| U.S. Courts | 31 (0.8%) | 36 (2.0%) |
| Other | 41 (1.0%) | 19 (1.0%) |
| TOTAL | 4,119 | 1,810 |

Note: Percentages do not total to 100% due to rounding.

somewhat surprising — and, for contemporaries, somewhat disappointing — answer was "hardly at all." In the first five years after the ending of appeals, one Supreme Court citation in every six was to the Judicial Committee. This was almost identical to the figure for the first half of Rinfret's chief justiceship, when appeals were still possible and the Judicial Committee was a superior court to which judicial deference was due. Even with the apron strings cut, the Supreme Court was not wandering very far.

Nor were references to other English courts reduced: they still accounted for two citations in every five. Even with the end of appeals to the Judicial Committee, the common law of Canada still had its roots deep in the English common law, and this necessarily made the House of Lords an important reference point. As well, the English courts had an excellent reputation for the crafted rigour of their judgments, although it should be noted that American courts, which also share the common law approach, almost never cite English authorities. In all, citations to English courts (including to the Judicial Committee) still accounted for more than one-half of all judicial citations.

Given the traditionalism of the contemporary judiciary and the important legal principle of *stare decisis* ("Let decided matters stand"), it is not surprising that the impact of the end of appeals was gradual rather than immediate, evolutionary rather than revolutionary; however, contemporaries held higher hopes and expressed disappointment. Professor Bora Laskin complained of "the conservative tradition of the Canadian legal profession reinforced by the awe and timidity of a colonial outlook"[24] and coined the phrase "the captive court" to describe the Supreme Court's continuing deference,[25] a captivity all the more frustrating now that the Supreme Court was "a free court subject only to self-imposed limitation."[26] And Professor Gilbert Kennedy bitterly criticized the Court's tendency to use the phrase "the English authorities have decided" as if it settled the matter beyond any need for discussion or explanation.[27]

A decrease in citations to English authorities would presumably have meant an increase in citations to the Supreme Court's own prior decisions, but this clearly did not happen either. Even though the Supreme Court's use of judicial authorities was up significantly in the early 1950s (from about 400 per year to about 800 per year), the share that went to its own decisions was down from 26.2 percent to 21.7 percent. To those who hoped that the end of appeals would mean the prompt emergence of a purely Canadian jurisprudence crafted by Canadian judges to provide the focal point for the decisions of Canadian courts, this was a disappointing beginning.

It might at first glance seem peculiar that fully one citation in every six was to other (that is to say, lower) Canadian courts. In the normal expectation, precedent (like water) typically flows downhill; however, as H. Patrick Glenn points out, the history of the common law is organized less around courts of appeal ("a continental graft"[28]) than as a conversation of judges "engaged in a common, shared exercise."[29] The language of judicial citation is more egalitarian than the logic of an appellate hierarchy would suggest. When lower court judges are cited by the Supreme Court, their findings of law are taken very seriously and they are sometimes named, quoted approvingly, and explicitly preferred to the esteemed courts of other countries.[30]

The final two categories of citations are so negligible that they could almost be omitted, although this will be marginally less so for subsequent chief justiceships. Citations of American authorities were extremely infrequent — the average was well below one per month — even though two of the members of the Rinfret Court (Rand and Estey) took some of their legal training in the United States. Geographical proximity and common law practices notwithstanding, American law and American jurisprudence played only a limited role in the law courts of mid-twentieth-century Canada, and the preferred models were heavily English. Other citations (almost all of them to Australia and New Zealand) were also relatively infrequent.

In all, the citation patterns point to a Supreme Court that was drawing its doctrinal cues firstly from English sources (especially the

## Table 3.3

### Supreme Court of Canada Judges Most Frequently Cited by the Rinfret Court
### Reported Cases, Supreme Court of Canada, 1949–1954

| Judge | Number of times cited | Number of times named | "Score" |
|---|---|---|---|
| Duff[†] | 273 | 156 | 429 |
| Rinfret[*†] | 191 | 37 | 228 |
| Anglin[†] | 143 | 51 | 194 |
| R. Taschereau[*] | 75 | 7 | 82 |
| Kerwin[*] | 53 | 14 | 67 |
| H. Taschereau[†] | 40 | 16 | 56 |
| Strong[†] | 41 | 14 | 55 |
| Davies[†] | 40 | 11 | 51 |
| Fitzpatrick[†] | 35 | 15 | 50 |
| Newcombe | 33 | 10 | 43 |
| Rand[*] | 30 | 8 | 38 |
| Mignault | 27 | 11 | 38 |

* indicates a member of the current court.
† indicates a (past or current) chief justice.

Judicial Committee, the House of Lords, and the English Court of Appeal) and only secondly from Canadian sources (especially itself). There was only the smallest trace of foreign influences, bearing in mind that to the lawyers and judges of the time, English sources were not foreign but American sources were. If "you are what you cite," then our Supreme Court in the early 1950s was still mostly English.

### The Supreme Court Cites the Supreme Court: Who and What?

When the Supreme Court cited its own case law, whose decisions was it drawing upon? I take it as axiomatic that cases are cited because they are "good law" and because the person who wrote that statement of law draws respect. A closer look at the Supreme Court's citation practices will take us to these more respected contemporaries and predecessors.

Table 3.3 supplies that closer look. The first column is a simple count of the number of times that a particular judge was cited, either by direct quotation or by a more general reference to his reasons for judgment. The second column indicates how often that judge was specifically named in the course of the citation; I will take this as a measure of prestige or respect, the more so because the percentage of Supreme Court citations that specifically name the judge have shown a surprising consistency, both from one judge to another within a single chief justiceship and from one chief justiceship to another. William Landes, Lawrence Lessig, and Michael E. Solimine suggest that a prestigious judge's name may function as "a 'brand-name' or 'trademark' that signifies quality,"[31] and David Klein and Darby Morrisroe think that judges may "cite others by name as a gesture of respect."[32] That is to say, the more respected and influential the judge, the more likely he (or, more recently, she) is to be named. The third column generates a "score" (frequency of citation plus frequency of naming) that I will use to rank the judges.

The citations focus on former chief justices and a small set of the Court's current members (Rinfret, Taschereau, and Kerwin). If there was a home-grown jurisprudential "superstar" to whom citation practices lead us, then that person was former chief justice Duff. His decisions were cited half again as often, and his name attached to those decisions three times as often, as any other past or current member of the Court. These two factors combine to give him an "impact score" of just over 400, almost double that of the runner-up (Rinfret) or the third-place holder (Frank Anglin). This trio in turn had a massive lead over the third rank, comprised of current members Kerwin and Taschereau. This leading trio is hardly surprising: they represent the current and the two previous chief justices, their terms together covering three full decades. And this point is confirmed by the fact that the third rank of cited former members of the Court is made up of the four chief justices who preceded Anglin, their collective terms reaching all the way back to 1892.

The prevalence of former chief justices and (to a much lesser extent) of current members of the Court simply highlights the names of the two who were neither. Pierre-Basile Mignault, who served from 1918 to 1929, was a scholar and a jurist of note[33] who had emerged as "the first great defender of the civil law."[34] More surprising (indeed, almost inexplicable) is the relatively high profile of Edmund Newcombe, who sat on the Court from 1924 to 1931 after serving for thirty years as deputy minister of justice.

Another way to approach the question of judicial influence is to ask not which judges are cited most often but which judges wrote the most frequently cited decisions. Only twelve previous decisions of the Supreme Court were cited half a dozen times or more by the Rinfret Court; that is to say, the threshold for frequently cited cases was surprisingly low, at just over once every twelve months. This is largely because, compared with current practices, the Rinfret Court did not use very many judicial citations, and even when it did cite judicial authority, it did not cite its own decisions particularly often. Almost half of the most frequently cited decisions were delivered by Duff, who also wrote his own reasons in three frequently cited *seriatim* decisions, as well as a directly cited separate concurrence; he does not so much dominate as overwhelm. Several circumstances explain this preeminence: first, he was the immediately previous chief justice; second, he served longer than any other individual in the Court's history; and third, he was regarded by contemporaries as the most able judge ever to serve on the Court.[35]

Not too surprisingly, the considerations of frequently cited judges and frequently cited cases have taken us to the same place, and that place is occupied by Duff. One criterion of judicial greatness is surely the provision of the decisions and formulations of legal doctrine that live on in the subsequent reasons for judgment of the Court, the more so when that impact continues for an extended period. On this measure, Duff is the preeminent Canadian influence over the jurisprudence of the Rinfret Court; only Anglin and Rinfret himself (chief justices both) are remotely comparable.

Cited cases are a mixture of venerable, long-standing decisions and more recent decisions by the current Court. That the twelve most frequently cited judges are a mixture of past chief justices and current members demonstrates the presence of both elements, and the balance between them says something about the way the Court chooses between tradition and novelty. In general, we expect that more recent decisions will tend over time to replace older ones, either because the more recent ones clarify and consolidate earlier ones or because the prevailing understanding of the law changes to make the older decisions less persuasive, but it is important to get some objective measure of how fast this replacement process operates. One way of doing so is to think of "citability" as being like radioactivity in the sense that it decrease (decays) over time, and this mathematical measure allows us to suggest a "half-life" for any of the precedent-setting cases delivered by the Court.[36] For the Rinfret Court, the "decay curve" is rather flat, at about 3.5 percent a year, suggesting a very low rate of precedent replacement (only one-half of all citations to a specific case occurring within seventeen years of its being delivered) and a corresponding high citation profile for the major figures from even the Court's more remote past.

# Major Decisions of the Rinfret Court

Another approach to understanding the Rinfret Court is to look at its significant decisions. There are, of course, many different ways to generate such a list; my criterion is how often the Supreme Court itself has used these cases in subsequent decisions. In this and subsequent chapters, I will select two or three of the most frequently cited cases of each chief justiceship to examine them from a double perspective. First, each case will be briefly summarized, giving a sense of the Court's style and tone. Second, I will apply Claire L'Heureux-Dubé's observations about case comment, legal argument, and judicial decision gradually refining even a fragmented decision to "a few clear propositions of law."[37] An important question, and one to which this approach gives some objective access, is what "propositions of law" the Rinfret Court's major decisions have contributed to Canadian jurisprudence.

It must be conceded that the citation count for the most frequently cited decisions of the Rinfret Court is not particularly impressive. The single most frequently cited case has been cited only thirty-four times in the forty-six years since it was delivered — less than once per year. The cutoff point for the "top twelve" is only seventeen citations in almost fifty years. Most of the paint that the Rinfret Court splashed on the jurisprudential wall has either faded or been painted over, but this just makes it all the more important to see what remains. The fragmentation of the Rinfret Court is clearly indicated by the fact that more than half of the most frequently cited cases involved *seriatim* decisions. I will illustrate the *seriatim* process, and why it can be so frustrating, by more closely examining two cases.

The second most frequently cited decision is *Saumur v. Quebec*[38] in 1953. This was also, at ninety pages, the longest decision handed down by the Rinfret Court, more than five times as long as average. The background was the long-standing unpopularity within Catholic Quebec of the Jehovah's Witnesses, aggravated by the fact that the Witnesses saw themselves as having a religious duty to spread their views with persistence and energy — characteristically, by standing on street corners with copies of their periodical publications, as well as by door-to-door missions. Nor did it help that their views included unflattering opinions of the Catholic Church that were couched in flamboyant biblical terminology. The 1950s saw a series of regulatory attempts to limit the behaviour of the Witnesses, met by legal challenges that several times reached the Supreme Court. *Saumur* was one of them, challenging a municipal bylaw that prohibited the distribution of pamphlets in the streets without prior permission from the chief of police.

This was one of the rare cases heard by a full nine-judge panel. The oral arguments lasted seven days, and the Court took ten months to reach a conclusion. The three Quebec judges, joined by one of their colleagues, voted to uphold the validity of the bylaw. Rinfret (with Taschereau) complained about the case's "extravagante mise-en-scène" and wrote a vigorous nineteen pages arguing that the pith and substance of the bylaw was the control and regulation of public usage of the streets. This was clearly within provincial jurisdiction, as demonstrated by a string of Judicial Committee and Supreme Court decisions. Even if the issue of freedom of religion were relevant, which he felt it was not, this too would fall within provincial jurisdiction over "property and civil rights within the province." Cartwright (joined by Fauteux) similarly found in 9½ pages that provincial legislatures could give municipalities the power to pass such a bylaw, this validity flowing from provincial jurisdiction either over the use of the highways or over police regulations.

But Rand found the bylaw to be legislation in relation to religion and free speech, beyond provincial regulation because these are not matters of a local or private nature. His 8 pages of reasons focused on the problem of censorship and a concern that "a more objectionable interference ... can scarcely be imagined." Kellock (in 22½ pages) reached a similar conclusion, providing a lengthy examination of the Civil Code of Quebec and of Quebec case law to support it. Estey, in 6½ pages, suggested that the right to the free exercise and enjoyment of religious profession and worship came under federal jurisdiction by virtue of the "peace, order and good government" clause. Locke's 17 pages went further: he found that these were constitutional rights of all the people, implicit in the BNA Act's reference to a constitution "similar in principle to that of the United Kingdom." The implication was that the federal government could not legislate to limit these rights either, heady stuff indeed for the 1950s.

With eight votes registered, the battle seemed fairly joined. Four judges (including all three Quebec judges) found the restrictions to be a valid exercise of provincial jurisdiction. Four judges (for four quite different reasons) found them to be unconstitutional. On which side would the ninth judge come down? The answer is — "neither." In 5½ pages, Kerwin focused his attention on Quebec's Freedom of

Worship Act (a continuation of a pre-Confederation statute), which he found rendered the bylaw inoperative insofar as it applied to the proselytizing activities of the Witnesses, although in all other respects the bylaw was valid. And given the even split of the more polarized positions, Kerwin's reasons for judgment became the decision of the Court.

*Saumur* splendidly illustrates why the Supreme Court received mixed reviews in the 1950s. On the one hand, it asserted a national vision of civil liberties over provincial parochialism, which struck a strong chord in the aftermath of the Second World War. On the other hand, it did so at the cost of a deep and visible division between its French- and English-Canadian judges, and the jurisprudence underpinning the outcomes was "confusing and inconclusive."[39]

Alberta's recent excitement over video lottery terminals (VLTs) gives *Johnson v. Attorney-General of Alberta*[40] an element of déjà vu. It involved The Slot Machine Act, an Alberta statute that provided that no slot machine "shall be capable of ownership, nor shall the same be the subject of property rights within the Province," meaning that the police could confiscate them whenever they found them. The only issue before the Supreme Court (although this did not prevent a wordy detour into the appropriate powers of provincial magistrates) was whether the act was valid provincial legislation or an infringement of federal jurisdiction over the criminal law. Clearly, the province had attempted a cute legal manoeuvre, evading the then-current constitutional definition of a criminal law as a prohibition enforced by a penalty. But the manoeuvre could be too transparent to be effective, because confiscation of property is sometimes a penalty and because the legislation adopted the Criminal Code definition of "slot machine." This is, in fact, what the seven-judge panel (sort of) found, restoring the trial judge's prohibition order.

But the reasons create confusion. Locke wrote 14 pages presenting the act as a violation ("it would be difficult to find a more direct encroachment") of the exclusive jurisdiction of Parliament regarding the criminal law, and therefore null and void. Cartwright reached the same conclusion in 2½ pages, but referred to Locke's decision only to pick up on his description of the legislative history of the act, not to endorse the reasons; and Kellock's single paragraph signed on not to Locke but to Cartwright. Meanwhile Rand, in 4 pages, redescribed both the act and the relevant provisions of the Criminal Code, found them essentially similar, and therefore declared the statute inoperative (but not *ultra vires*) on the grounds that the duplication would "introduce an interference" with the administration of the Code. On the other hand, Estey, in 8 pages of dissent, wrote that the provincial legislation was valid because it did not meet the Court's current definition of a criminal offence (a prohibition accompanied by a penalty), and Kerwin (curtly endorsed by Taschereau) wrote 5 pages reaching the same conclusion without once mentioning Estey (or vice versa). It is clear that Mr. Johnson won his case (by the narrowest of majorities), but it is not clear whether the provincial legislation was unconstitutionally null and void or merely "inoperative," there being only three judges on a seven-judge court to support the stronger conclusion.

Curiously, when this case was cited recently, it was to support the proposition that the regulation of gaming activity has a clear provincial aspect, even though it can also be addressed by federal criminal legislation.[41] On the contrary, Locke (surely the most plausible candidate for the leading decision for the result) said exactly the opposite, declaring that "the exclusive jurisdiction to legislate in relation to gaming lies with Parliament." The only judge dealing with the matter as overlapping jurisdiction subject to federal paramountcy was Rand, but not one of his colleagues explicitly agreed with him. L'Heureux-Dubé's comments notwithstanding, it would seem that the distillation of core meanings from lengthy decisions is not rocket science.

## The Most Influential Judges of the Rinfret Court

Like most professors, I certainly hope that my ideas will not only be published but will also be picked up by my colleagues. I am sure the same is true of judges, who seek not only to reach the fairest result in the immediate case, but also (at least some of the time) to do so in ways that prove persuasive and useful to other judges. The paradoxical feature of the doctrine of precedent is that judges limit their own creativity by accepting as authoritative the earlier decisions of other judges, and yet in the process, they create the precedents that will be treated as authoritative in future years. The practice of following precedent is forward-looking as well as backward-looking, because "today is not only yesterday's tomorrow; it is also tomorrow's yesterday."[42]

But this means that the methodology of the previous section can be turned around. When they cite the precedents that anchor their current decisions, the judges of the Supreme Court are implicitly "voting" for the most useful and authoritative decisions (and thereby for the most useful and authoritative members) of the current and

## Table 3.4

### Frequency with which Members of the Rinfret Court Are Subsequently Cited Reported Decisions, 1949–1999

| Judge | Number of times cited | Number of times named | "Score" |
|---|---|---|---|
| Rand | 129 | 82 | 211 |
| Cartwright[†] | 118 | 48 | 166 |
| Fauteux[†] | 114 | 32 | 146 |
| Rinfret[*] | 108 | 29 | 137 |
| Kerwin[†] | 94 | 30 | 124 |
| Kellock | 90 | 22 | 112 |
| Taschereau[†] | 77 | 22 | 99 |
| Estey | 50 | 24 | 74 |
| Locke | 54 | 13 | 67 |

* indicates the current chief justice.
† indicates future chief justices.

past Courts. But at the same time, each member of the current Court and each decision that the members deliver is also a candidate for the similar "votes" of future judges in future decisions. Table 3.4 ranks the judges of the Rinfret Court in terms of how often they were cited and named in subsequent decisions by the Supreme Court. Rand leads in the absolute frequency of citations, but even more decisively in the frequency with which he was identified by name; he is trailed by Cartwright and Fauteux, with Locke and Estey at the bottom of the table. To keep the playing field level, the count is limited to the decisions and reasons delivered by each individual between 1949 and 1954 and does not include citations to previous or subsequent decisions delivered under other chief justices.

To concede the obvious, the numbers are small. Even Rand, the Rinfret Court's citation leader, has been cited for the decisions he delivered over this five-year period fewer than three times per year since 1954, and at the other end of the table, Locke has managed barely once per year. Three different factors could explain this. First, it could be that the calibre of the Rinfret Court was not particularly high, its precedential track record suffering from the mediocrity of qualifications and performance that have plagued the Supreme Court for much of its existence. Second, it could be that the judges are handicapped by the fact that this Court and its immediate successors used judicial citations (and particularly the Court's own citations) more sparingly than have recent Courts. Third, it could be that a major shift in the style and direction of Supreme Court jurisprudence has undercut the usefulness of the decisions of the Rinfret Court. Or, of course, all of the above.

## Conclusion

The newly supreme Supreme Court did not have a fast start out of the gate. Although the gradual evolution away from a full-fledged *seriatim* style continued, the Court frequently delivered divided decisions, this tendency being more pronounced on the most important cases. This fragmented style blunted the Court's impact and leadership. Because the members never engaged each other's arguments directly — indeed, often never even acknowledged the ideas of their colleagues — the result was less a conversation building toward a conclusion than a series of disconnected monologues. It might be that all the reasons had essentially the same information, but you have to read all of them in order to find out that you only really needed to read one of them.

To the extent that such a fragmented and many-voiced Court had leaders, the strongest candidates were both from Ontario: Kerwin and Kellock (second and fifth in seniority), in that order. But they were less partners than rivals, more likely to disagree with each other than any other pairing on the Court. Kerwin generally prevailed by virtue of a loose voting bloc that included the three Quebec members; Kellock relied on a more eclectic mix. Over the following decades, however, neither one of them has accounted for the larger part of the Rinfret Court's own citation track. Rand's frequently solitary, independent course is now cited more often than either of the Ontario judges.

Its new-found supremacy did not alter the Court's citation style, which was still heavily focused on the English courts. The language of the citations reinforces the impression of the number count, being less a critical examination of a reasoned argument than an admiring invocation of highly respected authority. When the Court was not citing English authorities, it was citing Canadian cases — usually its own, and preeminently those of previous chief justices, especially Duff; however, there was also a pronounced readiness to cite the decisions of lower courts, and to pick up on their suggestions about the proper reading of law and doctrine. Conversation rather than strict hierarchy marks this style.

This is not to say that the Court made no move from under the shadow of Judicial Committee precedents. In constitutional law, for example, *Johannesson v. West St. Paul*[43] (dealing with federal jurisdiction over aeronautics) began the evolution of modern jurisprudence on the meaning of "peace, order and good government." And *Saumur* was one of several cases evincing the postwar concern with protecting civil liberties, although it is not clear from these few pieces what the assembled jigsaw puzzle might look like. These were not dramatic statements of a new-found independence, but tentative signs of the beginning of a less spectatular but nonetheless significant evolution.

In retrospect, it is not surprising to find more continuity than innovation in the first five years of the Court's new-found supremacy. The chief justice who started the new era had already served on the Court for a quarter century, half a decade of that as chief justice. A majority of his colleagues had ten years or more of experience on the Court, and the judges filling the two new seats were "old school" appointments, with political connections, limited judicial experience, and modest reputations. It takes more than the end of further appeals to transform the way a court operates, the way its members think about their role and their responsibilities. On the evidence of the first five years, the ending of appeals was far from the major leap forward that many had hoped for.

# The Kerwin Court:
# July 1954 to February 1963
# "The Technician"

Rinfret reached retirement age on June 22, 1954, and nineteen-year veteran Patrick Kerwin became chief justice a week later, at the age of 64. This represented little more than the simple operation of the seniority principle, the more transparently so given that Kerwin was the only member of the Court appointed by a Conservative prime minister (Bennett) in 1935; however, he had also clearly been (along with Kellock and, on different criteria, Rand) one of the leading members of the Rinfret Court. He was considered an able judge and a capable administrator; it showed the tenor of the time that the most controversial aspect of his appointment was the fact that a Catholic had succeeded another Catholic as chief justice.

One problem was his poor health, causing rumours that he would soon be retiring, and although in fact he served almost nine years before his death (slightly longer than the average tenure for a chief justice), these rumours meant that the Court operated against a background of uncertainty. But the major cause of instability was rapid turnover: his chief justiceship saw no fewer than five appointments. If some degree of turnover is generally good for any institution, too much too can quickly become disruptive — for example (as with the Martland/Judson/Ritchie trio), when a full third of the Court is replaced in a space of sixteen months.

The subtitle of this chapter ("The Technician") refers to the decision-making style of the period, quite different from what we see today. To describe a current member of the Court as demonstrating a "purely mechanical jurisprudence" would be taken as severe criticism. For the Kerwin Court (and earlier), most judges would have taken it as a compliment, because they saw their work as the rigorous application of a professional technique to disputes that arose against the background of law. I will expand on this distinction at the end of the next chapter, as we stand on the threshold of its total eclipse.

The Kerwin Court presided over the Canada of the Diefenbaker interlude — the surprising minority government of 1957, the record-setting landslide of 1958, and the collapse to minority government status in 1962. Kerwin died two months before the election that returned the Liberals to government; indeed, the frantic efforts to save the Conservative government in its closing days included serious proposals to make John Diefenbaker the new chief justice. In the confusion, the Conservatives left both the appointment of a new chief justice and the appointment of a replacement for Kerwin to the Pearson government. The election in 1960 of Jean Lesage's Liberals in Quebec signalled the beginning of the Quiet Revolution that utterly transformed English–French and Quebec–Canada relations. In terms of world politics, the major events were probably (at one end) the Anglo-French invasion to secure the Suez Canal, culminating in the United Nations's signal success in establishing an international peacekeeping force, and (at the other) the intensification of the Cold War when the Soviet Union embarrassed the United States by shooting down Francis Gary Power's U-2 "spy plane." In the United States, John Fitzgerald Kennedy became the first Catholic president in 1960 and promptly faced the Cuban Missile Crisis, and Earl Warren became chief justice of the United States just one year before Kerwin's appointment, although the emergence of the solid voting majority that constituted the Warren Court awaited the appointment of Arthur Goldberg in 1962.

## The Personnel of the Kerwin Court

The continuing members of the Court were (in order of seniority) Kerwin, Taschereau, Rand, Kellock, Estey, Locke, Cartwright, and Fauteux; by the time of Kerwin's death in February 1963, only Taschereau, Cartwright, and Fauteux remained.

**Douglas Charles Abbott** was appointed on July 1, 1954, to replace Rinfret. His was one of most controversial appointments in the history of the Supreme Court and is generally regarded as "the last of the obvious political appointments"[1] — it was the first appointment straight from the federal cabinet since that of Louis-Philippe Brodeur in 1911 and the most clearly partisan appointment since that of Fitzpatrick in 1906. Abbott was from Montreal, 55 years of age, and a McGill graduate who had studied law in France for one year. He had been a Liberal member of parliament since 1940 and a member of the government since 1945; at the time of his appointment, he had been finance minister for more than seven years, and there was some concern that he had not been active in the practice of law for more than a decade. He was a well-respected politician and widely thought of as possible successor to Prime Minister St. Laurent, so much so that his departure from politics for the Court came as a surprise. He was not the first English-speaking Quebecker ever appointed, but he was the first Quebec Protestant. The Duplessis government, which had clashed repeatedly with the federal Liberals over the previous two decades, found the appointment offensive and provocative, and the Canadian Bar Association criticized the use of political considerations.

**Henry Gratton Nolan** was appointed by the St. Laurent government on March 1, 1956, "yielding to the demands of Alberta."[2] He replaced Saskatchewan's J.W. Estey, who had died on January 22. Nolan was 61 years old when he was appointed, a popular and respected Calgary lawyer, and the first Rhodes Scholar (Alberta and Saskatchewan & University 1915) of the five who have ever been appointed to the Court. Just over a year later, however, he suffered a heart attack, and he died on July 8, 1957, having served the fourth shortest term (after John Armour, Albert Malouin, and David Mills) in the Court's history.

**Ronald Martland** was appointed to the Supreme Court on January 15, 1958, replacing Nolan. Fifty-one years old and also a Rhodes Scholar (Alberta & Hertford 1928), he was the Diefenbaker government's first Supreme Court appointment. He was a prominent corporate lawyer who had practised law in Edmonton and an expert in matters relating to natural resources, with no strong partisan connections and no prior judicial experience. Although at least initially Wilfred Judson had a higher profile, I will try to demonstrate that Martland's was one of the two pivotal appointments (Laskin being the other) since 1949.

**Wilfred Judson** of Ontario was appointed on February 5, 1958, replacing Kellock. (The official reason for Kellock's unexpected retirement was poor health, but it was widely thought that the real reason was his unhappiness at having to serve with — let alone under — Kerwin.) Born and educated in England, Judson had been a member of the Ontario High Court for seven years after practising in Toronto, and he was an expert in the equity law of wills and estates; he breaks the string of appointments without prior judicial experience. He was 55 years old when he took his seat on the Court.

**Roland Almon Ritchie** was appointed on May 5, 1959, to replace Rand (who had reached retirement age on April 17). Ritchie had practised law at Halifax; he was only 48 years old when appointed and had no judicial experience. The Martland/Judson/Ritchie trio represents an important legacy of the Diefenbaker government, both because of the length of their service (together they served almost seventy years on the Supreme Court, a "three in a row" total exceeded only by the 73½ years for Sir Wilfrid Laurier's appointment of Fitzpatrick, Duff, and Anglin in 1906–9) and because of the extent to which they formed an unusually coherent and stable voting block.

**Emmett Matthew Hall** was appointed on November 23, 1962, replacing Locke. He had just turned 64, making him the oldest appointee since Robert Smith in 1927, and he was the first western Roman Catholic appointed to the Supreme Court. Born in Quebec, he was educated in Saskatchewan and practised law in that province, where he was a law-school classmate and long-time friend of Diefenbaker. He had been a judge for five years, as chief justice of the Saskatchewan Court of Queen's Bench and then (briefly) chief justice of the Court of Appeal. He was the first member of the Supreme Court to have previously served as the chief justice of both a provincial trial court and a provincial court of appeal (Willard Z. Estey in 1977 was the second).[3]

A former member of the Saskatchewan Law Reform Commission, Hall brought to the bench an unusual record of social activism. When appointed, he was chairing the federal Royal Commission on Health Services, whose report led to the national medical care scheme, and he also served on the Ontario Royal Commission on Education (which produced the Hall-Dennis Report), the critical turning point in the 1970s reform of the Canadian education system. Hall had a reputation as a champion of civil liberties, making him the "odd one out" of the Diefenbaker appointees (which is why I do not suggest a "Diefenbaker quartet"). His judicial style and temperament has been linked with Duff and Rand[4] as well as with Laskin.[5]

The new appointees, like the judges they replaced, were successful white males typically in their 50s (Ritchie somewhat younger, Hall somewhat older), and the average age of the Court oscillated in the low 60s. All were from the country's two dominant ethnic groups, although the appointment of a Protestant anglophone from Quebec changed the ethnic balance and drew criticism in that province. In the closing days of the Rinfret Court, five members had no previous judicial experience and four had only limited experience; nine years and six appointments and one chief justice later, the same generalization still applied. The Rinfret Court had one member, Rand, with a reputation as an intellectual and an innovator; the Kerwin Court had one member, Hall, with a reputation as a law reformer.

## The Caseload of the Kerwin Court

The reported caseload of the Kerwin Court was somewhat higher than that of the Rinfret Court, although still well below the figures for more recent years. There were 758 reported panel decisions in the almost nine years of Kerwin's chief justiceship, or about 85 per year — roughly 30 percent higher than the figures for 1949–54. As noted earlier, these are "soft" numbers because not all decisions were reported, but it seems reasonable to assume that most were and that much of the apparent increase is genuine. We are still far from the burgeoning caseload that led to the reforms of the 1970s, but the steady caseload increase points in that direction.

Private law cases — disputes between natural persons and/or commercial companies — continued to account for most (54%) of the cases, public law (non-criminal disputes involving government) made up almost exactly one-third of the caseload, and criminal cases were the smallest category at about one-twelfth. These proportions are essentially unchanged from the Rinfret period. It was still the case that the Court's major work was the resolution of disputes between private actors. Private law decisions tended to be the shortest (just over 10 pages of text) and criminal law decisions the longest (at 12½ pages). Overall, the Kerwin Court wrote shorter decisions than the Rinfret Court (11 pages, down from 16), but much of that reduction reflects the decline of dissents and separate concurrences discussed later in this chapter.

Continuity applied as well to the sources from which appeals rose to the Court. Ontario and Quebec still accounted for about half of all appeals, the four western provinces for just under a third, and the federal Exchequer Court for one-fifth. The Atlantic provinces still lacked full-time specialized courts of appeal, relying instead on *en banc* panels of trial judges. This may explain why there were so few appeals from the region — proportionately even fewer than for the Rinfret Court and less than population share alone would lead one to expect. Ontario and Quebec remained among the stronger (that is to say, the least frequently reversed) of the appeal courts; British Columbia replaced Manitoba as the most frequently reversed.

What is different is the Kerwin Court's overall reversal rates, which were fully 10 percent lower than those of the Rinfret Court. This striking variation demonstrates why the reversal rates are not a reliable indication of merit: it is hardly credible that the collective provincial appellate bench was 10 percent "better" in 1954–63 than it had been in 1949–54, which means that, for example, the 5 percent spread between the reversal rates of the Quebec and Saskatchewan Courts of Appeal may not mean anything either. This drop was the most pronounced for public law appeals (which succeeded one-third of the time under Kerwin, half of the time under Rinfret) and the least so for criminal law appeals (virtually unchanged at 42 percent).

In general, then, despite its high personnel turnover, the performance of the Kerwin Court represents business as usual, although with a slightly larger caseload, significantly shorter decisions, fewer reversals of provincial appeal court decisions, and (as we will see) less-fragmented decisions.

## Decision-making by the Kerwin Court

The Kerwin Court was somewhat less divided than its predecessor; over its nine years, there were on average about two opinions delivered for each decision, down from almost three for the Rinfret Court. Unanimous opinions accounted for roughly one-half of all the cases, almost exactly double the proportion for the Rinfret Court. Conversely, there was a drop from 40 percent to about 15 percent in the proportion of cases in which the Court was so badly divided that not even a majority of the panel supporting a single outcome plus reasons. And *seriatim* decisions (drawing frequently repetitive and always overlapping reasons from most of the judges on the panel) accounted for only one case in every twenty-five, down from one case in every six for the Rinfret Court. The journey from confused plurality to concise clarity described by L'Heureux-Dubé[6] was clearly well under way, although it still had some way to go — the more so because the most serious fragmentation was often occasioned by the major cases.

The year-by-year figures suggest a clear break between an early and a late Kerwin Court. For the first four years, the number of opinions delivered per case averaged about 2½, with judges dissenting just over half the time and (on average) more than one separate concurrence per case. For the last five years, the number of opinions per case fell to about 1½, with judges delivering dissents just over a third of the time and separate concurrences slightly more often. This is all the more persuasive because there is an obvious explanation, namely the major change in personnel in 1958. Not only did one-third of the Court change in just over a year, but for the first time since Kerwin's own initial appointment in 1935, the appointments were made by a government that was not Liberal and by a prime minister who was neither King nor St. Laurent. One of the visible results of this reduced fragmentation was shorter decisions: the average fell from 12.3 pages for the first four terms to 10.1 pages for the last five. The average size of a panel remained low — indeed, even lower (at 5.38) than it was for the Rinfret Court (at 5.53). For both periods, criminal cases tended to be heard by the largest and private law cases by the smallest panels, but the private law cases that divided the Rinfret Court the most now divided the Kerwin Court the least.

The question of fragmentation is important because appeal courts do more than resolve the immediate case before them. If that was their only function, it would make little difference whether they handed down one set of reasons or several, or whether they gave much in the way of reasons at all. But today we think it their simultaneous and more important duty to provide leadership to the lower courts. This leadership is accomplished through the reasons for the outcome, discursive explanations that lay out the principles, the mitigating factors, and the trade-offs against other rules. But different sets of reasons, more or less parallel but differing in emphasis or detail, make it difficult for the lower courts to know where they are being led, particularly if those varying reasons never acknowledge or respond to each other.

It is still the case that the type of law explains only a very small part of the variation between cases. For both chief justiceships, Rinfret's and Kerwin's, public law cases fell in-between for both panel size and frequency of separate opinions; however, for both we are looking at variations on a theme rather than at different tendencies for different types of law.

Talking of "the Court" is, of course, simply a composite way of talking about the various individuals who serve on the Court. It is not "the Court" but an individual judge who decides to sign on to another judge's reasons, to dissent, or to write a separate concurrence, and this information is presented in Table 4.1. Because the judges appear in order of their appointment, reading the table from top to bottom is also something of a movement through time.

If the Court became less fragmented, this must mean either that some continuing judges were writing their own reasons less often

# Table 4.1

## Dissents, Concurrences, and Decisions, by Judge
## Reported Supreme Court Decisions, 1954–1963

| Judge | Panels | Wrote decision | Contributed to decision | Divided panels | With majority | Conc. | Diss. |
|-------|--------|--------|--------|--------|--------|--------|--------|
| Kerwin C.J. | 392 | 26.0% | 47.4% | 233 | 60.1% | 26.6% | 13.3% |
| Taschereau | 445 | 16.6% | 26.5% | 226 | 71.7% | 19.9% | 14.2% |
| Rand | 237 | 19.8% | 65.4% | 180 | 35.0% | 48.3% | 16.7% |
| Kellock | 110 | 25.5% | 61.8% | 83 | 45.8% | 47.0% | 7.2% |
| Estey | 53 | 18.9% | 41.5% | 39 | 59.0% | 30.8% | 10.3% |
| Locke | 439 | 14.6% | 46.5% | 268 | 39.2% | 42.2% | 18.7% |
| Cartwright | 520 | 15.4% | 46.3% | 289 | 34.6% | 33.9% | 31.5% |
| Fauteux | 446 | 15.9% | 24.7% | 214 | 72.0% | 17.3% | 10.7% |
| Abbott | 456 | 12.3% | 20.2% | 227 | 71.8% | 17.2% | 11.0% |
| Nolan | 49 | 14.3% | 22.4% | 36 | 59.0% | 33.3% | 5.6% |
| Martland | 317 | 18.3% | 24.9% | 115 | 64.3% | 23.5% | 12.2% |
| Judson | 310 | 26.1% | 31.9% | 129 | 72.1% | 12.4% | 15.5% |
| Ritchie | 230 | 18.7% | 27.8% | 84 | 65.5% | 22.6% | 11.9% |
| Hall | 12 | 8.3% | 33.3% | 7 | 42.9% | 14.3% | 42.9% |
| ALL | 4016 | 18.0% | 36.2% | 2143 | 55.8% | 28.3% | 15.9% |

(possibly influenced by a new chief justice) or that the new judges wrote less often than the people they replaced. The first possibility can be discarded immediately. Of the continuing members of the Rinfret Court, we can still say that the Quebec judges were the least active and Rand and Kellock the most active in writing dissents and separate opinions. If the Kerwin Court was less fragmented than its predecessor, this was not because of the performance of the continuing judges.

The differences grow from the performance of the new judges. Abbott, the first to join the Court, fits the generalization of the Quebec judges (and therefore prevents it from being only a generalization about French-Canadian judges); he signed on with the majority more often than any other judge except Fauteux, and he wrote less often than any other judge. But there was a dramatic shift when Estey, Rand, and Locke were replaced by the "Diefenbaker trio," each of whom signed on with the majority more frequently than anyone else on this or the previous Court and each of whom wrote separate opinions much less frequently than average. I have characterized this change as "less fragmentation," which puts a positive spin on it; Snell and Vaughan speak instead of the departure of "intellectually self-confident men" and their replacement by "younger justices with limited judicial experience,"[7] which is a more critical reading. Either way, it was unclear at the end of the Kerwin Court whether this was a transitional effect explained by a significant cadre of new and inexperienced judges or a permanent shift in the way the Court delivered its decisions.

## Voting Blocs on the Kerwin Court

The Kerwin Court was less fragmented than its predecessor, but it still divided frequently on its reasons for judgment. Crudely put, it was still prone to split, but when it did so, the pieces tended to be larger. The question is whether these pieces tended to involve identifiable blocs of judges.

The figures from Table 4.1 support the idea that Kerwin generally led his own Court. He was part of the majority more than three-quarters of the time, just over the all-Court average, and he wrote for the majority in just over one-quarter of his panel appearances, more than anyone else on the Court. In all, he delivered over 100 decisions for the majority, more than any other justice. Similar observations can be made of Kerwin's performance on the Rinfret Court, and they suggest that Kerwin was the leader both of the Rinfret Court and of his own.

But if Kerwin led, who followed? Given the turnover on the Court, the answer to this is complex. Initially, Kerwin's major support came from the trio of Quebec judges: Taschereau, Fauteux, and Abbott, each of whom signed on with Kerwin in just over 70 percent of their panel appearances. (I must note, however, that they signed on with each other even more often, about 80 percent of the time, and this is a point I will pursue later.) This group seems to have been the core of the early Kerwin Court. The use of smaller panels makes it unnecessary to look for a fifth member to give "control" of a nine-member Court; if there was such a fifth member, it was probably Estey, who joined with Kerwin more than two-thirds of the time. (With Estey's departure, Nolan seems to have taken his place not only on the Court but also on the edge of this dominant group.) But every one of the judges I have named signed Kerwin's reasons for judgment more often (and most of them much more often) than he signed theirs, which supports the notion that Kerwin led the group.

Cartwright is best described as being on the fringes of the "Kerwin core" in a more complex way: he did not sign on with Kerwin particularly often (in just over half of his panel appearances), but he had somewhat higher agreement rates with all the others. This suggests that he was less a solid member of the group than a competitor (mostly with Kerwin and mostly unsuccessfully) in setting the Court's focus and direction. It is striking that he was the member of the Kerwin Court most likely to dissent, doing so 17.5 percent of the time (just over double the all-Court average). Of the other members of the Court, only Locke and Rand dissented in more than 10 percent of their appearances. There is a curious ambivalence to Cartwright's position on the edge of the Kerwin group: he both signed on with and dissented from the Kerwin core more often than Estey did.

At the other end of the Court were Kellock and Rand, although it is probably more accurate to think of each being in his own separate corner, given that they signed on with each other in barely half of their panel appearances. Kellock's disagreements with — even dislike of — Kerwin were widely known and were the generally accepted reason for his unexpected early retirement. Rand continued his independent course from the Rinfret Court, writing (sometimes a decision, usually a separate concurring opinion, rarely a dissent) in two-thirds of his panel appearances. But for both, this was neither polarization nor isolation: Kellock delivered decisions for the Court more often than anyone except Kerwin himself, and Rand was not far off that mark either.

Locke's role is even harder to characterize. He signed on with Kerwin less often than did anybody except Kellock and Rand, but he also joined Rand and Kellock less often than did anyone else on the Court. It seems to me that the best way to characterize the early Kerwin Court is as a core of four (Kerwin plus the three Quebec judges), with two members on the edge of the group (Cartwright and Estey, later Nolan) and the other three (Kellock, Rand, and Locke) as independent outlyers.

But this is the early Kerwin Court, with its large contingent of continuing members. By February 1958, Kellock and Estey were both gone, the former replaced by Judson and the latter (via Nolan) by Martland. A year later, Rand had been replaced by Ritchie. (Hall's replacement of Locke occurred so late in the Court that I shall leave its impact for the next chapter.) The impact of the "Diefenbaker trio" can be summarized briefly: first, they formed an unusually cohesive group, signing on with each other in about 80 percent of their appearances (almost 90 percent for Martland/Ritchie); and second, they had very high agreement rates with the Quebec trio and with Kerwin, so much so that we can speak of a coherent seven-member group rather than two three-judge fragments plus Kerwin. But somewhat curiously, Kerwin is the least firmly attached to the group; with each of the other six, he has the lowest agreement score.

In general terms, this is what we would expect from a period of rapid turnover. The American literature generally suggests the presence of a "freshman effect" involving a tendency to keep a low profile and to follow the dominant group, at least during a transition period. Of course, this presupposes that there is a dominant group to follow, something which was more true of the Kerwin Court than it had been earlier. This freshman effect would be exaggerated by the limited judicial experience of the new members. But this impression is partly belied by the performance of Judson, who was, if anything, the leading member of the new core group; this is unusual — indeed, for the Supreme Court, unprecedented — for a "rookie."

Two questions remained at the end of the Kerwin Court. The first was whether the large group that centred the Court (consistently anchored by the high agreement rates among the three Quebec judges) would hold together as the freshman effect faded and the new members gained confidence and experience. And the second, assuming that the group did hold together, was whether Judson would continue to lead it.

## Citation Practices of the Kerwin Court

Judicial citations are the visible track of the sources from which the Supreme Court draws its authority: just as nutritionists say that "we are what we eat," I have suggested that "judges are what they cite." On this criterion, the Kerwin Court, like the Rinfret Court before it, was still strongly English.

### From where did the Supreme Court Get its Citations?

The largest single source of judicial authority was English courts other than the Judicial Committee, primarily the House of Lords and the English Court of Appeal. Many citations were to decisions from previous decades, even previous centuries; the median date (the year for which there is one earlier citation for each more recent one) for an English citation was 1908. The Judicial Committee still accounted for about one citation in every eight, a surprisingly high total given the very limited caseload of that body. In all, English citations accounted for almost half of the Supreme Court's use of judicial authority. At the same time, there was some movement: if English citations seem

### Table 4.2

### Citations to Judicial Authority by the Kerwin Court Reported Decisions, 1954–1963

| Source | Number | Frequency | Median Date |
|---|---|---|---|
| Judicial Committee | 503 | 13.2% | 1926 |
| Supreme Court of Canada | 1098 | 28.7% | 1944 |
| Other English Courts | 1286 | 33.7% | 1908 |
| Other Canadian Courts | 816 | 21.4% | 1938 |
| U.S. Courts | 57 | 1.5% | 1923 |
| Other | 58 | 1.5% | 1933 |

to have been high at 47 percent, this was still lower than the Rinfret Court's 59 percent. References to all Canadian courts rose from 38 percent to 50 percent, and references to the Supreme Court's own earlier decisions rose from 22 percent to 29 percent. References beyond the English and Canadian judiciary were still negligible: 1.5 percent to American sources and an almost identical 1.5 percent to everything else (still mainly Australian).

### *The Supreme Court Cites the Supreme Court: Who and What?*

But if the Supreme Court was citing itself more often, what did these citations look like? A simple count suggests that the Kerwin Court focused somewhat more on its current members than did its predecessor; the twelve most frequently cited judges were the eight continuing members of the Rinfret Court and four of the five most recent chief justices (see Table 4.3). These top twelve judges accounted for 75 percent of all citations, but the top three for barely one-third, suggesting a somewhat less concentrated focus. The twelve most frequently cited judges for the Rinfret Court included six former chief justices and four members of the current Court; for the Kerwin Court, the same count gives us four former chief justices and eight members of the current Court.

Again, Duff delivered more of the frequently cited cases than any other individual, followed by former chief justice Rinfret and future chief justice Cartwright. Only two decisions of the Kerwin Court itself made the list (and this at the bottom), although almost half of the most frequently cited cases were delivered by judges still serving on the bench. It is also significant that a list of all the cases most

### Table 4.3

### Supreme Court of Canada Judges Most Frequently Cited by the Kerwin Court
### Reported Cases, Supreme Court of Canada, 1954–1963

| Judge | Number of time cited | Number of times named | "Score" |
|---|---|---|---|
| Duff[†] | 174 | 98 | 272 |
| Kerwin[*†] | 116 | 23 | 139 |
| R. Taschereau[*] | 90 | 10 | 100 |
| Rand[*] | 69 | 29 | 98 |
| Rinfret[†] | 83 | 13 | 96 |
| Anglin[†] | 59 | 27 | 86 |
| Cartwright[*] | 60 | 15 | 75 |
| Fauteux[*] | 46 | 11 | 57 |
| Kellock[*] | 41 | 14 | 55 |
| Locke[*] | 39 | 9 | 48 |
| Estey[*] | 25 | 7 | 32 |
| Fitzpatrick[†] | 25 | 7 | 32 |

\* indicates a member of the current Court.
† indicates a past or current chief justice.

frequently cited by the Kerwin Court would contain more English than Canadian cases — and that the list would be led by two Judicial Committee decisions.[8] We understate the traditionalism of the Court's citation practices if we focus only on its own self-citations.

The decay rate for the Kerwin Court was 10 percent, significantly higher than the Rinfret Court's 3.5 percent, which means that the typical Rinfret Court decision would receive one-half of its lifetime total of citations in the first 16 years, but the typical Kerwin Court decision would do so in only 6.6 years. This decay rate intrigues me because it gives an objective measure of an important aspect of the judicial role. Judicial citation is the practical application of the doctrine of precedent, the idea that judges ground their current findings on law and doctrine in the prior decisions of their own and other courts. In part, this is the simple common sense of drawing on the insights of others to supplement our own decision-making rather than reinventing the wheel. But in the common law, prior decisions are more than just encapsulated common sense — they are also *authority*. The core of the appeal to precedent is the notion that "the previous treatment of occurrence X in manner Y constitutes, *solely because of its historical pedigree,* a reason for treating X in manner Y if and when X again occurs."[9]

For much of the history of the common law, the emphasis was on landmark decisions, "which not only settle a particular point of law, but add to the general authority of judicial decisions because they seem to settle a problem with some finality."[10] But this means that new cases do not quickly replace old cases when those old cases are landmark decisions. And the more the judge builds the reasons for judgment around such time-tested decisions, the more he denies himself and his current colleagues the active, creative role of *making* the law, as opposed to the more passive role of *interpreting* the law.[11] But this is what the decay rate is all about: it measures how quickly new case law is replacing old case law. The high decay rates of recent years suggest conscious judicial creativity; the low decay rates of the Rinfret and Kerwin Courts suggest a deliberate traditionalism.

## Major Decisions of the Kerwin Court

The Kerwin Court is interesting for what it did, but it is important for what it left behind, which is to say for its major decisions, the ones that left an enduring fingerprint on Canadian law.

*Roncarelli v. Duplessis*[12] was one of a string of civil rights decisions handed down by the Supreme Court in the 1950s, and like *Saumur* (discussed in the previous chapter), it involved the Quebec government's strong antipathy to the proselytizing activities of the Jehovah's Witnesses. This particular case involved the proprietor of a Montreal restaurant who had frequently (some 380 times) provided security for the bail required of arrested co-believers. The Liquor Commission of the Province of Quebec, on the instructions of the premier, cancelled Mr. Roncarelli's liquor licence and barred him forever from holding such a licence. Mr. Roncarelli brought an action for damages against the premier, which succeeded at trial but was reversed on appeal.

Martland (with Locke) provided a close review of the facts established at trial, specifically the fact that the Liquor Commission had acted on the instructions of Premier Duplessis, acting in his capacity as attorney-general of the province. He cited English case law both on the limits to the discretion of a body like the Liquor Commission and on the principle that the power of an independent commission must be exercised by that body and not by anyone else. The combination of these two principles clearly established Duplessis's liability (reversing the appeal court's decision), and Martland also saw fit to set the damages higher than those awarded at trial. Kerwin wrote briefly to stress Duplessis's direct involvement and otherwise agreed with Martland.

Rand (with Judson) also supplied a redundantly complete recital of the facts. His argument was generally parallel to that of Martland, although more explicitly related to social context and policy concerns, looking forward to consequences and not just backward to precedents. The broader context was the fact that "the field of licensed occupations and businesses of this nature is steadily becoming of greater concern to citizens generally." He enunciated a general principle that no legislative act can "be taken to contemplate an unlimited arbitrary power exercisable for any purpose" and "'discretion' necessarily implies good faith in discharging public duty." And the language used was (as was usual for Rand) more emotionally charged: Duplessis's action was described as "arbitrarily and illegally attempting to divest a citizen of an incident of his civil status."

Abbott agreed with Martland, Rand, and Kerwin as to the outcome, but he wrote his own brief reasons without explicit reference to any of them. He concluded that Duplessis had brought about the cancellation of the liquor licence without statutory authority and that no notice was necessary for the suit because Duplessis had no reasonable grounds for his action. His general style was one of flat declaration rather than explanation.

Taschereau's dissent focused on Roncarelli's failure to give the notice required by the Quebec Code of Civil Procedure before suing a public officer performing his functions; this, he found, constituted a total bar to the claim. Furthermore, he disagreed that Duplessis had done anything wrong in advising the director; the resulting decision remained that of the director, not of the premier, and the premier's advice had been appropriately rendered. Fauteux, writing his own dissent, conceded that the Commission had "abdicated" its responsibility such that the decision was — wrongfully — made by Duplessis; however, he agreed that the absence of notice was a bar to the claim and also insisted that the premier's actions had been undertaken in complete good faith.

Cartwright, also in dissent but following a different line, provided yet another close recital of the facts. For him, it was critical that the legislature provided no rules to guide the Liquor Commission, from which it followed that the commission enjoyed an unfettered discretion. He expressed doubts as to the wisdom of such a delegation but not as to the power of a legislature to grant it. He thought the commission was acting in an administrative rather than a quasi-judicial role, in which case the Court could not even ask whether there existed reasonable grounds for the action;[13] but even if the role were quasi-judicial, then the Court could review (and possibly reverse) the commission's decision — but he was "far from satisfied" that there were any grounds for an action for damages. Finally, unlike most of his colleagues, he attached little importance to the communications from Premier Duplessis, the director being entitled to seek advice from another public official.

This case illustrates several features of the Kerwin Court. The Court sometimes fragmented badly, even on important full-Court decisions, when the benefits of a more unified decision were the most obvious. It struggled toward a strong position on civil rights, but (as under Rinfret) at the cost of leaving the French-Canadian judges in dissent, an isolation softened by Cartwright's dissent (here as in *Saumur*) but heightened by the "defection" of the anglophone Quebec justice. And there is a sharp difference between the flatly mechanical decisions of judges such as Martland and Abbott and the more open-textured, policy-directed analysis of judges such as Rand. The case also demonstrates that the "proto-blocs" discussed earlier have "soft" boundaries: it is curious that Judson signed on with Rand and Locke with Martland rather than the other way around.

The second case, *O'Grady v. Sparling*,[14] dealt with the constitutional problems created when the federal and provincial legislatures generate overlapping rules. Crudely put, the federal government has jurisdiction over the criminal law and the provincial governments have jurisdiction over the streets and highways; but some crimes involve automobiles and highways — and worse yet, sometimes both the federal and the provincial governments will identify, and use their jurisdiction to pursue, a problem such as dangerous or drunk driving. Generally, Canadian courts (like the Judicial Committee before them) have not worried about the overlap unless one level of government is requiring what the other forbids, but this is a recurrent controversy and one that the Supreme Court has frequently had to revisit.

One of these occasions was *O'Grady v. Sparling*, heard by a full nine-judge panel in 1960. A person charged under the Manitoba Highway Traffic Act with driving without due care and attention argued the invalidity of provincial legislation because Parliament had "occupied the field" when it created the crime of criminal negligence in the operation of a motor vehicle. The majority decision was written by Judson, with Kerwin, Taschereau, Fauteux, Abbott, Martland, and Ritchie. Judson denied that a valid federal law was enough to invalidate any provincial law dealing with the same matter, and he also denied that there is a "general domain" of criminal law that the constitution assigned to the federal Parliament, let alone one that shifted when Parliament expanded its legislative activities. The overlap between the two pieces of legislation was clear (but not complete, given that the provincial law included, as the federal law did not, the notion of "inadvertent negligence"), but "there is no conflict between these provisions in the sense that they are repugnant." It was enough that "the two pieces of legislation differed both in legislative purpose and legal and practical effect," and the appeal was dismissed. Only two earlier judicial decisions were considered in any detail, the first being a 1958 decision by the Ontario Court of Appeal (which reached a similar conclusion) and the second being the Supreme Court's own 1941 decision in *Egan*.[15]

Cartwright (with Locke) dissented. For one thing, Cartwright and Locke read *Egan* more narrowly than did the majority. For another, although they conceded that there was "little authority precisely on the point," they argued that federal criminal jurisdiction "must include the power to decide what conduct shall not be punishable ... as well as to decide what conduct shall be so punishable." This meant that the majority was wrong to find the provincial legislation to be more clearly legitimate because it went further than the federal legislation — the "inadvertent negligence" point. In fact, this point cut precisely the other way and triggered concerns about paramountcy: Parliament could have gone further but chose not to, and this "negative implication" was decisive. Finally, Cartwright and Locke thought the Court should take "judicial notice" of social facts, specifically the fact that Parliament had identified the number of automobile accidents occurring on the highway as a matter calling for national action.

This decision also demonstrates several features of the Kerwin Court. Most obvious is the decreasing fragmentation of the Court, with two clearly confronting views. The second is the fact that Judson, a new judge, was writing the majority decision (and demonstrating the emerging dominant bloc) in a case important enough for a nine-judge panel. The third is the "flatness" of the reasoning — the problem "is precisely the same" as one previously considered; the provincial legislative power "is undoubted." The fourth is the isolation of Cartwright and Locke, the only justices examining the issues in terms of policy consequences or social facts. In the end, the twenty-year-old rule from *Egan* was affirmed, but the case was still important because the stakes were so high. The test for paramountcy remained the simple one: Can the competing federal and provincial enactments live together and operate concurrently? Effectively, this is still the test today (even if *Egan* is more likely than *O'Grady* to be cited to make this point), although Bora Laskin (writing then as professor rather than as justice) grumbled that it is questionable whether it is "good policy in a federal system" to use such a casual formula.[16]

The third case, *R. v. George*,[17] involved a man accused of robbery with violence who was acquitted at trial on the grounds that he was too intoxicated to form the intent to commit the crime. The Crown appeal (dismissed by the British Columbia Court of Appeal) was based on the argument that the trial judge had failed to consider the included offence of common assault. A five-judge panel split three ways on outcome plus reasons, although in such a way as to create little ambiguity. Fauteux (with Taschereau) focused on whether the wording of the Criminal Code *required* the trial judge to consider the included offence, regardless of whether the Crown drew specific attention to it in the trial, or whether it merely *permitted* the trial judge to do so as an exercise of discretion. This argument had persuaded a divided British Columbia Court of Appeal, but Fauteux rejected it on the basis of an English decision that found that "so long ago as the year 1693," it had been judicially determined that "may" means "shall" (that is, that permission implies requirement) when a statute "authorizes the doing of a thing for the sake of justice."[18] The second question, whether intoxication precluded intentional robbery with violence but included common assault, was dealt with even more briefly and again on the basis of an English decision: "The rules for determining the validity of a defence of drunkenness have been stated by the House of Lords in the well known case of *Beard*."[19] Those rules made a distinction between crimes of *specific* intent — there is more to the crime of robbery than simply taking an object that does not belong to you — and crimes of *general* intent — the crime of common assault involves little more than bashing someone very severely. The Kerwin Court accepted that a person might be so drunk as not to be able to form the intent to steal something (as distinct from just taking it), but not so drunk as to be able to apply physical force other than intentionally. Indeed, this was so self-evident that Fauteux did not even send the case back for retrial but simply substituted a finding of guilt for the trial judge's acquittal and imposed a sentence of time served.

Ritchie (with Martland) wrote additional reasons that simply paralleled Fauteux in more mechanical language without in any way acknowledging the echo. On the permission/requirement issue, Ritchie simply declared that under the Criminal Code, "the learned trial judge was under a duty" to consider the included charge; and on the intention issue, he pointed to *Beard* as directing the conclusion that the trial judge's decision "constitutes a finding that the respondent violently manhandled a man and knew that he was hitting him." As to the outcome, he agreed with Fauteux. Locke alone dissented, finding on the basis of an earlier (1939) decision by Duff that the Crown's silence meant that it acquiesced in dropping the included charge and disagreeing that the earlier English decisions had any bearing on the question of requirement versus permission. This being the case, the central legal principle involved was whether a person could be subjected to "a succession of trials for the same offence," and Locke thought this would be contrary "to the public interest."

There are several elements of interest in the decision. The first is the transparent tone of "the English authorities have decided," with Fauteux explaining and Ritchie flatly declaring that the issue is settled beyond discussion by the precedents. Only Locke brought up policy issues and implications ("the public interest"), only Locke looked more closely at the English decision to see how far its shadow really reaches, and only Locke linked the matter to explicit legal values and principles. The second is the way that Ritchie/(Martland) simply duplicated Fauteux/(Taschereau) without adding anything significant; conferencing after oral argument (which the Supreme Court would not adopt for another decade) would presumably have created a four-judge majority decision with a single dissent. Finally, this case foreshadows the controversial 1992 Supreme Court decision in *R. v. Daviault*,[20] in which a divided Court found that contrary to *R. v. George* (and to an intervening case, *Leary v. The Queen*,[21] which had become the leading case on the issue), the defence of intoxication should be capable of being put before the jury even for a criminal charge involving general rather than specific intent. Part of the reason for this shift may be that the Kerwin Court saw the issue as one of whether the degree of drunkenness "created a condition tantamount to insanity," while the Lamer Court in 1992 was looking for parallels with the condition of automatism.

## The Most Influential Judges of the Kerwin Court

As suggested previously, judicial decisions not only highlight (through their use of citations) the most useful decisions and the most respected judges from the past, they also present themselves for the similar consideration of future judges. Table 4.4 demonstrates how often each judge was cited and how frequently each judge was directly named for decisions handed down during Kerwin's chief justiceship. This table contains an additional column, because unlike the "natural" Court of Rinfret, the Kerwin Court saw a considerable turnover. Half of the members of the Court served for the entire period, but others left the Court partway through (such as Estey), were appointed only in the closing days of the chief justiceship (such as Hall), or had their service cut short by death (such as Nolan). The shorter the service, the harder it is for an individual to have made an impact; the fourth column acknowledges this "handicap" by giving the number of days that each individual served under Kerwin and expressing it as a percentage of Kerwin's tenure as chief justice.

In absolute terms, the citation count and the overall "score" are led by the current chief justice and a future chief justice (Cartwright); however, taking into consideration the varying periods for which each member served changes the picture considerably. Rand stands fourth for absolute frequency of citation and a clear first for being named directly; extrapolated over a full 3138 days rather than the 1761 days that he actually served, he would have far outpaced both Kerwin and Cartwright. Almost as striking is the performance of one of the judges of the Diefenbaker trio, namely, Judson: his Kerwin Court decisions have been cited even more often than those of Rand, although he is directly named less often. Projecting his performance over the full period would put Judson second only to Rand, a striking accomplishment for a judge in his first few years on the Court. Martland's initial appearance is rather less dramatic, but correcting for the time served would put him comfortably in fifth place on the table. Leaving out the trio whose service period is too short to be comparable (Nolan, Estey, and Hall), Kellock and Abbott stand out as the members of the Kerwin Court who had the least enduring impact on the law.

## Conclusion

The previous chapter suggested that the Rinfret Court did not use its new independence to strike out in a bold new direction. That same comment can be extended to the Kerwin chief justiceship, which is

## Table 4.4

### Frequency with which Members of the Kerwin Court Are Subsequently Cited Reported Decisions, 1954–1999

| Judge | Number of times cited | Number of times named | "Score" | Days served (%) |
|---|---|---|---|---|
| Kerwin* | 238 | 64 | 302 | 3138 (100%) |
| Cartwright† | 204 | 77 | 281 | 3138 (100%) |
| Rand | 164 | 105 | 269 | 1761 (56%) |
| Judson | 188 | 73 | 261 | 1823 (58%) |
| Fauteux† | 160 | 46 | 206 | 3138 (100%) |
| Locke | 129 | 57 | 186 | 2999 (96%) |
| Taschereau† | 112 | 41 | 153 | 3138 (100%) |
| Martland | 96 | 39 | 135 | 1844 (59%) |
| Abbott | 50 | 30 | 80 | 3138 (100%) |
| Ritchie | 45 | 21 | 66 | 1369 (44%) |
| Kellock | 36 | 17 | 53 | 1294 (41%) |
| Nolan | 16 | 2 | 18 | 494 (16%) |
| Estey | 12 | 4 | 16 | 570 (18%) |
| Hall | 0 | 0 | 0 | 71 (2%) |

* indicates the current chief justice.
† indicates future chief justices.

hardly surprising given that Kerwin had been the leading member of the Rinfret Court.

The turnover as the Court renewed itself after the stability of the Rinfret years intensified rather than challenged this tendency. Gone were the colourful figures, such as Rand, Kellock, and Locke, who broadened the debate by presenting their own somewhat different approach in dissent or, more often, in separate concurrence. The new members of the Court, either because of their "juniority" or because of their different orientation to the judicial role (a question only time could answer), tended instead to contribute to a more unified decision-delivery style. The results of that shift are no longer appreciated; as Dale Gibson wrote in 1975, "(i)t is unlikely that anyone will ever feel nostalgic about the Supreme Court's performance during the 1960's."[22] In general terms, it meant shorter decisions, fewer citations, and (because of more unified decision delivery) less articulation of alternative or minority viewpoints on the legal issues. This might not have mattered if the Court had been more discursive in explaining itself, but its formal mechanical approach did not accomplish this; at the extreme, it approached (in Dale Gibson's telling phrase) "empty exercises in formal logic."[23]

This accentuation of style did not involve a shift in focus or direction. The Kerwin Court continued the work begun by the Rinfret Court in the gradual and cautious evolution of a Canadian jurisprudence that was not simply an echo of previous or current English decisions, and this is demonstrated by the "footprints" the Court has left in the form of its frequently cited decisions. With regard to constitutional law, for example, the *Stevedores Reference*[24] saw a slightly expanded view of the federal jurisdiction over navigation and shipping, and the *Farm Products Reference*[25] similarly contributed to a more robust view of the federal trade and commerce power. Meanwhile, the decisions in *Switzman*[26] and *Roncarelli* represented a tentative activism with regard to civil liberties, although this still did not build toward a clear position and it tended to reveal serious fault lines between the Quebec judges and the rest of the Court.

The Court's citation practices remain strong focused on the Judicial Committee and the other English courts, but this was beginning to shift toward the use of Canadian authorities, especially the Supreme Court itself. And the most prominent of those Canadian authorities was still former Chief Justice Duff, although by the end of the Kerwin Court, only a single member of the Court (Taschereau) had personally served under Duff. Reliance on Canadian authorities from a time when the Supreme Court was subject to appeal to the Judicial Committee may have been a roundabout way of remaining reliant on the Judicial Committee.

The Kerwin Court represents the first renewal of the Supreme Court. The early Kerwin Court, like the Rinfret Court before it, was almost entirely staffed by judges appointed in the 1940s, established in their ways and approaching the end of their careers. The later Kerwin Court was dominated (in numbers if not always in performance) by newly appointed judges. By comparison with the exactly contemporary Warren Court in the United States (and I cannot help assuming that the comparison coloured public perception of the Canadian Court), the Kerwin Court was still bland and gradualist, avoiding the strong policy role that the USSC had embraced. Hence this chapter's subtitle: a narrow and technical, rather than a broad and policy-oriented, approach was still the rule. There was, however, some incremental engagement of the potential for a truly supreme Supreme Court.

# The Taschereau/ Cartwright/Fauteux Court: April 1963 to December 1973 "The Caretakers"

Despite designating the chief justiceship as the appropriate time unit for discussing the Supreme Court, I will nonetheless treat the three chief justiceships that divide the Kerwin Court from the Laskin Court as a single composite period. Let me defend this decision.

First, these judges' terms as chief justice were unusually short. Cartwright served the shortest chief justiceship in the Court's history, the only one of fewer than 1000 days. Combined, the three lasted 10 years and 8 months — about the same as Duff, Rinfret, or Laskin, and slightly longer than Kerwin. Only five chief justices since 1875 have served terms shorter than 5 years; this composite period includes three of them. At no other time would a dozen years have included the entire term of two successive chiefs.

This is what happens when the chief justiceship is a reward for longevity, which has been the Canadian tradition, violated only twice before 1970. Bushnell[1] and Snell and Vaughan[2] indicate that all three times, the decision to make the most senior judge the new chief justice was treated routinely, despite health concerns (Taschereau) or impending retirement (Cartwright and Fauteux). One result has been short chief justiceships: in 1999, both the USSC and the Supreme Court of Canada were serving under their sixteenth chief justice, although the USSC is almost a century older.[3] Another is that people come to the leadership of the Court at the end rather than at the beginning of their energetic service, distracted by impending retirement and sometimes by poor health. The subtitle of this chapter is a little unfair — Cartwright made significant changes to the Court's procedures — but it correctly suggests another implication: the chiefs were not the Court's "real" leaders.

Second, these three were the only members of the Rinfret Court still serving at the end of the Kerwin Court. Taschereau had been appointed in 1940, Cartwright and Fauteux in 1949; they constituted, in Bushnell's phrase, the "old guard" on the Court.[4] Only with their departure would a second generation of judges tackle the challenges and opportunities of final appellate authority.

Third, apart from the centre chair, the decade saw very little change in membership. The only people to leave the Court were Taschereau and Cartwright (along with Hall in the closing months); the only new appointments were their replacements, Louis-Philippe Pigeon and Bora Laskin (along with Brian Dickson, also in the closing months). This continuity in personnel had very practical implications: the real focus of the decade was not the three individuals who rotated through the chief justiceship, but the three who formed the solid bloc at the centre — not Taschereau, Cartwright, and Fauteux, but Martland, Ritchie, and Judson. But this again unifies the three chief justiceships into a single period and justifies their coverage in a single chapter.

Historically, this Court corresponds with a period of contested Liberal dominance in national politics — "dominance" because they formed the government for the entire period and "contested" because only one of the four elections resulted in a majority. The early years saw the Gerda Munsinger affair, triggered by accusations that members of the Diefenbaker cabinet had jeopardized the security of Canada through their liaisons with a known security risk; it directly affected the Court when Wishart Spence conducted a one-man inquiry into the incident. International politics were dominated by the Vietnam War, which began to wind down in the closing years of the Fauteux Court. American politics ran the sequence from the Kennedy assassination, through Lyndon B. Johnson's single term, to Richard Nixon's reelection in 1972 and the Watergate scandal that began to unfold shortly afterward. The baby boomers came of age (or at least of college age); their protests and their challenges to established institutions defined a decade, even as their numbers began to transform postsecondary institutions and the workplace.

# The Personnel of the Taschereau/Cartwright/ Fauteux Court

The continuing members of the Court (in order of seniority) were Taschereau, Cartwright, Fauteux, Abbott, Martland, Judson, Ritchie, and Hall, but the period saw four new appointments.

**Wishart Flett Spence** of Ontario was appointed on May 30, 1963, replacing Kerwin. The first appointment of Lester Pearson's Liberal government, he had served for thirteen years as a judge of the Ontario High Court, before which he had practised law in Toronto and taught part-time at Osgoode Hall.[5] Both his academic connection and his reasonably lengthy judicial service marked departures from several decades of Supreme Court appointments. He was also unusual in having done postgraduate study in law in the United States, receiving a master's degree from Harvard; among his postpatriation predecessors, only Rand and J.W. Estey studied in the United States, although several subsequent members of the Court have done so. Spence was 59 years of age when appointed.

**Louis-Philippe Pigeon** was appointed on September 21, 1967, replacing Taschereau. He was the first of the series of Court-transforming appointments made by Pierre Trudeau (as minister of justice and as prime minister), and he was therefore indicative of the type of person who would be sent to the Court. Sixty-two years of age, he had practised law at Quebec City. He had no judicial experience, but had been a teacher of constitutional law at Laval University and an expert in the civil law, and he had served as a legal adviser to Jean Lesage. His reputation as a legislative draftsman and constitutional expert answered a growing desire for a more scholarly Court. The dominant civil law jurist during his years on the Court, he had a "pragmatic and incisive mind" and was "painstaking and meticulous in his work if somewhat ponderous,"[6] but notwithstanding his Liberal political connections, "his view of law and the legal process was definitely conservative."[7]

**Bora Laskin** was appointed on March 23, 1970, replacing retiring Chief Justice Cartwright. The 57-year-old son of Russian Jewish immigrants, he was the first person appointed to the Court who was not from either of the two major charter groups or a Christian. He was also an unusual choice in that he was identified almost completely as an academic — accepted, indeed, as one of Canada's foremost legal scholars — and lacked any major experience in private practice, something that had long been considered indispensable for service on the Court. He was the fourth member of the Court to have studied in the United States, having done a master's degree at Harvard before becoming a full-time professor of law at the University of Toronto and Osgoode Hall Law School. His appointment to the Ontario Court of Appeal in 1965 had also been controversial, and his service on that court was noted for his frequent dissenting judgments on a court that before and after him almost invariably delivered unanimous decisions. He was widely published as a law teacher, emphasizing an activist approach to the judicial role and a centralist vision of the constitutional division of powers. In retrospect, of course, it is easy to see this appointment as a critical turning point, but it was not clear at the time that he would have such an impact. Bushnell makes the point by comparing Laskin's appointment with that of Mills (who served from February 1902 to May 1903), also an intellectual and a constitutional scholar to the exclusion of private legal practice and also American-trained, but who was at best a "might have been" or a "lost opportunity" rather than a major influence.[8] As will be discussed below, Associate Justice Laskin (as distinct from Chief Justice Laskin) began with the frequent dissents that had marked his service on the Ontario Court of Appeal; only time would tell whether these would represent frustrated isolation or a foreshadowing of the Court's future.

**Robert George Brian Dickson** was appointed on March 26, 1973, becoming the fiftieth person to be appointed to the Supreme Court. Dickson, from Manitoba, replaced Saskatchewan's Emmett Hall, maintaining the western representation on the Court while continuing the tradition of rotation among the western provinces. Dickson was born and raised in Saskatchewan but attended the University of Manitoba and its law school, returning from wartime service in the Royal Canadian Artillery to practice corporate law in Winnipeg. He was appointed to the Manitoba Court of Queen's Bench in 1963 and elevated to the provincial Court of Appeal in 1967 before joining the Supreme Court at the age of 55.

Although the Taschereau/Cartwright/Fauteux Court had relatively little turnover (apart from a last-minute flurry that saw Hall replaced by Dickson and Abbot's unexpected retirement the same day that Fauteux retired early), the limited changes were enough to change the appearance of the Court. For the first time, the Court had a member who was neither French nor British, neither Protestant nor Catholic. The new appointments also tilted the balance toward judicial experience; over the previous twenty years, only a single appointment (Judson) had had as much prior service on the lower benches as Laskin or Spence. Finally, three consecutive appointments with strong academic credentials — in Laskin's case, to the virtual exclusion of practical legal experience — gave the Court a scholarly component that it had never before enjoyed. The question for the following decade was whether the changes would transform the Court or set the stage for internal conflict.

## The Caseload of the Taschereau/Cartwright/ Fauteux Court

The caseload of the Taschereau/Cartwright/Fauteux Court was slightly higher than that of the Kerwin Court, at about 100 cases per year. This said, there is little else to distinguish the two periods. The Exchequer Court accounted for about one-fifth of the caseload, and the two central provinces (with two-thirds of the population) accounted for just under one-half. Reversal rates were marginally higher, but no more so that could be explained by normal variation. The Ontario Court of Appeal was reversed the least often (38.2% of the time) and the Manitoba Court of Appeal the most often (49% of the time). There was an apparent deterioration in the performance of the Atlantic appeal courts, reversed one-quarter of the time by the Kerwin Court and three-quarters of the time now, but this is the product of a double illusion. First, for much of the period, there were no full-time courts of appeal in the Atlantic provinces, and even at the end of the period, when there were only two, appeals in those provinces were handled instead by *en banc* panels of trial judges. There could be no institutional failure because there were no institutions to fail. Second, the numbers involved — just over two dozen for each period — are too small to support meaningful generalization.

Private law appeals still accounted for a narrow majority of the caseload (50.2%), followed by public law appeals (32.6%) and criminal appeals (17.2%); all of these proportions are little changed from the Kerwin Court. For the first time, however, the reversal rates for criminal appeals (at 39.5%) were lower than those for public or private law cases (43.4% and 42.7%, respectively); this is a distinction that would persist. Out of a total docket of just over 1000, the three largest groups of cases were business and economic cases (294), tax cases (262, mostly involving income and corporation tax), and transportation cases (176, mostly involving automobiles). The low criminal caseload again meant that there was less in the way of serious violent crime cases than one might have expected: over eleven years, only 31 murders and 9 rapes.

## Decision-making by the Taschereau/Cartwright/ Fauteux Court

Average panel sizes remained low for the Taschereau/Cartwright/Fauteux Court, at just under 5.5. This suggests that five was the "normal" panel size, with larger panels for those cases that seemed to raise more important issues.[9] The full nine-judge panel was used for fewer than 10 percent of all cases — again, a striking contrast to the practices of the USSC, where a panel of fewer than the full nine judges has long been unusual. One reason for the small panels may have been the growing caseload: smaller panels gave the justices a more manageable workload.

As seemed to be promised by the more unified decision-making style of the closing years of the Kerwin Court, the Taschereau and Cartwright Courts continued to write fewer dissents, and especially fewer separate concurrences, than had been the practice in the early postwar years, although this was less true of the Fauteux Court. The evolution is striking. One-half of the decisions of the Rinfret Court were accompanied by more than two sets of reasons, and one-half of those had more than three. For the Kerwin Court, only one-fifth of decisions had more than two sets of reasons, and one-half of those more than three. But for the Taschereau/Cartwright/Fauteux period, only one case in twelve had more than two sets of reasons, and only one-third of those had more than three. Unanimity (especially unanimity at any cost) is not always good, and dissension is not always bad; the issues that come before the Supreme Court are too important for this to be credible. The point is that a more coherent focus for even divided decisions, with two sides addressing each other over a clear point of disagreement, provides more effective communication and leadership, and it was the practices of the Taschereau/Cartwright/Fauteux Court that first achieved this focus.

There is a rather obvious reason for this evolution. It was under Cartwright that the Court began the practice of regular judicial conferences after oral argument.[10] The point of conference is to have a preliminary discussion on the merits and, on the basis of the commonality or the division of opinion, to tentatively assign the responsibility for writing. If several judges are in fundamental agreement on outcome and reasons, it is more efficient for one of them to write the draft judgment for circulation and comment, and the same is true for judges who find themselves in the minority. This move toward collegiality, toward a consultative process leading to a coherent institutional position, is a major step away from the anarchic independence of the *seriatim* judgment. It seems surprising that it took the Supreme Court of Canada so long, the more so when U.S. Chief Justice John Marshall is widely famous for the parallel reform at the beginning of the nineteenth century.[11] On the other hand, the High Court of Australia had still not taken the step toward regular conferencing as late as the 1990s.[12]

But notice that the move is not neutral. The *seriatim* court is well-suited to applying long-standing legal principles to immediate disputes: if several judges pursue independent enquiries and reach the same outcome supported by similar reasons, this demonstrates that previously established neutral principles direct a particular outcome. In redundancy lies reassurance; in decentralized fragmentation lies protection. The conferencing court is better suited for coherent, systematic leadership and, particularly, for innovation. Which of these two is the better vehicle for the judicial function depends on what it is that you think judges ought to be doing. And this makes it rather ironic that a Court dominated by the traditional view should have made the move toward conferencing and the concomitant increasing unanimity of judgments. Ultimately, a more forceful and innovative chief justice would use this to take the Court in quite a different direction.

Table 5.1 looks at the participation of each member of the Court during the Taschereau/Cartwright/Fauteux period; as in other chapters, the table has a temporal dimension, because it adds new members in the order of their appointment. From the beginning of the period not very many of the judges dissented or wrote separate concurrences very often. Somewhat surprisingly, the major exception is the second of the three chief justices — this even though Cartwright frequently wrote for the Court and led the Court to the conferencing style that promotes more unified decisions. For the 40 percent or so of panel appearances that involved divided decisions, no member of the early Court was as likely as Cartwright to differ either from the reasons or from the outcome reached by the majority. Equally surprising is the fact that Judson was almost as likely to write or to join dissenting opinions — surprising because his first years on the Court suggested that he was a rising star with a leading role and because the central thrust of the Kerwin Court had been the Diefenbaker trio plus the Quebec trio.

## Table 5.1

### Dissents, Concurrences, and Decisions, by Judge
### Reported Supreme Court Decisions, 1963–1973

| Judge | Panels | Wrote decision | Contributed to decision | Divided panels | With majority | Conc. | Diss. |
|---|---|---|---|---|---|---|---|
| Taschereau | 159 | 13.2% | 17.0% | 57 | 82.5% | 3.5% | 14.0% |
| Cartwright | 404 | 29.0% | 46.8% | 157 | 48.4% | 19.7% | 31.8% |
| Fauteux | 425 | 21.6% | 24.7% | 146 | 78.1% | 7.5% | 14.4% |
| Abbott | 485 | 13.6% | 17.1% | 164 | 77.4% | 3.7% | 18.9% |
| Martland | 671 | 19.7% | 24.3% | 240 | 82.5% | 6.3% | 11.3% |
| Judson | 677 | 18.5% | 27.3% | 269 | 64.7% | 5.6% | 29.7% |
| Ritchie | 707 | 17.5% | 24.3% | 262 | 73.7% | 11.5% | 14.9% |
| Hall | 643 | 15.2% | 20.4% | 218 | 63.8% | 8.3% | 28.0% |
| Spence | 689 | 12.6% | 24.5% | 274 | 55.1% | 10.9% | 33.9% |
| Pigeon | 354 | 23.7% | 37.6% | 130 | 54.6% | 13.1% | 32.3% |
| Laskin | 185 | 18.9% | 44.9% | 84 | 31.0% | 19.0% | 50.0% |
| Dickson | 11 | 18.2% | 18.2% | 2 | 100.0% | 0% | 0% |
| ALL | 5410 | 18.2% | 26.7% | 2003 | 65.8% | 9.5% | 24.7% |

The table also makes it obvious that something important was happening in the early 1970s. At first glance, there seems to have been a central core to the Tachereau/Cartwright/Fauteux Court, built around Martland, Ritchie, Abbott, Taschereau, and Fauteux, but excluding Hall and all the more recent appointments, especially Laskin. This could be an indication either of an impending major shift (if the dissents and separate concurrences flowed from a common set of concerns) or of persisting low-grade fragmentation (if they did not). A closer consideration of these two alternative possibilities follows.

## Voting Blocs on the Taschereau/Cartwright/Fauteux Court

The nature of the post-Kerwin Court hinged on two questions: First, would the six-judge voting block hold together when the Diefenbaker trio gained confidence and experience? Second, if it did hold together, who would lead it? The answer to the first question is simple: the bloc held together extremely well. The Quebec trio remained solid, the three inter-judge pairings signing on together an average of 88 percent of the time; the Diefenbaker trio similarly held firm, signing on together 86 percent of the time (with Judson being the weak link). But the cross-trio pairings within the six-judge group were higher yet, averaging 89 percent, and the main explanation for this is the very strong rate of agreement between Martland and each of the three Quebec judges. (Only five two-judge pairings showed an agreement rate over 90 percent; the strongest was Martland/Ritchie at 93.5 percent, the next three linked Martland to each of the three Quebec judges, and the last joined Fauteux/Abbott.)

The answer to the second question is more complex. These patterns highlight the central role of Martland, but not in the sense that Martland always led and everyone else followed. In general, if Justice A frequently agrees with Justice B, then there are three possible explanations: A is following B, B is following A, or both are following someone else. But if we can make the same observation about Justice A and Justice C, and then again of Justice A and Justice D, and then again of Justice E, it becomes increasingly clear that there is something very significant about Justice A. Martland *was* Justice A. Four members of the Court (Taschereau, Fauteux, Ritchie, and Pigeon) agreed with Martland more often than with anyone else; one (Cartwright) gave Martland his second highest agreement rate; and for the remainder (Abbott, Spence, Judson, Hall, and even Laskin), Martland ranked third. All of these except Laskin and Pigeon signed on with Martland more often than vice versa, which rules out the possibility (surely a remote one in any event) that Martland was a passive follower.

It seems to me that the best explanation is to see Martland as having gradually made himself the focus around which the Court frequently organized itself. Over these eleven years, he wrote more decisions than anyone else on the Court. Equally revealing is that he wrote separate opinions (dissents or separate concurrences) less often than anyone else on the Court except Taschereau and only half as often as the all-Court average. In this respect, his performance is reminiscent of Kerwin, who arguably led the Rinfret Court before becoming chief justice himself, except that Martland's leadership was of an increasingly unified Court and his supporting coalition seems to have been both larger and more solid. For reasons that go beyond mere seniority, there are grounds for thinking of Martland as a "chief justice in waiting" — and down this track lie the problems of the next decade.

The centre of gravity of the Taschereau/Cartwright/Fauteux Court was Martland; his closest ally was Ritchie, closely followed by the Quebec trio of Fauteux, Abbott, and Taschereau and then, more tentatively and less reliably, by Judson. When Pigeon replaced

Taschereau, the alliance became a little weaker (the agreement rates between Pigeon and the other members of the group put him just outside Judson), but Pigeon was still more likely to sign on with Martland than with any other member of the Court. Cartwright was on the fringes of this group; his most reliable ally was Hall, but Martland was second. This situation of being on the fringes of the fairly solid core of the Court helps to explain Cartwright's somewhat anomalous position: on the one hand, he delivered much more than a one-ninth share of the decisions; on the other hand, when the Court divided, he was usually outside the core and frequently in dissent.

If this was the "in" group, what did the "out" group look like? At first glance, the "decision-making" table (Table 5.1) seems to point to a group of later additions who wrote more than their share of dissents and separate concurrences. Hall and Spence were there from the beginning; they were apparently joined by Pigeon and then by Laskin, which logically sets up a 5–4 confrontation, with everything hinging on the next appointment. But this appearance is misleading, mainly because of Pigeon; if he did not simply replace Taschereau within the core group, neither did he make common cause with any of the other outsiders. Laskin drew Pigeon's support less often (and Martland did so more often) than did any other member of the Court.[13] Laskin's numbers clearly put him in his own corner for the three years that he was on the Court, frequently dissenting and often doing so alone. His most reliable support came from Hall (who sided with Laskin on almost 60 percent of the divided panels on which they sat) and, to a lesser extent (45 percent of divided panels), from Spence. But this "proto-faction" challenging the Martland/Ritchie core lost one-third of its membership when Hall retired early in 1973, and whatever may have been the case during the Laskin Court itself, the Laskin/Spence agreement rates between 1970 and 1973 were modest rather than impressive. Laskin's early participation shows him on the fringes of the Fauteux Court, frequently dissenting, more ready than anyone else to write separate opinions, less likely to sign on to the decision of any of his colleagues. In this sense, he looks very much like Rand, although Rand served on more routinely fragmented Courts while Laskin was much more the "odd man out."

But the important questions, of course, are what these voting patterns mean and what is at stake if one group rather than another tends to prevail most of the time. The next chapter will describe the "Laskin Revolution" that transformed the Supreme Court, but we can only really talk about a revolution if we can describe the old regime that was displaced. Commentators often contrast "the sixties" with "the fifties." For example, Gibson describes the judges of the sixties as "showing a much greater tendency to concur silently and to employ the 'formal manner' of reasoning with no indication of the policy considerations underlying their decisions."[14] He concludes: "If Mr. Justice Rand embodied the spirit of the fifties, Mr. Justice Ronald Martland seems to have been the archetypal judge of the sixties."[15] Similarly, Paul Weiler suggests that "the philosophical orientation of the Supreme Court changed direction sharply, sometime around the year 1960,"[16] this shift involving a move from a policy-oriented to a formalist style.

My own take is somewhat more nuanced. I would say that there was a centre of gravity to the jurisprudential style of the Supreme Court from (at least) 1949 right through until late in the Laskin Court. The changes in the chief justiceship were simply episodes within this general continuity. The major difference between the sixties and the fifties was the loss of the mildly independent voices on the edge of the Court (Rand, Kellock, and Locke), who frequently broadened the debate without constituting the central direction of the Court. In the sixties, these figures had been replaced by new judges who joined, and then embodied, the more traditional style.

The central elements of this continuity were firm fidelity to the established principles of the law and a scrupulous regard for the hierarchical structure of the courts. The greatest virtue of the law was predictability enhanced by a strict adherence to the prior decisions of higher courts, which means embracing both the binding authority of the Supreme Court's own prior decisions and the continuing rigour of the Judicial Committee's prepatriation cases. (Not until 1976 would the Supreme Court, in the person of Chief Justice Laskin, declare that previous Judicial Committee decisions were no longer necessarily binding.) "We once thought X, but we now say Y" is the very antithesis of predictability and therefore to be avoided. Somewhat paradoxically, this decision-making style combines a readiness to find strong statements of basic principle in prior decisions with a reluctance to make any such statements "up front" in the immediate case. This makes these decisions rather dull reading, and it is sometimes perplexing to follow through on a citation by reading the earlier case from which the principle is ostensibly drawn.[17]

Something of the mood and the philosophy of this approach can be found in a 1950 decision[18] delivered (for a unanimous Court) by Chief Justice Rinfret:

It is fundamental to the due administration of justice that the authority of decisions be scrupulously respected by all courts upon which they are binding. Without this uniform and consistent adherence the administration of justice becomes disordered, the law becomes uncertain, and the confidence of the public in it undermined. Nothing is more important than that the law as pronounced, including the interpretation by this Court of the decisions of the Judicial Committee, should be accepted and applied as our tradition requires; and even at the risk of that fallibility to which all judges are liable, we must maintain the complete integrity of the relationship between the courts.

The term that describes this style is *formalism,* because it involves a reliance on formal and mechanical rules for extracting meaning from written documents, including statutes and the written document that is the constitution. Bushnell cogently contrasts this formalist approach to interpretation with the more recent *contextualist* approach that requires the Court to look at social context and legislative history and practical impact of a statute; but the Taschereau/Cartwright/ Fauteux Court exhibited a "demonstrated hostility" to litigants seeking to present evidence of legislative facts.[19] The result is a curious flatness in the mode of judicial explanation: the text is rigorously examined and court decisions bearing on it are tersely cited, not as a springboard to a consideration of the real-world implications of the rule but as constituting the conclusion in themselves. For Gibson, this style is characterized by "cautious pragmatism" and "terse and technical exposition"[20] that could collapse into "empty exercises in formal logic."[21]

But if the objectivity of complete predictability is the goal, rather than the more subjective exercise of discretion, then this is best served by a formalist procedure that treats statutes and constitutions as documents to be interpreted mechanically and that refuses to "look behind" the statute to find things that do not appear on its face. At the heart of formalism, suggests Frederick Shauer, "lies the concept of decisionmaking according to rule."[22] Judges write their opinions "as if there is already an established legal rule which binds them" and which "is applied because the law requires it, not because the judges believe it is a desirable rule."[23] The core of this process is the self-limitation of the judicial decision-maker, who is consciously and voluntarily constrained from looking at the broader issues and implications that the contextualist sees as an interpretive element of the law itself.

This style is exemplified by an article that Pigeon wrote before joining the Court: "The question is, not what may be supposed to have been intended, but what has been said."[24] The givenness of the text constitutes "a fundamental rule of legal interpretation," and for Pigeon "law emanates from the inherent words of a text" rather than from any potentially subjective exploration of the drafter's intent.[25] This creates a narrow focus that takes the statute (or the section of the constitution) at its absolute face value, as the words appear on the page, rather than creating a discretionary zone that permits the shading of meaning in order to arrive at a preferred policy outcome. This is no longer the way we think of the judicial role — as L'Heureux-Dubé says, the "modern contextual approach" is today "the standard, normative approach to judicial interpretation"[26] — but it is a coherent and intellectually defensible position that long directed many of the members of the Supreme Court. And it represents the "before" to which the Laskin Revolution is the "after."

## Citation Practices of the Taschereau/Cartwright/ Fauteux Court

Because I have emphasized the continuities between the Taschereau/ Cartwright/Fauteux Court and its predecessors and stressed the revolutionary transformations yet to come, it is rather surprising to note that this Court's citation practices differ in ways that are intriguing and promising.

### *From where did the Supreme Court Get its Citations?*

The basic pattern of the Taschereau/Cartwright/Fauteux Court's citation practices is shown in Table 5.2, but of course, the meaning lies in the way these numbers compare with the predecessor Rinfret and Kerwin Courts. There are several important trends.

First and most important, the legacy of the Judicial Committee was finally fading; its proportion of total citations was down by almost half. This is all the more significant because the citations-per-year count of the Taschereau/Cartwright/Fauteux Court was actually lower than that of the Kerwin Court (about 400 per year, down from 500 per year), so it is not the case that a strong ongoing presence was simply being diluted by higher volumes. The fact that the median date of a Judicial Committee citation was virtually unchanged suggests that the cited cases were being drawn from the same general

### Table 5.2

### Citations to Judicial Authority by the Taschereau/ Cartwright/Fauteux Court Reported Decisions, 1963–1973

| Source | Number | Frequency | Median Date |
|---|---|---|---|
| Judicial Committee | 300 | 7.6% | 1927 |
| Supreme Court of Canada | 1538 | 38.8% | 1954 |
| Other English Courts | 997 | 25.2% | 1925 |
| Other Canadian Courts | 963 | 24.3% | 1951 |
| U.S. Courts | 121 | 3.1% | 1943 |
| Other | 44 | 1.1% | 1929 |

pool and not from the ongoing jurisprudence of the Judicial Committee flowing from its continuing relationship to countries such as Australia.

Citations to other English courts were also down, from just over one in every three to just under one in every four. The median date of an English decision had come forward almost two decades from the citations of the Kerwin Court, not only keeping pace with the passage of time but pulling closer, which suggests that the venerable common law precedents were being supplemented — it would be too much to say "replaced" — by citations to more contemporary English decisions and to judges such as Lord Denning.[27]

The flip side of the falling rate of citation to English authorities was an increase in the citation to Canadian authorities, primarily to the Supreme Court itself. Citation to prior Supreme Court decisions was now the largest single category among the sources of judicial authority, having jumped fully 10 percent (from 29% to 39%) since the Kerwin Court. The median date for a Supreme Court citation had also continued to move forward to 1954 — that is to say, to after the end of appeals to the Judicial Committee, although the average age of a Supreme Court citation was unchanged from the Kerwin Court.

Citations to other (lower) Canadian courts also increased modestly, enough for them to exceed the count for all English courts other than the Judicial Committee. As indicated earlier, these citations should not be thought of as perfunctory or as the pointing out of lower-court mistakes. Canadian sources, which had provided just over one-half of the judicial authorities of the Kerwin Court, now provided closer to two-thirds. The centre of gravity of Canadian jurisprudence was clearly shifting away from its English origins.

Citations to other sources (including the United States) remained so low as to be negligible. To be sure, the percentage share of American citations had doubled, but this was only from 1.5 percent to 3.1 percent (from six references a year to eleven), so it would be unrealistic to read very much into this. The gradual but pronounced decline of British influence was being filled, not by another external source, but from within. The residual "other" category remained even lower, still comprised of sporadic references to Australian and New Zealand courts.

### The Supreme Court Cites the Supreme Court: Who and What?

As shown in Table 5.3, the Taschereau/Cartwright/Fauteux Court marked another milestone: for the first time, Duff was displaced from the top spot for simple citation count, although he was directly named frequently enough to edge out Cartwright for the highest "score." Again, the list is dominated by most of the current members, including all three of the chief justices, and by former chief justices (Duff, Kerwin, Rinfret, Anglin). Rand alone made the top twelve despite being neither a current member nor a chief justice. All three members of the Diefenbaker trio (and Hall as well) are on the list, and their leader is clearly Judson. As for the Rinfret and Kerwin Courts, the list is dominated by current members and recent chief justices, with the balance continuing to swing toward the former.

The cases most frequently cited by the Taschereau/Cartwright/Fauteux Court no longer included a single decision by Duff but were instead dominated by the string of postwar chief justices. More than one-half of the dozen most frequently cited cases were handed down in the 1960s (but only three after Taschereau became chief justice), and one-half had been delivered by judges still serving on the bench; conversely, only three predated the end of appeals to the Judicial Committee. It is still the case that half-a-dozen English decisions would also have made the list had the count included cases from all sources, but (unlike for the earlier Courts) they would not have swamped the list.

I had expected that the citation patterns would lead me to a small core of pivotal decisions, gradually changing as some cases dropped off and others (presumably, but not necessarily, newer) were added, but the most frequently cited decisions of these successive chief justiceships show no such core. The explanation is rather obvious:

## Table 5.3

### Supreme Court of Canada Judges Most Frequently Cited by the Taschereau/Cartwright/Fauteux Court Reported Cases, Supreme Court of Canada, 1963–1973

| Judge | Number of times cited | Number of times named | "Score" |
|---|---|---|---|
| Duff[†] | 144 | 92 | 236 |
| Cartwright[*†] | 160 | 62 | 222 |
| Kerwin[†] | 133 | 48 | 181 |
| Judson[*] | 105 | 46 | 151 |
| Fauteux[*†] | 111 | 36 | 147 |
| Martland[*] | 92 | 32 | 124 |
| Rinfret[†] | 87 | 34 | 121 |
| Rand | 65 | 39 | 104 |
| R. Taschereau[*†] | 65 | 29 | 94 |
| Anglin[†] | 59 | 33 | 92 |
| Ritchie[*] | 57 | 24 | 81 |
| Hall[*] | 43 | 11 | 54 |

\* indicates a member of the current Court.
† indicates a past or current chief justice.

the jurisdiction of the Supreme Court covers all lower courts and all areas of Canadian law. Within any specific area of law, there may well be a handful of leading cases; current examples would include the "family law trio,"[28] the "damages trilogy,"[29] the "bankruptcy quartet,"[30] and the "administrative tribunal Charter trilogy."[31] So many streams, however, were feeding into the Supreme Court caseload that no small set of decisions could anchor the doctrinal explanations, at least not (as we shall see) until the rise of Charter jurisprudence and the handful of "mega-precedents" around which it is organized.

The concept of a decay rate assumes that the typical Supreme Court decision will gradually be cited less often as it gets older and that the rate of that decline is more or less constant. The higher the decay rate, the more rapidly the Court is replacing long-standing landmark decisions with more recent reformulations or clarifications. In this respect, the Kerwin Court (with a decay rate of 10%) was demonstrably more ready to use recent precedent than was the Rinfret Court (with a decay rate of 3.5%). But the Taschereau/Cartwright/ Fauteux Court refutes the appearance of a trend; its decay rate was lower than the Kerwin Court's, but not so low as the Rinfret Court's. At 6.7 percent, it suggests that the average Supreme Court decision would receive one-half of its lifetime citations within 10 years (up from 6.6 years for the Kerwin Court). The swing from English to Canadian citations suggests that the Court was responding to a developing Canadian jurisprudence, but the low decay rate suggests that it was not doing so in a consciously innovative way and that the Canadian precedents on which it drew tended to be somewhat dated.

## Major Decisions of the Taschereau/Cartwright/ Fauteux Court

The most frequently cited decisions of the Taschereau/Cartwright/Fauteux Court show both continuity and innovation in the way the Court organized itself to deal with major issues. *Drybones*[32] is perhaps the most famous — or at least, most widely recognized — of the Taschereau/Cartwright/Fauteux Court's decisions, representing the highpoint of the Court's Bill of Rights jurisprudence. It involved a man convicted for being "an Indian[33] unlawfully intoxicated off a reserve,"[34] the charge deriving from s.94(b) of the Indian Act. On appeal, Mr. Justice W.G. Morrow of the Territorial Court had reversed and acquitted, on the grounds that the provision violated the Canadian Bill of Rights, and his decision was upheld by the Northwest Territories Court of Appeal.

The Supreme Court divided on the issue, a nine-judge panel delivering five different sets of reasons for judgment, three of which were dissents. The majority decision was delivered by Ritchie, joined by Fauteux, Martland, Judson, and Spence. In what would today count as a very terse explanation, taking up only 5½ pages,[35] he conceded that the Bill of Rights did not explicitly authorize the Courts to invalidate statutes but simply gave advice on how to interpret them, but he concluded that it would "strike at the very foundations" of the Bill to ignore it whenever the "plain meaning" of a statute suggested something else, and he also rejected the "frozen rights" argument that would have the effect of protecting people against future rights violations but not against past ones. He was drawn to this conclusion, however, only because the statute made it "an offence punishable by law" for some Canadians to do something that Canadians of other races could do with impunity, and he did not "by any means" intend his comments to apply to the Indian Act more generally. In the course of his argument, he cited very little case law, except to explain how this case fit in with the prior decision of *Robertson & Rosetanni v.*

*The Queen.*[36] Hall wrote an even briefer, single-page separate concurrence, the main thrust of which was to place the case against the
background of American jurisprudence, specifically the "historic
desegregation case" of *Brown v. Board of Education.*[37]

The dissenters took a narrower view. Cartwright, in two pages,
saw no language specifically instructing the courts to ignore statutes
or to declare them inoperative simply because their plain language
infringed on declared rights or freedoms, and he acknowledged the
"error in my reasoning" when he had suggested otherwise in *Robertson & Rosetanni.* Pigeon's somewhat longer remarks (almost four
pages) gruffly endorsed the "frozen rights" concept as well as affirming legislative supremacy: "There can be no doubt that in enacting
legislation Parliament is presumed to be aware of the state of the
law." And Abbot's terse single paragraph in dissent described the
Bill of Rights as no more than a "canon or rule of interpretation" for
legislation.

At first glance, this is very promising, a firm stepping stone to a
robust reading of the Bill of Rights; the Diefenbaker trio was solidly
on side, even delivering the decision, and unlike in the major civil
rights cases of the 1950s, a senior French-Canadian judge had joined
them. In fact, it did not turn out this way, and *Drybones* stands almost
on its own as a Bill of Rights success. Ritchie and his allies meant
exactly what they said; they found it offensive to think that if two
men, one of whom was an Indian, stood side by side and committed
identical acts, then the Indian could be charged and the other could
not; but in any less clear-cut situation, the Bill was a simple guide
to interpretation.

*Calder v. Attorney-General of B.C.*[38] was one of the first Canadian
cases to raise the matter of Aboriginal title to land. The Nisga'a tribe
in northern British Columbia had never been conquered and never
signed a treaty. Concerned that the provincial government was permitting commercial activities (mineral exploration, forestry rights,
and tree farm licences) within the territory that they considered their
own, they approached the courts for a declaration that the Aboriginal
title to their ancient tribal territory had never been lawfully extinguished. When they lost in the lower courts, they brought their claim
before the Supreme Court, which split over the issue.

Judson, with the support of Martland and Ritchie (the full Diefenbaker trio), found that the Nisga'a were not covered by the Royal
Proclamation of 1763, which recognized Aboriginal title and a duty
to negotiate, because they had not come under British sovereignty

until 1846. He conceded that there was an Aboriginal title — "The fact is that when the settlers came, the Indians were there, organized in societies and occupying the land as their forefathers had done for centuries. This is what Indian title means ..." — but a series of proclamations by the colonial government indicated that it had "elected to exercise complete dominion over the lands in question, adverse to any right of occupancy which the Nisga'a Tribe might have had," and because the Aboriginal title was "dependent on the goodwill of the Sovereign," these actions were sufficient to extinguish the Aboriginal right. The Nisga'a claim was therefore refused.

On the other side, Hall, with Spence and Laskin, wrote longer reasons that disagreed on all fronts. He thought that the Royal Proclamation did apply (the relevant phrase being "all the Lands and Territories lying to the Westward"), and in any event, the treaty process in the western provinces was a "gross fraud" unless there was an Indian title to be extinguished. But such a title can be extinguished only by treaty or by specific legislation; ordinances by the governor are not enough, particularly in the absence of specific authorization from the British Crown. Therefore, the Nisga'a claim was upheld.

Both judicial trios agreed that there was an Aboriginal title that could survive the establishment of British sovereignty. They differed on whether that title had subsequently been extinguished and also on whether the Royal Proclamation of 1763 applied west of the Rockies. With a three–three tie, the issue was joined and the question was which side Pigeon would come down on; the answer was neither. Pigeon found that British Columbia (unlike the federal government and most provinces) had never passed legislation removing its sovereign immunity from being sued without giving its permission. There having been no such permission, the Court had no jurisdiction to grant the declaration. Although he was "deeply conscious of the hardship involved" in this finding, he had no choice.

This nicely shows the Court in transition. In some ways, it was the Court's style on major cases from Rinfret on. There was a panel so badly divided that it could not produce a majority behind a reasoned outcome, and the deciding vote was cast in such a way that it did not address, let alone fully resolve, the issues that divided the rest of the panel. A fundamental issue was addressed in ways that would prove fruitful for later Courts, raising arguments and problems that remain cogent, but the final decision was driven by a mechanical reasoning process that focused on technical details and resolutely ignored practical consequences. In other ways, this is the "new" style of the Court emerging: fundamental issues are addressed, and disagreements take the form of the two sides hearing and responding directly to the points raised by the other, canvassing English, American, Canadian, and Australian jurisprudence, as well as a wide range of historical documents. The decision is also modern for the fact that it is so long — almost 120 pages. Its inconclusive result notwithstanding, *Calder* was a springboard to the jurisprudence of the 1980s and 1990s in a way that *Drybones* could not be.

*The Queen v. Wray*[39] was one of the last decisions of the Cartwright Court; indeed, by the time the decision was delivered on June 26, 1970, Cartwright had been retired for three months. This was a murder case in which the police had persuaded the accused to sign a statement; although their methods meant that the statement was not admissible in evidence, the statement gave the police information that allowed them to recover the murder weapon. The question was whether the weapon could be admitted as evidence. The trial judge said that it could not and therefore directed a verdict of not guilty; the Crown appealed all the way to the Supreme Court.

In this the age of the Charter, of course, the question would be different (not "did the judge have discretion" but "was the evidence capable of being admitted") and the answer would be easy (it was not); but this was 1970, not 1982. Martland, with the support of Fauteux, Abbott, Ritchie, and Pigeon, found that the trial judge's discretion did not stretch as far as this particular judge had suggested. The argument proceeded by the way of a close examination, including lengthy quotation from a series of decisions of the House of Lords, the Judicial Committee, and a number of Canadian courts. It concluded by making a distinction between unfairness in the method of obtaining evidence of "unimpeachable probative value" (in which case the evidence should be admitted) and "unfairness" in the actual trial, involving evidence of "little probative value, but of great prejudicial effect" (in which case the evidence should be excluded). Both of these followed from the notion of a fair trial and neither involved a discretionary authority by the trial judge. Cartwright, on the other hand, went through precisely the same cases and found a thread of argument growing out of the principle that no accused person is bound to incriminate himself, leading to the conclusion not only that a discretion exists for the trial judge but that its exercise is not open to review on an appeal by the Crown. Hall and Spence each wrote brief separate dissents, agreeing with Cartwright and emphasizing some points in his analysis.

Martland's decision in *R. v. Wray* is still one of the most frequently cited decisions of the period, but in a way that illustrates the Court's change in direction. In the recent case of *R. v. Burlingham*,[40] for example, L'Heureux-Dubé, in dissent, criticized her colleagues for their decision regarding the exclusion of evidence; the charge that their position was "reminiscent of *Wray*" was a rebuke stinging enough to draw the unusual response of having one member of the majority (Sopinka) write a short supplementary comment refuting the accusation.

## Most Influential Members of the Taschereau/Cartwright/Fauteux Court

The decisions handed down by the Taschereau/Cartwright/Fauteux Court have (as of June 30, 1999) been cited just over 2000 times, and just over 700 times, the specific judge who delivered the reasons was identified by name. As in earlier chapters, the citation count and the naming count have been turned into a notional "score" that ranks the members of the Court. And as with the Kerwin Court, the modest degree of turnover calls for a fourth column that indicates how much of the combined chief justiceship each individual judge served.

The most influential judges on the Court were two members of the Diefenbaker trio (Ritchie and Martland, almost tied in the standings) and two of the three chief justices (Cartwright and Fauteux), with Cartwright's showing being significantly more impressive, given that he served for less than two-thirds of the period. This confirms my general description: Martland/Ritchie tended to lead the Court, especially when it divided, but as much in cooperation with as "over the top of" the chief justice of the day.

At the other end of the table (leaving out Dickson because of his short service) is the continuing low profile of Abbott. Even more striking is Taschereau's dismal showing, which remains marginal even when discounted for the fact that he served just over one-third of the period. This confirms the concerns with his health and other problems that made his selection as chief justice problematic, the contrast heightened by the greater relative prominence that he had shown on earlier Courts. Judson places in the middle of the table, but this still marks a striking slide from his stellar performance in the closing years of the Kerwin Court. Laskin was clearly beginning to leave a mark on the Court's jurisprudence that his apparent isolation

## Table 5.4

### Frequency with which Members of the Taschereau/Cartwright/Fauteux Court Are Subsequently Cited Reported Decisions, 1963–1999

| Judge | Number of times cited | Number of times named | "Score" | Days served (%) |
|-------|------|------|------|------|
| Ritchie | 310 | 103 | 413 | 3897 (100%) |
| Martland | 316 | 96 | 412 | 3897 (100%) |
| Cartwright* | 245 | 93 | 338 | 2526 (65%) |
| Fauteux* | 225 | 71 | 296 | 3897 (100%) |
| Judson | 209 | 74 | 283 | 3897 (100%) |
| Spence | 175 | 66 | 241 | 3859 (99%) |
| Pigeon | 163 | 66 | 229 | 2284 (59%) |
| Hall | 156 | 55 | 211 | 3600 (92%) |
| Laskin[†] | 136 | 66 | 202 | 1370 (35%) |
| Abbott | 69 | 25 | 94 | 3897 (100%) |
| Dickson[†] | 38 | 14 | 52 | 271 (7%) |
| Taschereau* | 11 | 3 | 14 | 1592 (41%) |

* indicates the current chief justices.
† indicates future chief justices.

in the decision-making process did not suggest; extrapolated over a full 3900 days, he would have led the Court.

## Conclusion

The Taschereau/Cartwright/Fauteux period generally represents a formalization and intensification of the practices of the early 1960s. The trend toward more unified decisions continued, with fewer dissents, fewer separate concurrences, and shorter decisions. The motor of this development was the emergence of a stable bloc that provided the Court's centre of gravity, roughly the Quebec trio plus the Diefenbaker trio, although the replacement of Taschereau with Pigeon and the gradual detachment of Judson qualify this simplification. Martland and Ritchie were generally the leaders of this central bloc, which is not to deny the more contested influence of Cartwright. The emergence of this stable pattern was facilitated by slower turnover of one new face every three years, providing new blood without undermining stability and continuity.

The rotation through the chief justiceship of three very senior members of the Court would seem to militate against any development of a strong new direction — and yet Cartwright's institution of regular judicial conferencing after oral argument represented a critical change in the Court's operations. It facilitated the emergence of a coherent centre bloc whose very size had a stifling effect on the diversity of views that many had come to expect from the more fragmented early Court. It also pointed to a Court more capable of strategic coordination and, potentially, innovation. Nor does an emphasis on the solid central block deny the voices that spoke from the margins — Hall, Spence, and, eventually, Laskin.

If there was a central thrust or logic to the period, it is best captured by the notion of formalism discussed earlier — a strong commitment to *stare decisis,* combined with a narrow conception of the judicial function focused on textual analysis rather than on policy consequences. Certainly, this position was attractive to the Quebec judges, aware of the potential dangers of an aggressively innovative institution within which the Québécois point of view would always be outnumbered; *stare decisis* and strong textual analysis provide a good way of ensuring a truly supreme Supreme Court that would neither surprise nor upset. This predilection toward reticence nicely explains the Court's approach to the Canadian Bill of Rights, a document of ambivalent constitutional status that could have been rendered robust only by the exercise of a degree of long-term strategy and cautious flexibility that the Court had never yet achieved.

Paradoxically, the Court combined a strong emphasis on precedent with a significant shift in the sources from which those precedents were sought. For the first time, there was a sharp drop in both Judicial Committee and other English citations, the gap filled with the Supreme Court's own prior decisions. Those decisions were now more likely to be drawn from the Court's more recent decisions; although Duff remained the most frequently cited judge, the second rank was comprised of current members of the Court: Cartwright, Judson, Fauteux, and Martland. As with the adoption of conferencing, the Court's citations indicated a potential openness to a new role and style that was not yet being fully embraced.

In general, the Court's performance was low-key and low-profile; it was generally attacked more for what it had *not* done (or had not done sufficiently vigorously) than for anything offensive or controversial that it *had* done. On the constitutional front, it presided over "a considerable expansion of provincial legislative jurisdiction," although this generally took the form less of cutting back on explicitly federal jurisdiction than of permitting the provinces a de facto concurrent power in areas in which the federal government was not active.[41] With regard to civil liberties, the Supreme Court was "very unsympathetic"[42] — this in contrast to the somewhat tentative but mildly promising string of civil rights cases the 1950s.

The Taschereau/Cartwright/Fauteux Court represents the clear emergence of a new status quo, a solid dominant block on the Court behind the clear leadership of Martland and Ritchie. At the same time, however, it included a significant minority fragment increasingly organized behind Laskin, the man (to exaggerate only slightly) who taught the Ontario Court of Appeal how to write dissents. Laskin could have been a latter-day replay of Rand, a significant voice from the margin of the Court, but instead he was about to become the surprise choice for the new chief justice. As a result, the new status quo for the Court was about to turn into the new battleground, with the role, status, and direction of the Court hanging in the balance. The truly supreme Supreme Court was finally becoming a major player in Canadian public life, but the transition was far from smooth.

# The Laskin Court: December 1973 to March 1984 "The Revolutionary"

Bora Laskin's chief justiceship was a watershed; "before Laskin" and "after Laskin" are the periods into which the half-century divides. Turnover was one source of change (nine appointments in eleven years), particularly as Trudeau transformed the credentials of a typical Supreme Court justice, but it was several years before the revolving door gave Laskin effective control. He spent the early part of his chief justiceship writing vigorous dissents, some eventually becoming established doctrine[1] and some not.[2] Also important was the 1975 amendment to the Supreme Court Act, which expanded the Court's leave jurisdiction. Laskin had a major impact on the decision-making process, resulting in larger panels with less fragmentation of written decisions.[3] It was under his leadership that the Supreme Court emerged as a significant presence on the national scene: the decision in the *Patriation Reference*[4] was shown live on national television. Before Laskin, we did not, and after Laskin we do, take for granted a Supreme Court of leadership, innovation, and high visibility. This is what a true watershed looks like.

Laskin's chief justiceship was completely contained by Pierre Trudeau's tenure as prime minister of Canada: Laskin became chief justice during Trudeau's minority government of 1972–74 (followed by a majority win in 1974, the Joe Clark interregnum of 1979, and the majority comeback of 1980), and his chief justiceship ended a few weeks after Trudeau decided to step down during his February 29 "walk in the snow." Laskin was chief justice during both the 1976 election of the Parti Québécois (PQ) and the 1980 sovereignty-association referendum — that is to say, during the heightening of the tensions between Quebec and the rest of Canada that had been triggered by the 1960s' Quiet Revolution. Major news in international affairs included the Camp David agreement, which signalled a promising peace process in the Middle East, and the fall of the Shah of Iran. In American politics, the Laskin period began with the Watergate scandal, which eventually pushed Richard Nixon out of office, and ended with the Iran-Contra scandal that shadowed Ronald Reagan's second term. Energy prices soared when the petroleum-producing territories of the Middle East finally found a basis for cooperation, and the Canadian repercussions included conflict between the national government and the resource-rich western provinces, especially Alberta; the Laskin Court was called on to adjudicate some of the disputes arising from this conflict, which its decisions exacerbated.

## The Personnel of the Laskin Court

The continuing members of the Laskin Court (in order of seniority) were Martland, Judson, Ritchie, Spence, Pigeon, and Dickson; however, this was only the beginning of a lengthy list, because Laskin ultimately saw more new faces on the bench (eight) than any other chief justice in the history of the Court.[5]

**Jean-Marie Philémon Joseph Beetz** was appointed on January 1, 1974, one of the two Quebec appointments occasioned by the surprise double resignation of Fauteux (two years before compulsory retirement) and Abbott (six months early). Born in Montreal and educated at the University of Montreal, he went to Oxford as a Rhodes Scholar (Quebec & Pembroke 1951) before returning to Quebec to practise law. He worked in private practice for only a short time before joining the faculty of law at the University of Montreal, becoming dean in 1968. A colleague and friend of Trudeau, he served as an assistant to the Cabinet and then as constitutional adviser to the prime minister before being appointed in 1973 to the Quebec Court of Queen's Bench (since renamed the Court of Appeal). After only a single year in that position, he joined the Supreme Court at the age of 46, another academic lawyer on a bench that before the late sixties had seen few academics.

The second of the appointments, on January 1, 1974, was **Louis-Philippe de Grandpré**, the President of the Canadian Bar Association. Bushnell suggests that the duo of Beetz and de Grandpré represents an attempt by Trudeau to satisfy both the legal academics and the legal practitioners, the two "combatting elements within the profession."[6] De Grandpré was 56 years old when he joined the Court, with a solid thirty-five years of experience as a lawyer, and this "helped to compensate for the absence of such experience in both Beetz and the new chief justice."[7] The two appointments were generally welcomed in Quebec, but within four years, de Grandpré abruptly resigned, complaining of Laskin's style and of the Court's direction on constitutional matters.

**Willard Zebedee Estey** joined the Court on September 29, 1977, at the age of 57, replacing Judson. Born and educated in Saskatchewan, he completed graduate studies at Harvard and practised corporate law in Toronto. He was appointed to the Court of Appeal of Ontario in 1973, then was shifted to the trial bench to become chief justice of the High Court of Ontario in 1975, but moved again to become chief justice of the Court of Appeal in 1976. He was an outspoken individual who clearly represented the practitioner's side of the academic/practitioner divide. He was the son of James W. Estey, who served on the Supreme Court from 1944 to 1956, the two comprising the first (and so far the only) father/son combo in the history of the Court.

**Yves Pratte** was appointed on October 1, 1977, replacing de Grandpré. He had studied law at Laval University and the University of Toronto before embarking on a career in private practice and public service, including a term as chairman of Air Canada. He was appointed at the age of 52. The two 1977 appointments, Estey and Pratte, seemed a significant departure from the previous Trudeau pattern, distinguished as they were by corporate law expertise with no strong academic connection, and Pratte's was also criticized as a patronage appointment. He resigned in less than two years, pleading health reasons.

**William Rogers McIntyre** was appointed to the Supreme Court on January 1, 1979, replacing Spence. A native of Quebec, he attended the University of Saskatchewan and served in the Canadian Army in Europe before entering private practice in Victoria, B.C. His specialty was criminal law, and this was one of the reasons he was picked to replace Spence, who had had parallel expertise.[8] He was appointed to the Supreme Court of British Columbia in 1967 and elevated to the Court of Appeal in 1973, coming to the Supreme Court at age 60 with more than a decade of judicial experience. The appointment of a judge from B.C. to replace a judge from Ontario was a temporary departure from the convention of three judges from

Quebec, three from Ontario, and three from the rest of Canada,[9] a balance that was restored just over three years later.

**Julien Chouinard** was appointed to the Supreme Court by the short-lived Clark government. He took office on September 24, 1979, replacing Pratte. Born in Quebec, he studied at Laval and spent a year as a Rhodes Scholar at Oxford (Quebec & St. John's 1951) before being called to the bar in 1953. He served as provincial deputy minister of justice before running (unsuccessfully) for the Conservative Party in the 1968 election and was appointed to the Quebec Court of Appeal in 1975. Clark reportedly tried to entice him into the federal Cabinet during the summer of 1979, appointing him to the Supreme Court when that move failed.[10] Chouinard joined the Court at the age of 50.

**Antonio Lamer** was appointed on March 28, 1980, replacing Pigeon. Born in Montreal, he graduated from the University of Montreal and entered private practice as a criminal defence lawyer. He was active in the Liberal Party, but not to the extent of running for elected office. He was appointed to the Quebec Superior Court in 1969 and then served as vice-chairman and chairman of the Law Reform Commission of Canada after before being named to the Quebec Court of Appeal in 1978. He joined the Supreme Court at the age of 47. For much of the history of the Supreme Court, Lamer's background in criminal law would have made him unusual on the Court and would have specifically prepared him for only a small portion of the caseload; however, by 1980, the bench already had one criminal specialist (McIntyre), and its criminal caseload was steadily growing.

**Bertha Wilson** was appointed on March 4, 1982, replacing Martland. (The irony is obvious, the traditionalist being replaced by the feminist.) She was the first woman ever appointed to the Supreme Court of Canada, shortly after Sandra Day O'Connor became the first woman on the U.S. Supreme Court. Born and educated in Scotland, Wilson studied law at Dalhousie and practised law in Toronto until her appointment to the Ontario Court of Appeal in 1975. The appointment of a judge from Ontario to replace a judge from Alberta restored the regional balance of the Court, which had been disturbed by the 1979 appointment of McIntyre.

The justices of the Laskin Court demonstrated how Trudeau's influence had transformed the Court, the Jewish chief justice and the first woman justice constituting only the most visible dimensions of that influence. The judges of the Laskin Court were more likely than their predecessors to have done graduate study in law (many of them in the United States) and more likely to have taught law at the university level, making them "the most learned and scholarly group of justices ever to join the Supreme Court."[11] Most came to the Court with some judicial experience, and although none had ever held elected office, they demonstrated "a proliferation of non-elected government experience."[12]

## The Caseload of the Laskin Court

The most significant thing about the caseload of the Laskin Court is something that cannot be seen on any table analyzing that caseload because it determines the size of the table itself. For much of its history, well into the postwar era, the caseload of the Supreme Court was relatively modest. The rising numbers of appeals through the late 1960s and into the 1970s — something that was true of the provincial appeal courts as well — provided one of the reasons for a major overhauling of the Canadian court system in general and the Supreme Court in particular. One of the most important elements was a revision of the Supreme Court's discretionary leave jurisdiction.

There are two ways in which a case can come before the Supreme Court for review. The first is by *right*: some cases raise issues such that the Supreme Court must hear them if either of the parties want the case to be heard. The second is by *leave*: virtually any case can rise from a court of appeal to the Supreme Court upon application to the Court for leave to appeal, although most applications are refused. A 1975 amendment to The Supreme Court Act shifted the balance between these two access routes. To put it very simply, before 1975, there was a right to appeal on any civil case involving more than $10,000 and on any criminal case involving a capital crime; after 1975, there was instead a right to appeal on any criminal case involving a dissent on a matter of law within the court of appeal.[13]

Increasing the discretionary leave jurisdiction has two implications for the Court. The first is that it keeps the caseload smaller, allowing the Court to give more careful attention to the cases that it does hear.[14] The second is that it gives some control over the timing on "hot" issues — the Court can wait until the case law has built up in the lower courts, until the "right" case comes along, until informed public opinion is beginning to gel, or whatever. The Court grants leave if the legal issue is of sufficient importance to be considered by the highest Court, but this does not involve any assessment of how likely the appeal is to succeed, which means that "a denial of leave to appeal does not imply that the leave-denying panel of the Supreme Court thought that the lower decision was rightly decided."[15] The Laskin Court was the first to have such a wide degree of control over its own agenda.

The current procedure works unevenly, because more criminal defendants have an appeal by right in provinces such as Manitoba and Quebec where dissents are more common than in provinces such as Ontario and Nova Scotia where dissents are rare. The 1975 reforms took the Supreme Court only part of the way to the USSC's totally discretionary control over its own docket. As it is, the Supreme Court before 1975 was hearing about 85 percent appeals by right and 15 percent appeals by leave, and these proportions almost reversed themselves after 1975[16] (although the proportion of appeals by right has recently been somewhat higher).

That said, the visible impact of the expanded leave jurisdiction has been modest. The volume of the caseload has not come down; it reached about 100 cases per year during the 1960s and has been at least that high ever since. At best, the new measures prevented the continued expansion of the caseload (and resulting diffusion of the Court's energies) that might otherwise have occurred. The fact that appeals by right have been eliminated for civil appeals but still exist for criminal appeals may partly explain why the balance between the two has been shifting away from private law and toward criminal law, although private law cases were still the largest category (and criminal appeals the smallest) for the Laskin Court.

There was also some change at this time in the sources of appeals to the Supreme Court. For some reason, the number of appeals from Quebec rose almost to match that from Ontario, but this proved to be a short-term aberration rather than a long-term shift. There were also proportionately more appeals from the Atlantic provinces, which may simply reflect the fact that New Brunswick and Nova Scotia now had full-time specialized appeal courts (since 1967), with Newfoundland following suit in 1974. These increases were offset by a drop in the number of appeals from the federal courts — as anticipated, given that taking pressure off the Supreme Court's caseload was one reason for replacing the single-tier Exchequer Court with the trial and appeal divisions of the new Federal Court. The Courts of Appeal of Ontario and British Columbia were reversed the least often by the Laskin Court (about 40% of the time), and those of Manitoba and Saskatchewan were reversed the most often (about 60% of the time).

Appeals succeeded slightly more often than had been the case for the previous twenty years, but the difference was small — 45 percent compared with 42.3 percent for the Taschereau/Cartwright/Fauteux Court and 38.9 percent for the Kerwin Court — and the change in reporting practices (all Supreme Court decisions being reported since 1970) means that the two periods may not be strictly comparable. This apparent increase applied to all three types of law, but there were continuing signs of a clear divergence between the lower reversal rates for the increasing proportion of criminal appeals (35.6%) and the higher reversal rates for public and private appeals (48.3% and 50.1%, respectively). Whatever the cause (and the remaining appeal-by-right cases may account for some of it), this pattern has persisted.

Viewed through the window of the caseload, the world of the Laskin Court looks very much like the world of the previous Courts. Out of a caseload of 1000, the largest single category was still economic and business-related cases (125 examples), tax cases (137, mostly corporate and income tax), and transportation cases (132, three-quarters of which involved automobiles). Curiously, although criminal cases increased only modestly as a share of the total caseload, major crimes were up sharply; there were 73 murder cases and 17 sexual assault cases in just over 10 years.

## Decision-making by the Laskin Court

Two major trends, larger panel sizes and greater unanimity, were evident from the start. The long-standing practice of the U.S. Supreme Court has been for all nine judges to sit on virtually every appeal on the merits, this contrasting with the Canadian practice of normally using five-judge panels, with larger panels for particularly important cases. The decision as to the size of the panel and the assignment of specific judges have been at the discretion of the chief justice — which meant that there were no formal barriers to larger panels once Laskin decided he wanted them. The Court did not move all the way to the American practice, however. The general rule since Laskin seems to have been seven judges as the normal panel size, with nine-judge panels for unusually important cases and five-judge panels for more routine ones.

Crediting Laskin for the move toward greater unanimity is somewhat paradoxical: he was often called "The Great Dissenter," particularly in the first half of his chief justiceship. To some extent, this sobriquet reflects the changing norms of the Court. Laskin actually signed on to the majority decision more often than Fauteux or Kerwin and almost as often as Cartwright; his relative independence stands out because of the increasing solidarity of his Court in the delivery of reasons for judgement.[17]

It is generally agreed in the American literature that a key factor in the frequency of dissents and concurrences is the influence of the chief justice.[18] Through techniques that include formal and informal sanctions, good personal relations, personal example, persuasion and compromise, and the strategic use of opinion assignments, a chief justice can promote unity or not, as he proposes and as fortune disposes.[19] Laskin's success is all the more striking given that the U.S. Supreme Court after World War II had demonstrated a pronounced "practice of individualism in the formulation of expression of judicial opinions"[20] in which dissents became the norm and unanimous decisions were unusual. Despite this highly visible contrary example, Laskin's efforts culminated in a more unified Court than Canada had ever seen before (or has seen since).

The average panel size for the Laskin Court was 25 percent larger (that is, the panels included about 1½ more judges) than before. Notwithstanding this greater opportunity for disagreement, the frequency for both separate concurrences and dissents was virtually unchanged. In the decade before Laskin, the Court delivered an average of 1.49 reasons for judgment with an average panel size of 5.44, which means that the judges wrote reasons in just over one-quarter (26.8%) of all their panel appearances. For the Laskin Court, the production of 1.39 reasons for judgment with a panel size of 6.82 means that the judges on that Court wrote their own reasons in just over one-fifth (20.4%) of all their panel appearances. Perfect unity (one set of reasons per case) would have had judges writing in about one panel appearance in seven (14.7%). Separate concurrences were only half as common as dissents, which means that on many panels the majority and minority for the result coalesced behind a single set of reasons. Even divided decisions could increasingly be seen as a debate between two organized points of view, rather than as a bewildering set of fragments.

Dissents and separate concurrences were both slightly more likely in criminal cases than in the other types, but this is almost entirely a function of the fact that, on average, the criminal cases drew the larger panels.[21] In all areas of law, the Laskin Court was much more unified than the Rinfret or Kerwin Courts and as or more unified than the Courts of the preceding period — again, bearing in mind that

## Table 6.1A

### Dissents, Concurrences, and Decisions, by Judge Reported Supreme Court Decisions, 1973–1978

| Judge | Panels | Wrote decision | Contributed to decision | Divided panels | With majority | Conc. | Diss. |
|---|---|---|---|---|---|---|---|
| Laskin | 466 | 31.1% | 47.9% | 222 | 45.9% | 12.2% | 41.9% |
| Martland | 497 | 17.3% | 24.5% | 218 | 66.1% | 14.2% | 19.7% |
| Judson | 352 | 4.8% | 7.4% | 162 | 73.5% | 5.6% | 21.0% |
| Ritchie | 507 | 12.6% | 17.6% | 212 | 68.4% | 13.7% | 17.9% |
| Spence | 469 | 11.1% | 19.6% | 209 | 53.6% | 7.2% | 39.2% |
| Pigeon | 559 | 15.0% | 23.1% | 226 | 69.5% | 13.3% | 17.3% |
| Dickson | 569 | 13.2% | 19.2% | 226 | 63.3% | 7.5% | 29.2% |
| Beetz | 539 | 6.1% | 9.6% | 219 | 66.2% | 17.8% | 16.0% |
| de Grandpré | 319 | 17.9% | 28.8% | 147 | 53.1% | 15.0% | 32.0% |
| Estey | 192 | 11.5% | 16.7% | 69 | 62.3% | 7.2% | 30.4% |
| Pratte | 181 | 11.0% | 14.9% | 59 | 74.6% | 10.2% | 15.3% |
| McIntyre | 66 | 18.2% | 19.7% | 23 | 73.9% | 4.3% | 21.7% |
| ALL | 4716 | 14.1% | 21.3% | 1992 | 62.7% | 11.6% | 25.7% |

dissents and separate concurrences both became less frequent toward the end of Laskin's chief justiceship.

But the composite numbers for the Court are simply the aggregate of the performances of the individual members, and these performances are shown in Tables 6.1A and 6.1B. For this chapter (but no other), the dynamics of the Court are best revealed by subdividing the period, using the 1979/80 term as the dividing point. And I will stress in advance that there are two different aspects to the evolving decision-making practices that stand in paradoxical juxtaposition. The first is the steady increase in unanimous decisions: in about 60 percent of their panel appearances for the first six years and in more than 80 percent for the last four years, judges spoke with a single voice. But the second is the fact that when the Court divided, it did so along rather consistent lines. This is demonstrated by the fact that of the initial (top nine) members of the Court, there was one set of people who dissented about 15 percent of the time and another set dissenting twice as often. Most prominent among the frequent dissenters were Chief Justice Laskin, Spence, and Dickson — the so-called "L-S-D Connection."[22] At first glance, de Grandpré seems to be a fourth member of the outsider group, but I will show later why this is an incorrect reading. On the other hand, the numbers for

## Table 6.1B

### Dissents, Concurrences, and Decisions, by Judge Reported Supreme Court Decisions, 1979–1984

| Judge | Panels | Wrote decision | Contributed to decision | Divided panels | With majority | Conc. | Diss. |
|---|---|---|---|---|---|---|---|
| Laskin | 210 | 44.3% | 46.7% | 37 | 75.7% | 2.7% | 21.6% |
| Martland | 184 | 26.6% | 30.4% | 32 | 59.4% | 12.5% | 28.1% |
| Ritchie | 282 | 10.3% | 14.9% | 56 | 57.1% | 8.9% | 33.9% |
| Pigeon | 41 | 24.4% | 26.8% | 7 | 85.7% | 14.3% | 0.0% |
| Dickson | 351 | 12.3% | 17.7% | 68 | 64.7% | 14.7% | 20.6% |
| Beetz | 293 | 7.5% | 9.6% | 58 | 63.8% | 22.4% | 13.8% |
| Estey | 359 | 12.8% | 15.9% | 70 | 70.0% | 7.1% | 22.9% |
| McIntyre | 357 | 10.6% | 12.9% | 70 | 71.4% | 7.1% | 21.4% |
| Chouinard | 326 | 12.3% | 12.9% | 60 | 75.0% | 11.7% | 13.3% |
| Lamer | 243 | 11.5% | 16.9% | 48 | 60.4% | 20.8% | 18.8% |
| Wilson | 106 | 16.0% | 25.5% | 29 | 44.8% | 17.2% | 37.9% |
| ALL | 2752 | 15.1% | 18.5% | 535 | 65.8% | 12.3% | 21.9% |

Estey (who replaced Judson in 1977) do correctly identify a Laskin ally.

Nineteen seventy-nine and 1980 saw even more turnover: in January 1979, McIntyre replaced Spence; in September 1979, Chouinard replaced Pratte; and in March 1980, Lamer replaced Pigeon. This completely transformed the decision-delivering patterns on the Court. Laskin, who had previously been with the majority in a smaller proportion of divided decisions than any other member of the Court, now formed part of that majority more often than anyone else — and, disproportionately often, he wrote the reasons as well. Conversely, Martland and Ritchie, who during the first six years had dissented significantly less often than the all-Court average, now wrote or joined dissents more often than anyone else (at least until Wilson joined the Court). The beginning of the 1979 term was an unusually dramatic turnaround and, arguably, it was the appointment of Chouinard that tipped the balance.[23]

Bushnell tells quite a different story. For him, Laskin's early influence was demonstrated by decisions such as *Murdoch v. Murdoch* (1973)[24] and the *Anti-Inflation Reference* (1976),[25] but "as the Supreme Court moved into the latter half of the 1970s, the 'Laskin Court' evaporated, leaving once again the court of old."[26] This was exacerbated by Laskin's poor health after 1978, such that "Laskin in the end sank into the role of a dissenter."[27] I can only say that I see it differently.

For both subperiods, Dickson is the member of the Court whose numbers most closely approximate the all-Court figures, his membership in good standing in the L-S-D Connection notwithstanding. This shows that his relationship to Laskin was more complex than a simple story of the loyal understudy finally rewarded with the leading role. On many issues, Dickson was a solid ally for Laskin; but on others, some involving important constitutional matters, he clearly charted his own course. The most appropriate way to conceptualize this is to see Dickson toward the middle and Laskin on one "wing" of the Court (initially in the minority, latterly dominant).

## Voting Blocs on the Laskin Court

When Laskin became chief justice in 1973, the Court consisted of a trio of senior Diefenbaker-appointed justices (Martland, Judson, and Ritchie), a trio of justices more recently appointed by Liberal prime ministers (Spence, Pigeon, and Laskin himself), and a trio of junior judges appointed for or during the 1973 term (Dickson, Beetz, and de Grandpré). These nine constituted the Court for almost four full terms, until Estey and Pratte replaced Judson and de Grandpré for the 1977 term; the revolving door that gave the Court thirteen appointments in a dozen years had not yet begun to turn.

The focus of Trudeau's second term as prime minister was the patriation of the Canadian constitution, but his first term saw nothing less than the restructuring of the Canadian court system, especially the Supreme Court. Trudeau's efforts (as minister of justice and then as prime minister) were also directed toward changing the implicit job requirements of an appeal court judge. But if reconstruction represents progress for those who are driving the process, it looks rather different to those who contributed conscientiously to the institution that is being reconstructed. Friction within the Court seemed inevitable.[28]

At first glance, it seems an uneven contest — the unreconstructed "Diefenbaker three" against the "Liberal six" — but Table 6.1A shows that this is not how things unfolded, largely because the Liberal six turned out really to be the L-S-D Connection plus the "Quebec three." As shown in the previous chapter, Martland and Ritchie had worked very well with the Quebec judges of the Taschereau/Cartwright/Fauteux period, so the question was whether they could establish the same rapport with a new set of Quebec judges. Table 6.1A shows that they could.

My focus is on the divided decisions of the Laskin Court, although these fell from just over 40 percent in the mid-1970s to just under 20 percent in the early 1980s. Laskin versus Martland was not complete polarization but a more focused division, the major but not the only fault line on a Court with fewer fault lines than its predecessors; however, it supplies a critical part of the story of the Laskin Court, frustrating the chief justice on major issues such as the extent of federal jurisdiction over airports [*Construction Montcalm*][29] or Indian reservations [*Four B Manufacturing*],[30] or the constitutionality of patriation [*Patriation Reference*].[31]

The first step in unravelling the Court's voting alliances is to ask which combinations of judges tend to deliver the decisions for divided panels, which is the ultimate "cash-in" value of Table 6.1A's data on the frequencies of dissent and separate concurrence. By far the most successful combination over the Laskin Court's first four terms was one that includes six judges: Martland, Ritchie, Judson, Beetz, Pigeon, and de Grandpré. And the most frequent of the five-judge decision-delivering coalitions was those six less Beetz. Smaller panels mean that three- and four-judge combinations can also be effective, and the most frequent of these smaller groupings included the "excluded three" (Laskin, Spence, and Dickson) plus Judson, which puts an intriguing bracket around Judson's performance, to which I will return. That Trudeau's hand-picked chief justice could so often be painted into a three-judge dissenting corner suggests limits to the extent, or at least to the rapidity, with which a prime minister's appointing power can alter the direction of the Court.

A second way to unravel voting alliances is the American methodology that Paul H. Edelman and Jim Chen have melodramatically labelled "The Most Dangerous Justice."[32] They ask the slightly different question of how many of the actual decision-delivering coalitions include each judge, regardless of how often that coalition occurs. They call this phenomenon *flexible voting,* and they regard it as a kind of judicial power, typically wielded by more junior members who have not yet developed other resources, such as seniority. If we use this approach, Judson emerges as the most powerful member of the Court with a "Power Score" of 121 — which is to say that he was a member of 21 percent more decision-delivering coalitions than the average member of the Court. Laskin and de Grandpré emerge as the least flexible, with scores of 76 and 78 respectively, although I would suggest that they should be treated not as neighbours but as occupying opposite "wings" of the Court.

But, as Edelman and Chen caution, their "Power Score" reflects only an opportunity for influence and not necessarily its exercise. The Court's most "flexible" judges are in the best position to drive bargains with potential coalition partners for their support, in the form either of compromise modifications to the reasons for judgment or of gaining the writing assignment themselves.[33] But the measure generates a false positive for the person they label "Justice Milquetoast," sliding from one coalition to another without bargaining, always a passenger but never the driver. This description seems to catch Judson, the most likely to be with the majority of a divided panel but the least likely to write a decision. This characterization is supported by the fact that Judson often did not attend judicial conferences, either writing his own brief separate concurrences or silently signing on to the draft judgments that emerged from other chambers. This is in surprising contrast to the sparkling promise of his first years on the Kerwin Court.

A third way to penetrate the statistics is to look at two-judge agreement rates to see how often each pair of judges used the opportunity of serving on the same panel to sign on to the same set of reasons. This approach clearly shows the two wings of the Court. On the one side was Laskin, strongly supported by Spence (74.2% of the time) and only slightly less so by Dickson. On the other side was the Martland/Ritchie duo (71.3% agreement rate). Between them was the Quebec trio, anchored by Beetz/Pigeon (77.0% agreement rate), which was more than twice as likely (in the case of de Grandpré, more than four times as likely) to side with Martland/Ritchie as with Laskin. Finally, Judson was a sometime but not constant ally of the Laskin group, generally tending simply to side with (but not very often to create) the winner.

The departure of Judson and de Grandpré in 1977 created the opportunity for a major shift in Laskin's favour. Judson was more of a weathervane than a reliable ally, and de Grandpré was Laskin's most constant opponent, his resignation a protest against what he regarded as Laskin's "mindless centralization." Two strong supporters would give Laskin a narrow majority, and the person doing the appointing was the prime minister whose reconstructionist project had put Laskin in the chief justiceship. It did not turn out that way, however, indicating the limits to the power contained even in Canada's unilateral appointment process. W.Z. Estey did sign on with

Laskin and his allies most of the time, but Pratte did not, instead turning the Quebec trio into an even more solid bloc that now left Martland and Ritchie in the middle ground.

The Laskin breakthrough came with the next set of replacements: Spence replaced by McIntyre in January 1979, Pratte by Chouinard later that same year, and Pigeon by Lamer early in 1980. It has been suggested to me that Spence deliberately retired early so as to allow Trudeau to make the new appointment before the pending federal election. If so, the tactic was successful. McIntyre become a reliable Laskin ally (second only to Estey) on the divided panels that sank to their lowest level in the entire half-century. Ironically, the critical appointment was that of Chouinard, the only Supreme Court justice appointed by a Conservative prime minister in the twenty-three years between Diefenbaker's fourth appointee (Hall) and Brian Mulroney's first (Gérard La Forest). Chouinard broke the Quebec bloc and tilted the 5–4 balance toward rather than away from Laskin; Lamer's appointment six months later was the frosting on the cake.

Interestingly, under the Laskin ascendancy, the new minority simply shattered rather than retreating into steady dissent. Even on the increasingly infrequent divided panels, they often split. If there was a surviving core to the opposition to Laskin, it was Martland/Beetz — one from each of the Diefenbaker trio and the Quebec trio — with Ritchie taking a more moderate position. Martland's departure in 1982 (replaced by Wilson) left Laskin even more preeminent. Laskin's misfortune was that by the time he had a large-enough cadre of dependable allies, his health was failing. Still, the statistical evidence does not support Bushnell's conclusion that Laskin began as a reformer but "in the end sank into the role of a dissenter."[34] On the contrary, Laskin started off as a dissenter (writing or joining eighty-seven dissents in his first six terms as chief justice), but ended in poor health but firm control (writing or joining only eight dissents in his last four terms). Working over top of an essentially hostile majority for much of his term undoubtedly accounts for the limited impact of Laskin's decisions on current citation practices, as we will see later.

## Citation Practices of the Laskin Court

The "Laskin revolution" did not significantly touch the Court's citation practices. To be sure, the continuity in personnel makes dramatic transformation unlikely; Laskin's citation patterns are already part of the numbers for the Taschereau/Cartwright/Fauteux Court, and he

## Table 6.2

## Citations to Judicial Authority by the Laskin Court
## Reported Decisions, 1973–1984

| Source | Number | Frequency | Median Date |
|---|---|---|---|
| Judicial Committee | 732 | 7.7% | 1928 |
| Supreme Court of Canada | 3660 | 38.4% | 1965 |
| Other English Courts | 1838 | 19.3% | 1932 |
| Other Canadian Courts | 2806 | 29.4% | 1967 |
| U.S. Courts | 316 | 3.3% | 1958 |
| Other | 177 | 1.9% | 1957 |

had allies (Hall and Spence) whose writing often reflected a broader outlook than the formalism of their colleagues. Conversely, the dominant members of the earlier Court (and in particular the Diefenbaker trio) served under Laskin as well, and especially in the first half of his chief justiceship, they did a great deal of the writing. Both considerations would blur the edges of any change in citation practices.

### From where did the Supreme Court Get its Citations?

Even so, the consistency between two periods is striking. Judicial Committee citations had been declining for a quarter of a century; now they flattened out, remaining at about one in fourteen (see Table 6.2). Citations to the earlier decisions of the Supreme Court had been climbing just as steadily; now they flattened out as well. Nor was there any major increase in citations to U.S. authorities or to those of other countries, although the civil rights orientation of the Laskin Court might have tended to draw on such sources.

In only two respects did the general citation practices of the Laskin Court differ from those of its immediate predecessors. The first was a continuing swing away from the English authorities, this time in favour of other Canadian courts; all English authorities now accounted for about a quarter of all citations, and all Canadian authorities for more than two-thirds. Hierarchy notwithstanding, the Supreme Court often gives the findings of the lower courts the same close scrutiny and respectful observation that it gives those of the House of Lords or the U.S. Supreme Court; this shift is therefore not insignificant. The second was a sharp increase in the sheer volume of citations, from about 400 per year to 900 per year. In proportionate terms, neither self-citations nor American citations increased at all; in absolute terms, they more than doubled.[35]

## The Supreme Court Cites the Supreme Court: Who and What?

But if the Laskin Court was not citing prior Supreme Court decisions proportionately more often, it was certainly citing different prior decisions. Table 6.3 counts the total number of times that individual Supreme Court judges were cited by the Laskin Court and also the number of times that they were specifically named in that citation. For the first time since 1949, Duff was pushed out of top spot — although given the congestion at the top of the table perhaps we should say that he was sharing it with three members of the current Court. One of those three was Laskin himself, marginally in first place. Today it seems obvious that the recency of his service should give him an advantage over Duff, but no current member of the Court had accomplished this during any previous chief justiceship, and the fact that the lead was so modest says something about Duff and about the traditionalism of the Supreme Court. Also pushing the top of the list (marginally in second place) was Martland, the Laskin/Martland placing nicely symbolizing both the struggle that dominated the Court for a decade and Laskin's eventual victory.

The rest of the list is, again, comprised of current members of the Court and chief justices of the recent past. Martland's closest ally, Ritchie, is there, as is the harder-to-classify Judson; and Laskin's ally Dickson appears as well. The only one who is neither a current member nor a chief justice is Rand, a distinction he enjoyed for the previous period as well. The table also reveals a more egalitarian citation pattern. The spread between the first and the twelfth most frequently cited judges is barely two to one; for the Rinfret and Kerwin periods, this was the spread between the first and the second.

The decay rate for self-citations by the Laskin Court was 7.5 percent. This gives the typical case a citation half-life of 8.9 years, which means that half of all the citations a decision would ever receive came in the first nine years and a quarter in the second nine years. This in turn suggests a replacement rate for the leading precedents that was higher than that of the Taschereau/Cartwright/Fauteux period (with a half-life of 10 years) or the Rinfret Court (6.9 years), but lower than the Kerwin Court (6.6 years). The practical face of this gradual replacement was the continuing high profile of Duff and (to a lesser extent) of Rand, both of whom continued to be cited more

## Table 6.3

### Supreme Court of Canada Judges Most Frequently Cited by the Laskin Court
### Reported Cases, Supreme Court of Canada, 1973–1984

| Judge | Number of times cited | Number of times named | "Score" |
|---|---|---|---|
| Laskin[*†] | 294 | 96 | 390 |
| Martland[*] | 279 | 92 | 371 |
| Duff[†] | 228 | 142 | 370 |
| Pigeon[*] | 266 | 103 | 369 |
| Cartwright[†] | 213 | 91 | 304 |
| Ritchie[*] | 213 | 70 | 283 |
| Fauteux[†] | 201 | 59 | 260 |
| Judson[*] | 176 | 63 | 239 |
| Dickson[*] | 163 | 69 | 232 |
| Kerwin[†] | 154 | 71 | 225 |
| Rand | 137 | 81 | 218 |
| Rinfret[†] | 141 | 47 | 188 |

* indicates a member of the current Court.
† indicates a past or current chief justice.

frequently than even some reasonably long-serving members of the current Court.

## Major Decisions of the Laskin Court

The previous discussion centres around what the Laskin Court cited; the discussion that follows is concerned with what the Laskin Court did that subsequent Courts found worth citing. Dickson stands out, overshadowing his own chief justice and delivering six of the thirteen most frequently cited decisions of the Laskin Court, including three of the top four. Laskin himself wrote only two. McIntyre, who joined the Court more than halfway through the Laskin chief justiceship, puts as many decisions on the list as Laskin, presumably reflecting his criminal law expertise when criminal cases began to make up a larger part of the caseload. Laskin may have revolutionized the Court, but Dickson had the greater impact on the jurisprudence.

*Canadian Union of Public Employees Local 963 v. New Brunswick Liquor Corporation*,[36] the most frequently cited of the Laskin Court's decisions, is an example of Dickson's impact. The case involved a public service strike in New Brunswick, the question of

whether the statute allowed the employer to use management personnel temporarily to do the work of striking union personnel, and the
jurisdiction of the New Brunswick Public Service Labour Relations
Board. Put briefly, the board had said that management employees
could not do the work, and the New Brunswick Court of Appeal set
aside the order even though the statute said that the board's findings
were not subject to judicial review. Dickson wrote the reasons for a
unanimous nine-judge panel.

Cases of this sort are important because they involve the division
of labour between the formal court system and the specialized boards
and tribunals that have proliferated at both the federal and provincial
level since the Second World War. It does not seem acceptable that
the Courts should never "look over the shoulder" of an administrative
board,[37] but if they are too ready to substitute their own judgment,
we lose most of the boards' potential advantages of special expertise
and more flexible rules for procedure and evidence. To put it crudely,
the question is how badly a board has to botch things up before the
courts will step in, and *CUPE* is important (and frequently cited)
because it has become the landmark statement of the appropriate
modern standard.

Dickson conceded that the legislation was "very badly drafted"
and "bristles with ambiguities." But he went on to argue that the
privative clause (the provision that the board's decision is not subject
to review by a court) was "typically" found in labour relations legislation, and that the reasons for its inclusion were "straightforward
and compelling." Indeed, the "usual reasons for judicial restraint
upon review of labour board decisions are only reinforced in a case
such as this one." Therefore, the Court of Appeal was wrong to think
that the board's decision was subject to review for its correctness —
that is, for whether the court would have reached the same result.
Instead, the proper question was whether the Board's interpretation
was "so patently unreasonable that its construction cannot be rationally supported by the relevant legislation," and this (transparently) is
an easier test to pass, a higher threshold for review. But Dickson
pushed it a step further: the board's interpretation might appear
unreasonable in the light of private sector experiences, but not in the
context of the public sector, and he stressed the importance of seeing
the legislation as maintaining a balance between employer and employees in that context.

It is a little strong to call this "vintage Dickson" (*Hunter* is much
more readable),[38] but it was clearly a "modern" decision in everything

except its length (seven pages). There was a concern with general principles, an exploration of context, a consideration of real-world policy implications, and a discussion of the special circumstances of administrative boards in general and public sector boards in particular. Narrowly technical issues (such as the Court of Appeal's distinction between substantive issues and "preliminary and collatoral matters") were set aside as not being helpful, and citations were treated less as definitive authorities than as reasoned arguments that may or may not contribute usefully to the immediate issue. This was more "the Supreme Court deliberates" than "the authorities have decided."

The second case is *Kienapple*.[39] Bushnell saw the case as a major exercise in the law reform that Canadians had long awaited.[40] It involved an Ontario man convicted both of rape and of intercourse with a female under the age of fourteen. The issue was whether he could be convicted and sentenced twice "in respect of the same single act." Laskin (with Judson, Spence, Pigeon, and Dickson) found this to be simply another face of the more generally accepted principle that one could not be punished twice for the same offence and said that a developmental continuity with English law and with earlier Supreme Court decisions required that the appeal succeed.

Ritchie wrote the dissent for himself, Fauteux, Abbott, and Martland, flatly rejecting the argument: "twice for the same offense" was simply not the same thing as "twice for separate offenses arising from the same action," and on his reading, the English and Canadian case law established the former but did not justify the latter. Martland added further dissenting comments of his own. For one thing, he was concerned that the Court was deciding a matter that had not even been raised in the lower courts, something that appeal courts normally do not allow. For another, since the accused had received concurrent sentences, the majority's finding would not even reduce his time in jail, and this lack of practical effect made the decision an empty "academic exercise." Both concerns nicely demonstrate Schauer's point (quoted in the previous chapter) that formalism narrows the range within which the decision-maker operates.[41]

On the same day as the *Kienapple* decision, a decision was handed down by Fauteux for a five-judge panel that went exactly the opposite way, concluding that convictions for two offences arising from the same act did not mean that an accused was being punished twice for the same offence.[42] The contradictory decisions were embarrassing for the Court, but they illustrate the way the Court was "turning the corner." On my count, *Doré* has only been cited twice in the last twenty-four years, compared with forty times for *Kienapple*.

Bushnell complains that Ritchie gives no reasoning, just conclusions flowing from authorities.[43] Frankly, compared with contemporary decision-writing, Laskin held himself rather narrowly to a consideration of authorities. There was none of the purposive analysis that the Court now considers routine, no careful consideration of the context, no exploration of the policy implications of one decision over the other. The difference, narrow but significant, is that Ritchie was satisfied to stay within the limits laid down by the authorities — not all English, and some from lower rather than higher or coordinate courts. Laskin, on the other hand, was willing to look at a long-standing principle and wonder if the prevailing narrow reading of it was necessarily the most plausible and defensible. The distinction may not seem earthshaking, but the confrontation is significant.

## The Most Influential Judges of the Laskin Court

The decisions of the Laskin Court have been referred to 3360 times in subsequent Supreme Court decisions, suggesting a significant degree of continuing influence. As for the previous Courts, about one-third (1196) of these citations involved the specific naming of the cited judge. This data is collected in Table 6.4 below. As before, "number of times cited" and "number of times named" have been totalled to generate a "score" for each justice, and again, the turnover on the Court makes it useful to indicate how much of the total time span was served by each justice. For the Laskin Court, "number of times cited" and "number of times named" run so parallel to each other that the totalled score does not change a single ranking, something that is not generally true of the other chief justiceships.

Laskin has not been the most influential member of his own Court. Dickson leads the table in both the absolute frequency of citation and the number of times he was explicitly identified. When we look back at the similar tables for earlier Courts, we can see that he was the first to break the 1000 mark, although the different lengths of the chief justiceships and, above all, the changes in judicial citation practices preclude using these "scores" to compare individual judges from different periods. Some of Dickson's preeminence can be attributed to the light "shining back" from his subsequent strong leadership of the Court in the first years of the Charter era, but this simply shows the difficulty of constructing a truly level playing field.

## Table 6.4

### Frequency with which Members of the Laskin Court Are Subsequently Cited Reported Decisions, 1973–1999

| Judge | Number of times cited | Number of times named | "Score" | Days served (%) |
|---|---|---|---|---|
| Dickson[†] | 761 | 363 | 1124 | 3742 (100%) |
| Laskin[*] | 633 | 251 | 884 | 3742 (100%) |
| Pigeon | 344 | 134 | 478 | 2233 (60%) |
| Ritchie | 246 | 92 | 338 | 3742 (100%) |
| Martland | 225 | 73 | 298 | 2967 (79%) |
| Beetz | 193 | 93 | 286 | 3737 (100%) |
| Estey | 179 | 87 | 266 | 2370 (63%) |
| McIntyre | 197 | 59 | 256 | 1911 (51%) |
| Lamer[†] | 123 | 60 | 183 | 1459 (39%) |
| de Grandpré | 122 | 60 | 182 | 1369 (37%) |
| Spence | 121 | 46 | 167 | 1828 (49%) |
| Chouinard | 64 | 27 | 91 | 1654 (44%) |
| Pratte | 48 | 24 | 72 | 637 (17%) |
| Wilson | 24 | 10 | 34 | 753 (20%) |
| Judson | 7 | 1 | 8 | 1301 (35%) |

\* indicates the current chief justice.
† indicates future chief justices.

Noting Dickson's modest lead on the table is not to deny Laskin's considerable legacy. Chief justices do not always lead their Court in subsequent citation; Kerwin did (and Cartwright would have had I not folded him into a composite period), but Rinfret, Taschereau, and Fauteux did not. Since Laskin (some would suggest "since Cartwright," although I have reservations), we expect a visible prominence of the chief justice among his colleagues that is more than the traditional first among equals.[44] This is one of the many changes that mark the great watershed that is the Laskin Court.

Pigeon holds third place, a clear step below Dickson and Laskin but well above everyone else on the Court — all the more impressive given that he served barely half of the over ten years. This may reflect Pigeon's acknowledged expertise in the civil law. Apart from him, the lasting influence of the Quebec judges on the Laskin Court is modest; they have a much lower collective profile on the Court than was the case on previous Courts. This is clearly because of the rapid turnover among the Quebec members, the most disappointing aspect of Trudeau's string of appointments.

Martland and Ritchie are toward the middle of the table. At first glance, this is surprising: because they generally prevailed over Laskin in the first six years and lost out only in the last four, one would expect deeper footprints. But the victory of Laskin's contextualist style over Martland's mechanical style was not the swing of a pendulum; it was the turning of a corner. Martland and Ritchie were on the "other" side of the Laskin watershed in a way that transcends mere chronology. The *Wray* case, discussed at the end of the previous chapter, is a case in point — less for its finding (that the evidence should have been admitted) than for its mindset (in the absence of a clear legislative or common law mandate for trial judge discretion, it is not up to the Court to consider establishing a judicial one).

Judson's position at the bottom of the table speaks for itself. The limited length of his service is not an adequate explanation, because the same can be said of other judges who made a stronger mark (de Grandpré and Lamer in particular). Judson's first years had suggested an outstanding new judge with a glorious future on the Court. In fact, his impact began to fade almost immediately and vanished by the beginning of the Laskin Court.

## Conclusion

The Laskin Court clearly delivered on the hopes of those who wanted a powerful Court playing a strong public role. Not immediately, and not without resistance from within his own Court, Laskin changed the way that the Court operated (with larger panels and, eventually, greater unanimity) and the way that it approached its business (with more willingness to tackle law reform and more concern for policy consequences). A divided Court delayed, and illness cut short, the more sweeping changes he might have contemplated.

Turnover continued to disrupt the Court under Laskin. This was particularly true of the Quebec judges: the three Quebec seats on the nine-judge Court accounted for five of the eight new appointments. Only one (Beetz) served long enough or was accomplished enough to be a significant player on the Laskin Court, an unfortunate imbalance at a time when Quebec's place in Confederation became the major national issue.

The Taschereau/Cartwright/Fauteux Court had seen a new status quo establish itself, with the Diefenbaker trio (and particularly Martland/Ritchie) at its core; the Laskin Court saw waves of new appointments first frustrated by, and then ultimately overwhelming, this regime. The previous status quo was replaced by a more unified Court more dominated by the chief justice than ever before; however, the doctrinal footprints of that leadership are ambiguous — at first, because of opposition from Martland/Ritchie; later, because of ambivalent support from Dickson and Dickson's own somewhat different vision of Canadian federalism. On some fronts, Laskin rewrote the constitution like his professorial publications had suggested he would: the *Anti-Inflation Reference*[45] is a powerful statement of the federal "peace, order and good government" power, and *R. v. Wetmore*[46] is the culminating transformation of the federal prosecution power. On other fronts, such as the application of enclave theory to Indian reservations or airports, he was frustrated. The *Patriation Reference*[47] is the entire chief justiceship in miniature: Martland failed to get his way, but so did Laskin, and the federal government was not quite defeated yet not quite triumphant. Despite this nuanced result, the visibility of the Court and the prominence of Laskin drew the ire of provincial premiers; Section 92A of the Constitution Act 1982 was included specifically to reverse a Laskin decision.

The Laskin Court's citation practices continued the mild swing away from English authorities (still only a mild swing, despite Laskin's declaration that Judicial Committee decisions no longer constituted binding precedent), but did not move toward a stronger emphasis on its own prior decisions and did not shift the focus of self-citation significantly toward recent cases. Duff's predominance on the citation lists was broken, albeit only to the extent of his sharing top place. But when it came to the Laskin Court's own establishment of precedent for the future, Laskin was clearly eclipsed by his own successor.

By the end of the Laskin Court, it seems appropriate to speak of another renewal of the Court's membership; with Ritchie so close to retirement, only Dickson and an ailing Beetz remained from the first half of the Laskin chief justiceship. Yet this was the Court that would confront the critical new challenge of the Charter. Finally rising to long-standing expectations, the Court was about to face its greatest test.

# The Dickson Court: April 1984 to June 1990 "The Consolidator"

When Bora Laskin died on March 26, 1984, Dickson became the new chief justice. Ritchie was more senior, but he was 73 years old and in poor health and he retired later that year. A tradition of alternating Quebec and non-Quebec chief justices would have made Beetz, almost as senior and of comparable stature, the logical candidate; however, I think the notion of an English–French alternation is largely illusory, and the real tradition, rarely departed from, is one of seniority.[1] In this case, the seniority rule gave the centre chair to a highly respected member of the Court who had been one of its strongest leaders through the previous decade. One of Dickson's strengths was lucid exposition; I am struck by the number of lawyers and judges who have volunteered opinions about Dickson, often referring to some of his decisions not just as good law but also as unusually good writing.

The subtitle of this chapter derives from the triple challenge faced by Laskin's successor. First, Laskin had given the Court a high public profile, but the price was controversy. The challenge was to maintain both visibility and credibility, neither sliding back into obscurity nor squandering the Court's new-found prestige on ill-considered causes. Second, the new chief justice had to establish his own leadership over a Court that had been so dominated by Laskin as to have little shape or direction apart from him. But unlike the American practice in which the new chief justice is usually appointed from outside the Court, in Canada the new leader had to emerge from within the very Court that Laskin had so dominated. The third part of the challenge was the Canadian Charter of Rights and Freedoms, which became an entrenched part of the Canadian constitution in 1982. It is ironic that Laskin, the consistent defender of both national government power and civil liberties, did not live to deliver a single Charter decision.[2] This heightens the drama of the shift from Laskin to Dickson.

Dickson began in Laskin's shadow, but I do not want to make that shadow too deep or to place Dickson too far into it. Dickson had been part of the L-S-D Connection formed (usually in dissent) in the early 1970s, but there were significant differences between him and Laskin. Dickson's background was practical rather than academic, and his expertise was in corporate law rather than constitutional or criminal law. He had been one of the judges who split the difference between Laskin and Martland on the *Patriation Reference*. And on some of Laskin's innovations, such as the string of cases that link *Di Iorio*[3] to *R. v. Wetmore*[4] and essentially redefine the federal prosecution power, Dickson remained in such persistent dissent as to draw the veiled criticism of some of his colleagues.[5]

## The Personnel of the Dickson Court

The continuing members (in order of seniority) were Dickson, Ritchie, Beetz, Estey, McIntyre, Chouinard, Lamer, and Wilson, and there were seven further appointments.

**Gerald Eric Le Dain** was appointed on May 29, 1984, replacing Laskin. He was the last of the Trudeau appointments. An academic, he had taught at McGill University, had been dean of law at York University, and had served as a member of the Federal Court of Appeal for almost nine years. This combination of academic reputation and judicial experience makes him an excellent example of Trudeau's priorities in staffing the Court.

**Gérard V. La Forest** was appointed on January 16, 1985, replacing Ritchie. He was the first of a string of nine appointments by the new Conservative government of Brian Mulroney. The fifth Rhodes Scholar (New Brunswick & St. John's 1949) to be appointed to the Supreme Court, his background was primarily academic; he had taught law at the University of New Brunswick for twelve years and served as dean of law at the University of Alberta for two years. He had also worked in the federal Ministry of Justice and on the Law Reform Commission of Canada before being appointed to the New Brunswick Court of Appeal in 1981. He was the first francophone from outside Quebec ever appointed to the Court, and he probably rivals Laskin as the most distinguished academic ever to serve on the Supreme Court; his work on extradition law (like Laskin's book on constitutional law) continues to be used in revised and edited form and to be cited by the Court.

**Claire L'Heureux-Dubé** was appointed on April 15, 1987, replacing Chouinard after his death. She was born in Quebec City and studied law at Laval before entering private practice. She was appointed to the Quebec Superior Court in 1973 and to the Quebec Court of Appeal in 1979, joining the Supreme Court at the age of 59 with fourteen years of judicial experience. Although her legal practice covered several areas, her primary interest seemed to be family law matters, an unusual background for a Supreme Court justice.

**John Sopinka** was appointed on May 24, 1988, replacing W.Z. Estey after his unexpected retirement. Sopinka was a well-known Conservative lawyer from Toronto and the first "ethnic" member of the Court, drawing attention to this at his swearing-in by addressing the court in English, French, and Ukranian.[6] He had no prior judicial experience, the only such member on the Dickson Court, although this had been more common earlier. He was thought of as a "hard-nosed trial lawyer" in the Estey tradition rather than as an academic.

**Charles Doherty Gonthier** was appointed on February 1, 1989, replacing Beetz, who retired for health reasons. He was born in Montreal and studied law at McGill before entering private practice. He was appointed to the Quebec Superior Court in 1974 and to the Quebec Court of Appeal in 1988, coming to the Court with fifteen years of experience. He was 60 years old at the time of his appointment.

**Peter deCartaret Cory** was appointed to the Supreme Court on February 1, 1989, replacing Le Dain after his retirement (on the same day as Beetz) for health reasons. Born in Windsor, Ontario, he received his education at the University of Western Ontario and Osgoode Hall Law School and served in the RCAF. He was appointed to the Ontario High Court in 1974 and to the Ontario Court of Appeal in 1981. He was 64 years old when he joined the Court, the oldest appointee since Hall in 1962.

**Beverley McLachlin** was appointed on March 30, 1989, replacing McIntyre, who resigned "for no particular expressed reason" four years early.[7] Born in Pincher Creek, Alberta, she studied at the University of Alberta and taught on the law faculty at the University of British Columbia for seven years. She was appointed to Supreme Court of British Columbia in 1981 and to the Court of Appeal in 1985, and then returned to the B.C. Supreme Court as chief justice in 1988 before being appointed to the Supreme Court six months later. She was 45 years old at the time of her appointment, the youngest appointment since Robert Taschereau in 1940 (before she was born).

As these appointments continue to demonstrate, the modern criteria for service on the Supreme Court include either academic reputation or appellate judicial experience or both, and direct political connections have all but vanished. In addition, new conventions seem to have emerged. For one thing, the "new" Supreme Court includes women members, starting with Wilson in 1982 and rising to three with McLachlin in 1989. For another, there is an unusually high premium on prior service on appellate courts, the new "rule" seeming to be that at any given time the Court will include seven members elevated from the provincial courts of appeal, one from the Federal Court of Appeal, and one without prior judicial experience. In the past, there was a more even balance between promoted judges and "new" judges, the promoted judges generally had relatively little experience, academic credentials were rare, and political connections were important. And, finally, although there has been no Quebec anglophone appointed since Abbott in 1954, there appears to be a recent emphasis on the appointment of francophones from outside Quebec.

What the list also demonstrates is an important continuity between the Laskin and Dickson Courts, namely a very rapid turnover rate that has not been seen since the first decade of the century. The Dickson Court saw seven new faces in six years, a rate approached only by the early years of the Laskin Court (six new faces in six years). Newcomers, however competent and experienced, need to be "socialized" into their new role, to learn the work routine and the give-and-take with colleagues. The fact that the biggest rash of turnovers occurred toward the end of Dickson's chief justiceship meant that this problem (exacerbated by Dickson's own replacement) would be handed on to his successor.

## The Caseload of the Dickson Court

The caseload of the Dickson Court remained at the same level as the Laskin Court's, just over 100 per year; again, the expanded leave jurisdiction seems to have contained, not reversed, the caseload growth that caused concern in the early 1970s. Unlike earlier chief justiceships, the largest part of the caseload (37.1%) was made up of 245 criminal appeals, followed by public law (145), private law (138), and Charter cases (132). Private law and public law appeals were the most frequently successful (about half the time), with criminal law appeals (32.7%) and Charter appeals (31.8%) being reversed rather less often. Overall, the reversal rate was down about 5 percent from that of the Laskin Court, although this is partly because of the increase in criminal appeals, which tended under Laskin as well to have a lower reversal rate.

The numbers for the Charter appeals may well carry two surprises for many readers. The first is that they account for only about one case in five — the high profile and headline-grabbing power of many Charter decisions might have led us to expect a higher ratio. The second is the fact that the reversal rate on Charter appeals was so low, at less than one in three. But this simply demonstrates the real purpose of the expanded leave process: it allows the Supreme Court to focus its energy on a smaller set of cases. The critical criterion, however, is not whether it thinks the lower court may have erred; it is whether the matter is important enough to warrant the Supreme Court speaking out. Judicial leadership can be demonstrated just as effectively by affirming (and sometimes by carrying a step further) the legal analysis of the lower court; and in the process, the decision and its supporting reasons become binding law in the entire country.

Compared with previous chief justiceships, the Dickson Court saw proportionately fewer cases from Ontario and Quebec. The rule of thumb that works for most periods is that Ontario and Quebec, with two-thirds of the population, generate one-half of the caseload. This is already somewhat surprising: For one thing, one might have expected better correlation with population. For another, given that the economy has long been more concentrated in the two central provinces than the population has been, one might have expected this to be reflected in a caseload long focused on private law. For a third thing, mere physical proximity would seem to lower the threshold for appeals from Toronto and Montreal, compared with Halifax and Vancouver. But for the Dickson Court, the balance had swung even further, with Ontario and Quebec now providing just over 40 percent of the caseload. Appeals from the federal court were also down (from about 15% to about 10% of the total caseload), suggesting that the reforms of the 1970s continued to be effective.

One could almost suggest that there was an "Ottawa River effect," with the courts of appeal to the east having high reversal rates and those to the west low reversal rates. Only Manitoba and Newfoundland broke this pattern. The most striking aspect of this is the differential between the reversal rates for the Ontario and Quebec Courts of Appeal. These have long been the strongest in the country, by which I mean that they are among the courts least often reversed by the Supreme Court. The Ontario court may generally have performed slightly better (although during the Kerwin chief justiceship, the Quebec court was marginally ahead), but the differences have been too small to carry the weight of heavy conclusions. There are, of course, good reasons for expecting that these would be the strongest courts: the largest provinces have the largest and best-established cadres of lawyers, the widest and deepest pools of talent upon which to draw for judicial appointments. But this just makes it more perplexing that during Dickson's chief justiceship, the reversal rates of the Quebec Court of Appeal should have diverged so dramatically from those of its neighbour — from near-parity to being reversed almost exactly twice as often — without any sign of a transition. Nor is this a short-term aberration; it persisted for the Lamer Court as well.

At first glance, the answer would seem to lie in the divergence between Quebec and the rest of Canada that began with the Quiet Revolution in the 1960s; by the mid 1980s, presumably, the Quebec court was filled with individuals who had lived through, and been affected by, the transformation of Quebec. Certainly, a parallel development in the United States, with a string of popular political leaders at the state level aggressively challenging the long-standing jurisdictional pretensions of a national government, would eventually produce confrontations between the Supreme Court and the states' highest courts. But in Canada, the provincial superior courts are appointed by the same people who appoint the national high court, and most of the judges appointed to the Supreme Court in the last twenty-five years were elevated from provincial courts of appeal. Finally, the reversals have not involved the cases arising from Quebec's controversial language laws or related policies; on these, the Supreme Court has generally upheld the Quebec court while toning down the rhetoric. Because the easy answers do not work, the development remains problematic. And because frequent reversals would seem to be a green light for lawyers, it is curious that the volume of appeals from Quebec has not risen in response.

In terms of the kind of Canada that appeared through the caseload window, the Dickson Court docket was strikingly different from its predecessors'. The private law cases that had always made up the bulk of the caseload were down. But the flip side, flowing from the sharp increase in the proportionate numbers of criminal cases, was that the Dickson Court saw far more violence than had its predecessors. There were 64 murder cases, 11 of assault, 31 involving sexual assault, and 14 including fire and explosions. There were almost as many cases involving narcotics (47) as involving taxes, something that was not remotely the case for any earlier period. For most of the history of the Court, the most relevant legal expertise was some branch of corporate, business, or tax law; for the Dickson Court and since then, the single most relevant category is criminal law.

## Decision-making on the Dickson Court

A 1986 article by Madame Justice Bertha Wilson[8] has given us the best statement so far of the decision-making processes of the "modern" Supreme Court. I have already mentioned the basic features — significant advance preparation by the judges, the use of the give-and-take of oral argument, conferencing, and the circulation of written drafts — although Wilson is frustratingly cryptic about the way panels are set up and the way decision-writing is assigned. On these important questions, much ink has been spilled in the United States, but we are still very much in the dark in Canada.[9]

I suggested earlier that two major and highly visible dimensions of Laskin's leadership were larger panels and more unified decisions. The first question, then, is whether Dickson maintained this momentum, and the answer is yes, except for the Charter cases. The average panel size was down slightly, mostly related to the turnover of personnel. The number of opinions delivered per case rose gradually but steadily through the period. On all these measures, the Dickson Court was slightly below the Laskin Court, although well above any Court previous to that.

The most striking development was the return of the separate concurrence; these were about twice as common as for the Laskin Court, although they had been rising in the closing years of the Laskin Court as well. If all that mattered were winners and losers, then separate concurrences would not matter. But in a final court of appeal, especially one with significant control over its own agenda, the focus must be on the discursive explanations that cast their shadows forward. All judges know that unanimous decisions have the most impact, so they know that by writing their own supplementary or competing reasons, even in support of the same outcome, they weaken the decision and send signals to litigants and lawyers that there are issues here to revisit. Dissents, of course, indicate even more fundamental disagreement not just on the reasons but on the outcome itself. These too rebounded somewhat for the Dickson Court from the very low levels of the late Laskin Court, without becoming as frequent as they had been on the pre-Laskin Courts.

What explains this retreat from the increasingly unified Court is the new Charter cases.[10] It was the Charter cases that caused the divisions within the Court; remove these, and the Dickson Court would have been much more unified, much closer to the performance of the late Laskin Court (save for some increase in separate concurrences). Compared with the rest of the caseload, the typical Charter case was heard by a larger panel, drew more than half again as many sets of reasons for judgment, and saw at least twice as many judges writing or signing dissents or separate concurrences. Given the magnitude of the challenge, however, this seems more appropriate than surprising.

Against the background of this increasing disagreement, one small countertrend stands out, and this is the apparent emergence of a relatively new *per coram* style of judgment — a decision delivered by "the Court" with no indication of a specific lead author — which was used by the Dickson Court on more than fifty occasions.[11] At one time, I attached considerable significance to this development, the reasonable conjecture being that the point was to emphasis the Court's firm unanimity on basic issues,[12] but after closer investigation, I am no longer convinced. The large majority of these cases are curt, one-page dismissals of appeals by right, and only a handful carry any lasting significance.[13] There is no new trend here, neither one that builds over time nor one that uniquely identifies the Dickson Court, but the more prosaic observation holds that on major issues of unusual importance, the Court — to some extent under Laskin, particularly under Dickson, and less so under Lamer — has tried particularly hard to demonstrate solidarity and has occasionally (but only occasionally) succeeded.

A second correlate of the modestly increasing fragmentation of the Dickson Court emerges from Table 7.1, which shows the participation of each judge in the panels on which they served. Because this table lists the judges in the order in which they joined the Court, reading from top to bottom also gives some indication of trends over time. By and large, the more recent appointees (with the significant exception of Gonthier) wrote dissents and/or separate concurrences much more often than the judges they replaced. And this was particularly true of the three women judges, all of whom wrote their own separate opinions much more often than average. Of the three, only McLachlin wrote the opinion of the Court more often than the

## Table 7.1

### Dissents, Concurrences, and Decisions, by Judge
### Reported Supreme Court Decisions, 1984–1990

| Judge | Panels | Wrote decision | Contributed to decision | Divided panels | With majority | Conc. | Diss. |
|---|---|---|---|---|---|---|---|
| Ritchie | 23 | 8.7% | 13.0% | 5 | 80.0% | 0.0% | 20.0% |
| Dickson | 427 | 24.4% | 30.0% | 173 | 81.5% | 5.8% | 12.7% |
| Beetz | 295 | 11.2% | 17.3% | 80 | 66.3% | 20.0% | 13.8% |
| Estey | 196 | 15.8% | 25.0% | 57 | 64.9% | 17.5% | 17.5% |
| McIntyre | 366 | 14.2% | 23.0% | 122 | 63.1% | 16.4% | 20.5% |
| Chouinard | 168 | 11.3% | 13.1% | 39 | 76.9% | 5.1% | 17.9% |
| Lamer | 507 | 20.1% | 28.0% | 178 | 68.0% | 14.6% | 17.4% |
| Wilson | 532 | 13.2% | 29.7% | 204 | 51.5% | 19.6% | 28.9% |
| Le Dain | 228 | 11.0% | 16.7% | 60 | 73.3% | 20.0% | 6.7% |
| La Forest | 419 | 11.9% | 22.4% | 164 | 66.5% | 17.7% | 15.9% |
| L'Heureux-Dubé | 294 | 7.5% | 19.0% | 120 | 50.8% | 10.0% | 39.2% |
| Sopinka | 194 | 17.5% | 35.6% | 84 | 50.0% | 27.4% | 22.6% |
| Cory | 160 | 15.6% | 23.1% | 58 | 72.4% | 8.6% | 19.0% |
| Gonthier | 154 | 9.7% | 11.7% | 61 | 88.5% | 3.3% | 8.2% |
| McLachlin | 110 | 19.1% | 35.5% | 44 | 56.8% | 15.9% | 27.3% |
| ALL | 4073 | 14.9% | 24.3% | 1449 | 65.2% | 14.8% | 20.0% |

all-judge average; both Wilson and L'Heureux-Dubé did most of their writing in dissent or in separate concurrence.

## Voting Blocs on the Dickson Court

Laskin worked toward — and ended by dominating — a more unified Supreme Court than had ever been seen before. In some respects, the Dickson chief justiceship represented a partial retreat. Laskin delivered the decision of the Court in 45 percent of all his panel appearances, almost double Dickson's rate. And the late Laskin Court (after the replacement of Pratte with Chouinard had given Laskin effective control) rendered non-unanimous decisions in only 20 percent of its cases; on the Dickson Court, this rose to 35 percent. Both of these figures suggest a Court that was no longer as firmly united by a single dominant vision. On the other hand, when the Court did divide (which it was now doing rather more often), Dickson was on the decision-delivering side of the divided panel even more often — more than 80 percent of the time, compared with Laskin's 75 percent.

The decision-delivery figures for the late Laskin Court suggest something of a one-man show; the Dickson figures show a chief justice more willing to share with his allies the delivery of decisions. The people who wrote the most decisions for the Dickson Court are easily identified: Dickson had 104 decisions, and Lamer was close behind with 102; Wilson was in third place with 70, and La Forest in fourth with 50. Leaving out the 55 *per coram* decisions, this means that four individuals combined for about 60 percent of all the authored decisions of the Court, half again as many as were authored by the other eleven.

From this information alone, we could equally well have identified either the bloc that centred the Court or the leading figures of the two or more factions competing for the leadership of a divided Court. Which of these two was indeed the case can be determined by examining the two-judge agreement rates. Specifically, which of his colleagues were most likely to sign on with Dickson when they served together on a divided panel? Of the people who served for any significant part of the period, the most frequent allies were (in order) La Forest, Lamer, and Wilson. Of the many other judges who came and went on the revolving-door Court, Chouinard was Dickson's most reliable supporter on the early Court, Gonthier and Cory on the later Court.

But if this identifies Dickson's most dependable allies, who were his opponents? The judges with the lowest agreement rates with Dickson were McLachlin, McIntyre, and Estey — not, of course, a triumvirate, because McLachlin replaced McIntyre when he retired, and by this time, Estey had already retired as well. Following through on McIntyre as the longest-serving member of this set reinforces the impression of an "outsider" group, because McIntyre's highest agreement rates were with precisely those members (such as Sopinka, LeDain, and Beetz) not bracketed with Dickson above.

This double set of observations reinforces the argument that Dickson was not simply a loyal Laskin understudy. His most reliable supporters were not the same people who had been Laskin's strongest allies, nor did he inherit Laskin's opponents. In the closing years of Laskin's chief justiceship, Laskin drew the highest levels of agreement from McIntyre and Estey. Conversely, during her first few years on the Court, Wilson joined the majority in fewer divided panels than any of her colleagues, very much the odd one out on a Court where dissents were otherwise declining. But the Dickson Court from the beginning showed a distinctly different configuration. His strongest supporters were newcomer La Forest and former dissident Wilson, and his lowest support rates came from the Laskin loyalists Estey and McIntyre. The only major carryover from the Laskin group to the Dickson group was Lamer. But the opposition bloc was not simply an eroding carryover from the earlier period; Sopinka/McLachlin was a voting alliance just as solid as that of Estey/McIntyre.

The Dickson Court saw the disintegration of the Quebec bloc that had been a more or less constant feature of the Court's voting patterns since 1949. Beetz signed on with Chouinard proportionately more often than with anyone else; indeed, their agreement rate of 78.8 percent on all divided panel appearances was the highest on the Court. But Beetz's agreement rate with Lamer was well below average, and Chouinard's replacement, L'Heureux-Dubé, was the one with whom Beetz agreed the least. Indeed, the Beetz–L'Heureux-Dubé agreement rate of 21.7 percent on divided panels is one of the three lowest two-judge linkages on the Court. Lamer did not sign on with Chouinard particularly often either, and he also agreed with L'Heureux-Dubé less often than with any other colleague. When Gonthier replaced Beetz, he agreed with Lamer no more often, and with L'Heureux-Dubé equally seldom, as his predecessor.

Perhaps the Quebec bloc vanished, particularly in relation to L'Heureux-Dubé, because there was a "women judges" bloc to which she could belong instead, consisting at first of two women and then (with the appointment of McLachlin two years later) of three. This is certainly one of the things that we might expect if women really do differ from men in the way that they perceive social conflict and the law,[14] if there are different legal issues (or different aspects of legal issues) to which they respond, if it is true that (as Bertha Wilson's classic article suggested) women judges "make a difference."[15] But this is not the case, at least not in any straightforward way. L'Heureux-Dubé was more likely to sign on with the two women judges than with any of her other colleagues, but this is more a question of how seldom she signed on with the others rather than how often she signed on with the women, which was rather less than half the time. Both Wilson and McLachlin had several more constant allies than L'Heureux-Dubé. And, the most telling point of all, the Wilson/McLachlin agreement score was one of the lowest on the Court. From time to time, the women judges closed ranks against the men, but this was an infrequent rather than a regular occurrence, and it tended to involve cases (such as *R. v. Keegstra*) that did not in any simple sense raise feminist issues. In the end, it is clear that there was no more a "women judges" bloc on the Court than there was a "men judges" bloc.

Despite the slight increase in voting fragmentation, Dickson and his allies maintained a control of the Court — not as obvious a control as Laskin's (because the decision writing was more evenly shared) but comparably effective. The "opposition bloc" seemed to be able to renew itself but not to grow in strength, McLachlin/Sopinka simply replacing Estey/McIntyre. But just as the Laskin voting blocs did not carry over into the Dickson Court, so the Dickson voting blocs did not carry over into the Lamer Court; neither among Dickson's allies (Lamer and La Forest) nor among his opponents (McLachlin and Sopinka) do the pairings accurately predict the partnerships of the 1990s.

## Citation Practices of the Dickson Court

With new personnel and new challenges, it is not surprising to discover that the Dickson Court was developing a new style of judicial citation, although not all of these differences lie in the most obvious directions.

### *From where did the Supreme Court Get its Citations?*

The citation practices of the Dickson Court confirm the continuing marginalization of Judicial Committee precedents, which dwindled to less than 3 percent of the total. In the early 1950s the Judicial Committee was cited almost as often as the Supreme Court itself; by the late 1980s, it was cited one-fifteenth as often. Citations of the other English courts were down comparably, to about one in every eight. The Rinfret Court cited English courts (including the Judicial Committee) about three times for every time it cited itself; for the Dickson Court, this ratio was almost reversed.

It was always a logical possibility that the decline of English citations would create a gap that would be filled from another logical source, the United States. After all, the United States is geographically adjacent, it is a common law country, it uses one of the official languages, it is a federal system with a division of jursidiction between two levels of government, and its Bill of Rights is in some sense the prototype on which twentieth-century entrenchments, including that of Canada, have been modelled. These arguments notwithstanding, American case law has not flowed into the gap left by the lower salience of English authorities, even with the Charter as a new crack through which that influence could have entered. To

## Table 7.2

### Citations to Judicial Authority by the Dickson Court Reported Decisions, 1984–1990

| Source | Number | Frequency | Median Date |
|---|---|---|---|
| Judicial Committee | 253 | 2.9% | 1922 |
| Supreme Court of Canada | 3342 | 38.9% | 1981 |
| Other English Courts | 1173 | 13.7% | 1948 |
| Other Canadian Courts | 3035 | 35.3% | 1978 |
| U.S. Courts | 615 | 7.2% | 1968 |
| Other | 170 | 2.0% | |

be sure, there was some increase in American citations, to about double the level of the Laskin Court, or about one citation in fourteen. But this total is still quite modest, even more so when we realize that it is to a range of U.S. courts (federal and state) and not just to the USSC. In fact, citations to the USSC were only about half again as frequent as citations to the Judicial Committee. This is a significant milestone in its own right, because it had not been true of any prior period of Supreme Court history, but it is scarcely the spectre of a new captivity.[16]

If U.S. authorities did not fill the gap, neither did those of other countries — not even, for example, Australia. In addition to the obvious list of similarities (British origins, English language, federal system, growing rights jurisprudence, issues of Aboriginal rights), Australia had now added a new-found liberation from the Judicial Committee, with the formal ending of those appeals in 1986.[17] This had no impact; citations to other countries, with Australia counting for the bulk of those, remained negligible.

Somewhat curiously, although the Dickson Court was now citing English authorities less, it was not citing itself more. The use of Supreme Court citations was unchanged as a proportion of the total, although it is worth noting that it was a steady share of a growing total, the Dickson Court citing about 1400 cases a year compared with the Laskin Court's 900. Although the numbers are too neat to take literally, the proportionate drop in Judicial Committee citations was made up by American citations (mostly to the USSC), and the decrease in other English citations was almost exactly offset by the increase in other Canadian citations.

The increasing frequency with which other Canadian courts were cited was an important development in itself. As I have already commented, when I read Supreme Court decisions, I am struck by the consideration that is given to the lower courts and the respect with which their contributions are acknowledged; there is nothing perfunctory about the way the Supreme Court uses these authorities. Indeed, they are sometimes explicitly accepted over what would at first glance seem to be preemptively authoritative alternatives (such as the House of Lords or the USSC). It is important to know that the Supreme Court under Dickson cited itself far more often than it cited any other single court in the world. But I think it is also important to notice that the second most frequently cited court was the Ontario Court of Appeal (with 605 citations), followed by the House of Lords (376), the USSC (367), the Quebec Court of Appeal (323), and the English Court of Appeal (313). The single judicial authority from outside of Canada who is cited most often is Lord Denning (72 citations, named 42 times — not quite enough to displace Fauteux from the Supreme Court of Canada influence table below, Table 7.3). But excluding the members of the Supreme Court itself, the most frequently cited judicial official in the world is Mr. Justice G.A. Martin of the Ontario Court of Appeal (cited 127 times, named 65), which would put him well up in that same table, behind Estey but ahead of Martland. If the purpose of ending appeals to the Judicial Committee was to create a body of law that would be drawn from Canadian sources, then citations to lower Canadian courts have to be counted as part of the fulfillment of that purpose.

## The Supreme Court Cites the Supreme Court: Who and What?

If the Dickson Court was not citing itself proportionately more often, it was citing itself in significantly different ways and emphasizing quite a different set of its current and previous members, as shown in Table 7.3.

There is nothing particularly surprising about this list: it includes the longer-serving current members, including the chief, the two most recent chief justices, and the longest-serving recent member. Compared with the parallel lists drawn up for the previous Courts, however, it is striking for two things. The first is the fact that the balance is tipped so dramatically away from previous chief justices and toward current members. Duff, who led the count for the first twenty-five years and was still in solid third place for the Laskin Court, has disappeared from the list, and even so recent a chief justice

## Table 7.3

### Supreme Court of Canada Judges Most Frequently Cited by the Dickson Court
### Reported Cases, Supreme Court of Canada, 1984–1990

| Judge | Number of times cited | Number of times named | "Score" |
|---|---|---|---|
| Dickson*† | 668 | 294 | 962 |
| Lamer* | 286 | 132 | 418 |
| Laskin† | 273 | 142 | 415 |
| McIntyre* | 186 | 72 | 258 |
| Wilson* | 169 | 85 | 254 |
| Ritchie* | 167 | 76 | 243 |
| Estey* | 139 | 63 | 202 |
| Martland | 131 | 47 | 178 |
| Beetz* | 114 | 48 | 162 |
| Pigeon* | 103 | 58 | 161 |
| La Forest* | 103 | 49 | 152 |
| Fauteux† | 96 | 24 | 120 |

* indicates a member of the current Court.
† indicates a past or current chief justice.

as Fauteux is barely clinging to the bottom place of the table. Only Laskin prevents a sweep by current members, and he is pushed to third place. The second is the extent of Dickson's preeminence; he has both more citations and more times that he is specifically named than the next two combined.

This point is reinforced by the fact that every one of these frequently cited cases was a decision of the Dickson Court itself. By contrast, the Laskin Court's top dozen included only two decisions delivered by the Laskin Court itself and one that predated the end of appeals in 1949, although the Laskin chief justiceship was more than half again as long as Dickson's. This is the practical face of saying that the Dickson Court's attention was focused on more recent case law, with a subsequent devaluing of the Court's more dated precedents.

The reason for this focus is absolutely transparent: it is the Charter. Except for the *Manitoba Language Reference,* every one of the top dozen most frequently cited cases is a Charter case. The great, historic mission of the Dickson Court — the grandiloquent language does seem appropriate — was to lay the groundwork for the interpretation of the new Canadian Charter of Rights and Freedoms and then to apply these first principles to a growing range of Charter issues. *Hunter v. Southam*[18] was the first major Charter decision; it dealt specifically with the issue of unreasonable search and seizure, but it was more important for having "first enunciated and applied the 'purposive' method that has served as the standard approach in the elaboration of Charter rights and freedoms."[19] *R. v. Oakes*[20] tackled the critical issue of what the "reasonable limits" qualifier in Section 1 of the Charter really meant and what argumentative steps a government must follow to establish the reasonableness of any impugned limit. *Big M*[21] was both the first case to have dealt with freedom of religion and an opportunity for Dickson to expand upon the process of analysis appropriate for "purposive" interpretation; *Edwards Books*[22] was the follow-up to *Big M*, as provinces attempted to put their own Sunday closing rules in the gap left by the striking down of the federal Lord's Day Act. *Therens*[23] dealt with the definition of "detention" and therefore with the conditions that trigger the legal rights of Charter Section 10. The *B.C. Motor Vehicle Reference*[24] began to define the meaning of "fundamental rights" in Section 7, *Collins*[25] is still regarded as "the quintessential pronouncement"[26] on the basic guidelines for excluding evidence under Section 24(2), and *Mills*[27] dealt with the question of appropriate remedies for Charter violations.

## Citation Practices and Decay Rates

The same point can be made again by noting that the decay rate for self-citations for the Dickson Court was 15.7 percent, so much higher than previous self-citation rates as to point to a complete change in the way that the Supreme Court approached its own case law. A decay rate of 15.7 percent means a half-life of only about four years, so that in the first four years a case will receive one-half (and in the second four years, one-quarter) of all the citations that are ever made to it. The speed with which a case reaches the point that it is rarely cited, and therefore the rate at which more recent decisions replace older (including not very old) decisions, had accelerated considerably. By way of comparison, the half-life of a Supreme Court citation for the Rinfret Court was seventeen years.

## Major Decisions of the Dickson Court

We can get a better feeling for the new style of the Court by looking at some of its more enduring and important decisions.

Despite its rather innocuous appearance, *Hunter v. Southam* was far from an ordinary dispute between two private individuals: "Hunter" was the appellant in his capacity as director of investigation and research of the Combines Investigation Branch and "Southam" was one of Canada's major newspaper chains. The case involved documents seized by the Combines Investigation Branch upon Mr. Hunter's authorization; Southam immediately applied for a ruling that the search violated the Charter. The oral argument was heard by a nine-judge panel in November, 1983, while Laskin was still chief justice; however, the *Supreme Court Reports* indicate that Laskin "took no part in the judgment" and the unanimous decision was handed down the following autumn by the new chief justice, Brian Dickson.

Dickson began with the flat statement of the novel status ("supreme law") of the Charter, proceeded to a recital of the facts, and then summarized the contending arguments. He acknowledged the absence of a textual context for the Charter right to freedom from "unreasonable search and seizure," and said that "it is clear" that neither a dictionary nor the traditional rules for interpreting statutes could adequately unfold its meaning, because "the task of expounding a constitution is crucially different from that of construing a statute." This task is different because a constitution "must be capable of growth and development over time to meet new social, political and historical realities often unimagined by its framers," with the judiciary as the "guardian of the constitution" in this growth. The double thrust of this declaration is important. First, it was squarely on the contextualist rather than the formalist side of the Laskin watershed; and second, it repudiated the long-dominant "watertight compartments" metaphor of the Judicial Committee in favour of the historically marginalized "living tree" metaphor.

Dickson "begins with the obvious," which is that the Charter "is a purposive document" whose purpose is to guarantee and to protect rights within the limits of reason and to constrain government actions inconsistent with those rights. But the English common law is not an adequate guide, because it articulates restraints on government searches in terms of the law of trespass, and this is too narrow. Dickson was more persuaded by the American approach, which treats this right as part of a right to privacy, although the broader Canadian wording "might protect interests beyond the right of privacy." He further followed American jurisprudence in finding that the balancing of the individual right to privacy with the government interest in carrying out a search must take place before the search. This means that a warrantless search (like the one contemplated in the Combines Investigation Act) is *prima facie* unwarranted and also that warrants must be approved by a neutral third party. As well, "Anglo-Canadian legal and political traditions point to a higher standard" than the Act's terminology of "there may be evidence."

As to the remedy, Dickson denied that the appropriate standards should be "read into" the existing legislation, such that the question in the immediate case would become whether the actual search would have satisfied such "re-structured" legislation. This is because "the courts are guardians of the Constitution," but "it is the legislature's responsibility to enact legislation that embodies appropriate safeguards" and "it should not fall to the courts to fill in the details that will render unconstitutional lacunae constitutional." Finally, he noted that Section 1 of the Charter permits "reasonable limits" to Charter rights, but left "to another day" the "difficult question" of how it would fit in with these and other sections of the Charter.

This case is a good illustration of the way in which the Dickson Court accomplished the "first phase" of Charter jurisprudence. A unanimous Court provided clear direction for future decisions. "Purposive" interpretation, "growth and development, the "living tree" metaphor, the court as "the guardian" — these terms are saturated with historic meaning and pregnant with future implications. The English common law past was cautiously held at arms length, to be distinguished rather than integrated, although the approving direct references to American jurisprudence made this case somewhat unusual. Finally, Dickson was careful not to bite off more than he can chew; he declined to "redraft" the legislation himself, and left "to another day" and another case the consideration of Section 1's "reasonable limits."

*R. v. Vaillancourt*[28] dealt with the notion of "constructive" or "felony" murder: the legal rule that if a death occurs as a result of a major crime, then all the persons involved in the crime are guilty of murder. Vaillancourt had been involved in an armed robbery during the course of which his accomplice (who escaped) killed someone; he appealed his murder conviction, alleging a Charter violation.

Lamer (with Dickson, Estey, and Wilson) described the beginnings of the concept of "felony murder" in the English common law; despite this concept's "questionable origins and subsequent criticisms," it was embodied in English and Canadian statutes in the nineteenth century. A review of other jurisdictions found the same concept in American law ("though it is said to be in decline") and in New Zealand and some Australian states (where it is "narrower" and abolition has been recommended). Supreme Court cases were cited to show that a criminal offence requires a "mental element" in the form of intentionality or recklessness and that the absence of this element violates constitutional requirements. This is even more so for crimes such as robbery and, particularly, murder that carry a special stigma, a moral blameworthiness. A second logical track led to the same conclusion, because the "presumption of innocence" in s.11(d) of the Charter requires proof beyond reasonable doubt. But "constructive murder" requires that a person be found guilty of murder once it is proven that he has taken part in a major crime resulting in a death, even if there remains reasonable doubt of any intention to cause death. (Vaillancourt testified, and gave some evidence, that he had reason to believe his accomplice's weapon was not loaded.) Lamer acknowledged Parliament's concern with discouraging the use of weapons in the commission of crimes, but this was not enough to uphold the law as a "reasonable limit" because the same purpose could be accomplished without invoking stigma-laden terms such as "murder." The appeal was allowed, the conviction was set aside, and a new trial was ordered.

La Forest echoed Lamer, with slightly more restraint. He agreed that a special stigma attaches to the crime of murder such that the principles of fundamental justice require an appropriate *mens rea,* although he was willing to settle for "a closely related intention," such as an intent to cause serious bodily harm combined with recklessness — that is to say, he split the difference between the existing statute and Lamer's standard of reasonable doubt versus objective foreseeability. This was enough for a finding of unconstitutionality, beyond the saving reach of s.1, because the challenged law would require a conviction for a purely accidental death. Beetz (with Le Dain) also concurred with the result, but for reasons that were even more self-contained: the impugned section violates the principles of fundamental justice in such a way as not to be saved by s.1, but this did not make it necessary even to consider (let alone to answer) the question of whether a conviction for murder could legitimately rest on anything less than proof beyond a reasonable doubt of subjective foresight. In other words, the current law could be found to be unconstitutional without necessitating spelling out in detail what it would have had to look like in order to be constitutional.

McIntyre, on his own, dissented. For him, it was enough that Parliament had decided to use the term "murder" to describe such a killing. This may be in some sense "illogical," but this is not at all the same thing as saying that it "violates" the principles of fundamental justice. He demonstrated both a willingness to defer to the legislature and a preference for a close rather than a generous reading of the constitutional text — what we might call Charter minimalism.

The differences among the three sets of reasons on the majority side demonstrate the way in which separate concurrences signal the gradations of opinion within a divided Court. Lamer, writing for not-quite-a-majority of the panel, gave a strong decision laying out a trail that Parliament must follow; La Forest almost agreed, although in a way that came a little closer to saving the legislation and widening Parliament's choices; and Beetz and Le Dain preferred to invalidate the current law on narrower terms, considering the further issues only when some subsequent case makes it necessary. In the light of hindsight, we can say that Lamer's "maximalism" would prevail, but decisions such as this also point to an alternate future in which the appointment of Beetz-like judges might have meant a Charter that evolved in much the same way but at a much slower tempo.

## Most Influential Judges of the Dickson Court

In the previous chapter, I mentioned that Dickson was the first to "score" more than 1000 for his subsequent influence. The figures in Table 7.4, then, are even more impressive: Lamer became the second, and Wilson the third, to break 1000, while Dickson went well over 1500. Part of this, of course, is the same phenomenon that explains why a loaf of bread or a chocolate bar costs so much more than it did when we were children — inflation. The Kerwin Court made about 500 judicial citations per year, and fewer than 150 of them were to Supreme Court decisions. By contrast, the Lamer Court (which made most of the citations to the Dickson Court) made about 1800 judicial citations per year, more than half of them to prior Supreme Court decisions. Taking this six-to-one ratio at face value, perhaps Rand's score of just over 200 (Table 3.3) is more impressive than it appeared at first glance.

The strong showing of the current chief justice and of the man who would replace him is not unexpected — at the least because since Laskin (possibly since Cartwright), the chief justice has led the Court in every sense. It is a little more surprising to see Wilson in a

## Table 7.4

### Frequency with which Members of the Dickson Court Are Subsequently Cited Reported Decisions, 1984–1999

| Judge | Number of times cited | Number of times named | "Score" | Days served (%) |
|---|---|---|---|---|
| Dickson* | 1217 | 473 | 1690 | 2263 (100%) |
| Lamer† | 815 | 327 | 1142 | 2263 (100%) |
| Wilson | 676 | 337 | 1013 | 2263 (100%) |
| La Forest | 587 | 248 | 835 | 1991 (88%) |
| McIntyre | 442 | 194 | 636 | 1763 (78%) |
| Le Dain | 212 | 113 | 325 | 1646 (73%) |
| Sopinka | 237 | 61 | 298 | 765 (34%) |
| Beetz | 199 | 91 | 290 | 1636 (72%) |
| Estey | 162 | 67 | 229 | 1464 (65%) |
| McLachlin | 152 | 43 | 195 | 457 (20%) |
| Cory | 146 | 43 | 189 | 514 (23%) |
| L'Heureux-Dubé | 107 | 42 | 149 | 1172 (52%) |
| Gonthier | 70 | 27 | 97 | 514 (23%) |
| Chouinard | 39 | 8 | 47 | 1023 (45%) |
| Ritchie | 4 | 1 | 5 | 195 (9%) |

* indicates the current chief justice.
† indicates the future chief justices.

strong third place, given the fact that she delivered less than her notional share of decisions and was frequently in dissent. Most dissents leave few precedential footprints, and this table helps to distinguish between dissents that are the last echo of a fading doctrine and those that represent the first articulation of an emerging viewpoint. Wilson's dramatic separate concurrence in *Morgentaler,*[29] for example, did not draw the signature of a single colleague, but today it is almost invariably Wilson who is cited, while the more constrained decisions have been left behind. Most of the other entries show the effects of the rapid turnover — long-standing members of the Court in their closing years or neophyte members still finding their footing. If there are two disappointments, they would be Beetz and Chouinard, although Lamer's place on this table (and that of many other judges in previous chapters) puts the lie to any suggestion that we can generalize this to a relative invisibility for Quebec judges.

## Conclusion

If the Laskin Court opened the door for a strong public role for the Court, it was the Dickson Court that stepped through. The major challenge was the Charter, and the major fear was that the Court would "wimp out" in the same way an earlier Court had done for the Bill of Rights; but in fact, the outcome was a firm statement of a powerful Charter with some (but not too many) showcase decisions to punch the point home. Although the Court retreated somewhat from the unified solidarity of the late Laskin Court and fragmented more on the Charter cases than on any other element of its caseload, it held together firmly enough to chart a clear course.

Turnover continued to be a problem, averaging one new face a year. Since the largest set of new appointments came in the last two years (four in a single twelve-month period), this was a problem that would carry over into the new chief justiceship. At the start of his term, Dickson had several colleagues in failing health; at the end, he had several colleagues who were still making the transition to the highest Court. This necessarily suggests an uneven sharing of the work, with the load falling disproportionately on the healthy senior judges, especially Dickson and Lamer; but it also suggests a lower degree of fragmentation, at least in transition.

The Charter dominated the agenda of the Dickson Court, but not to the exclusion of other issues; there were also a number of significant decisions in constitutional law. Although Dickson's approach to federalism was somewhat different from that of Laskin, it would be a mistake to turn him or his Court into provincialists, and the rebalancing of the constitutional division of powers continued. *Crown Zellerbach* (1989)[30] strengthened the "national dimensions" branch of the federal "peace order and good government" power; *AGT v. CRTC* (1989)[31] expanded federal jurisdiction over communications; and *GMAC v. City National Leasing* (1989)[32] breathed new life into the "trade in general" branch of the federal trade and commerce power, something that had been a dead letter for a century. *Guerin* (1984)[33] established the fiduciary relationship between Aboriginal peoples and the federal government, and *Valente* (1985)[34] was the Court's first exploration of judicial independence. But these were at best the second ring of the circus; the Charter clearly had centre stage.

By the end of the Dickson Court, there had been yet another almost complete turnover in the Court's membership; only Lamer (the new chief justice) and Wilson (who would leave within two years) had more than five years of experience. The initial Charter challenge had been successfully met; the next frontier was to be the Charter's equality rights, which came into effect three years after the rest of the Charter.

# The Lamer Court:
# July 1990 to July 1999
# "The Innovator"

Just as Rinfret's chief justiceship started before the end of appeals to the Judicial Committee, so Lamer's chief justiceship extends beyond the fifty-year point — but not far beyond, given the surprising announcement on August 21, 1999, that he would be stepping down on January 7, 2000, some nine years before compulsory retirement. The subtitle of this chapter, "the Innovator," identifies the new ground that the Lamer Court broke with regard to the criminal law and to equality rights under the Charter.

When Dickson retired at the end of the 1989–90 term, Antonio Lamer became chief justice, the last of Trudeau's judges presiding over a Court of eight Mulroney judges. Lamer was the logical successor in terms of both the "strong" tradition of seniority and the "weak" tradition of Quebec/non-Quebec alternation. He came to office as the senior member of an extremely junior Court, with only ten years of experience on the Court himself; in this century, only Fitzpatrick and Laskin have had less. And when he took the centre chair, the average length of tenure of the Court fell below four years for only the second time in this century (the other time being in 1906), although the average age of just under 60 was very close to the long-term average of 62.9. The lack of experience was, of course, a transitional problem — it corrected itself with an exceptionally low rate of turnover until 1997 — although it came at a very important time for the country and the Court.

When Lamer took office, the Meech Lake Accord had already failed and the constitutional process that was to end with the 1992 referendum on the Charlottetown Accord was just beginning. Lamer's tenure saw the utter collapse of the federal Conservative Party, the return to office of the Parti Québécois, and Quebec's second sovereignty referendum (which failed by a paper-thin margin). This last particular hot potato was eventually handed to the Supreme Court in the *Quebec Secession Reference*.[1] In international politics, the Berlin Wall was down, the Cold War was over, and the Soviet Union was falling apart, although the Gulf War was a warning that problems still remained. In the United States, the Republicans regained control of Congress but lost the presidency to Bill Clinton, who was reelected in 1996 just in time to confront the Monica Lewinsky scandal and an impeachment attempt. The baby boomers were by now looking at early retirement packages, although the demographics of longer life spans and lower birthrates meant that their political impact was not fading.

## The Personnel of the Lamer Court

The continuing members of the Court (in order of seniority) were Lamer, Wilson, La Forest, L'Heureux-Dubé, Sopinka, Gonthier, Cory, and McLachlin. There was only the most modest turnover until almost the end of the decade; the revolving-door Court of the 1970s and 1980s was no more.

**William Alexander Stevenson** was appointed to the Supreme Court on September 17, 1990, replacing Dickson. He had been appointed to the District Court of Northern Alberta on July 31, 1975, becoming a member of the Alberta Court of Queen's Bench when that court was established (by the consolidation of the District Court and the Supreme Court Trial Division) in 1979. In 1980, he was elevated to the Court of Appeal of Alberta, and he came to the Supreme Court at the age of 56 with fifteen years of distinguished judicial experience; however, he served less than two years before resigning for health reasons. His experience is a useful reminder of the stresses that accompany the Supreme Court's work; although Stevenson had been a senior member of strong provincial court of appeal, he had significant problems coping with the transition to the higher Court.

**Frank Iacobucci** was appointed on January 7, 1991, replacing Wilson. He was born in Vancouver and studied at the University of British Columbia before becoming a professor and then dean of the Faculty of Law at the University of Toronto. He served for three years as deputy minister of justice and deputy attorney-general of Canada and was a constitutional advisor to Prime Minister Mulroney during the time of the Meech Lake Accord, before being appointed chief justice of the Federal Court in 1988. He came to the Court at the age of 53 with less than three years of judicial experience.

John C. Major was appointed to the Court on November 13, 1992, replacing fellow Albertan Stevenson. Born in Mattawa, Ontario, he was educated at Loyola College (now Concordia University) and the University of Toronto before moving west to practice law in Calgary, where he was named Queen's Counsel in 1972. He served as counsel for the McDonald Commission on the RCMP, for the royal commission on the failure of the Canadian Commercial and Northland banks (the Estey Commission), and for the Code Inquiry. He was appointed to the Alberta Court of Appeal on July 11, 1991. Major was 61 years old with less than two years of judicial experience when he was apointed to the Supreme Court.

**Michel Bastarache** was appointed on September 30, 1997, replacing La Forest. He was born in Quebec City and educated at the University of Moncton, the University of Montreal, the University of Ottawa, and the University of Nice. He practised law in Moncton and in Ottawa, and also served as a law professor and dean at the University of Moncton Law School and the University of Ottawa. He was appointed to New Brunswick Court of Appeal in 1995, coming to the Supreme Court at the age of 50 with less than three years of judicial experience.

**Ian Cornell Binnie** was appointed to the Supreme Court on January 8, 1998, replacing Sopinka. He was born in Montreal and educated at McGill University, Cambridge University, and the University of Toronto, and he practised law in Toronto. He was a part-time lecturer at Osgoode Hall, served for a time as associate deputy minister of justice for Canada and as a constitutional advisor to the government of Newfoundland. He was 59 years old when appointed to the Court. Like the man he replaced, he had no prior judicial experience, reinforcing the impression that there is a modern convention that one member of the Court must be appointed (as the quaint legal phrase has it) "off the street."

In some ways, these appointments maintained the patterns of the post-Laskin (and post-Trudeau) appointments, marking this as a genuine institutional change and not simply the passing preference of a single prime minister. Several of the judges (La Forest among the continuing members, Iacobucci and Bastarache among the new ones) came to the Court with strong academic credentials, and although the holding of elected office now seemed to be almost a disqualification, several had experience in public service; however, there was much less emphasis than before on previous judicial experience; all but one (Binnie) were elevated from a court of appeal, but only Stevenson had as much as three years of experience. The monopoly of males of British and French descent has clearly been broken by L'Heureux-Dubé, McLachlin, and Sopinka among the continuing members and by Iacobucci among the new appointees. Louise Arbour, who took up her duties on September 1999, brought the number of women on the Court back up to its Dickson Court high of three.

## The Caseload of the Lamer Court

In all respects, the Lamer Court caseload was a simple continuation of the caseload of the Dickson Court. The Court still handled just over 100 cases per year, which we can probably take as the practical maximum load for the Court — anything larger simply contributes to backlog. And the largest block of cases (43.6%) still involved criminal appeals, followed by public law appeals (25.3%), private law appeals (16.3%), and Charter cases (14.5%). These proportions are not very different from those for the Dickson Court, except for a modest swing away from the latter two.

Ontario and Quebec still accounted for about 40 percent of the caseload, well under their share of the population — indeed, for the first time, British Columbia accounted for more appeals than Quebec, despite having only half Quebec's population. As with the Dickson Court, the Federal Court accounted for just under 10 percent of the caseload, although, as will be discussed later, the "second wave" of Charter cases was less likely to involve legal rights and more likely to involve the impact of federal legislation on equality rights, which means that the appeals that rose from the Federal Court were more likely than ever to be the major cases. Overall success rates for the Lamer Court were 5 percent higher (at 45%) than for its predecessor. The Alberta and British Columbia courts of appeal accounted for much of the difference: they were half again as likely to be reversed by the Lamer Court as by the Dickson Court. And the differential between the seldom-reversed Ontario Court of Appeal and the frequently reversed Quebec Court of Appeal, which first opened up under Dickson, remained large enough to take seriously.

The strongest correlate of the higher reversal rates was not region but subject matter. Neither private law nor public law appeals were much more likely to succeed with the Lamer Court, but criminal law reversals were up from 32.7 percent to 39.4 percent, and the Charter appeals that succeeded 31.8 percent of the time under Dickson were now half again as likely to succeed. It is tempting to interpret this as marking a new wave of Charter activism led from above, but (given that Charter cases fell as a percentage of total caseload from 20.0% to 14.5%) it may just mean that the Court was using its leave jurisdiction a little less permissively on Charter appeals.

What did the 1990s — the last decade of the first fifty years of supremacy, the end of the millennium — look like through the window of the Supreme Court caseload? Essentially, it looked like the world of the Dickson Court, with the evolution seen by that Court pushed one notch further. Economic cases were a modest rather than a major element of the caseload: business-related cases accounted for only 87 cases; tax cases were only slightly more numerous, with 92 examples; and the transportation category was proportionately at its lowest point in the period, with only 68 cases, still mostly dealing with automobiles. Conversely, crime, especially violent crime, continued to occupy a significant and growing share of the caseload: there were 107 murder cases, 98 sexual assault cases, 24 assaults, and 6 fires and explosions.

This growing criminal caseload, especially cases involving violence, was not a passing aberration; it characterized both the Dickson and Lamer Courts. Nor was this a Charter phenomenon now that the focus of the Charter caseload had shifted from legal rights to equality rights. Martland or Kerwin or Rand (to say nothing of Duff) would be genuinely surprised by the caseload under Lamer, so different from their emphasis on company law, tax law, and transportation law. Especially given the smaller panels, a member of the early Court would have seen barely one murder case and one other violent crime case in a year; members of the Lamer Court saw more in an average month.

## Decision-making by the Lamer Court

The late Laskin Court had shown the least fragmented Court in the Court's history, with the highest proportion of unanimous decisions, the lowest rates for dissents and separate concurrences, the smallest fragments when the Court divided. The Dickson Court receded slightly from these levels, and the Lamer Court continued the gradual retreat — and, as for the Dickson Court, this was primarily a function of the Charter cases.

The average number of opinions delivered per case rose slightly, from 1.58 to 1.69, but standing on its own, this is the poorest measure

## Table 8.1

### Dissents, Concurrences, and Decisions, by Judge
### Reported Supreme Court Decisions, 1990–1999

| Judge | Panels | Wrote decision | Contributed to decision | Divided panels | With majority | Conc. | Diss. |
|---|---|---|---|---|---|---|---|
| Lamer | 544 | 32.0% | 42.5% | 268 | 68.3% | 15.3% | 16.4% |
| Wilson | 22 | 22.7% | 59.1% | 16 | 50.0% | 50.0% | 0.0% |
| La Forest | 611 | 13.9% | 25.0% | 294 | 65.0% | 19.7% | 15.3% |
| L'Heureux-Dube | 694 | 8.9% | 29.7% | 337 | 39.5% | 28.5% | 32.0% |
| Sopinka | 679 | 20.8% | 31.2% | 307 | 65.5% | 16.3% | 18.2% |
| Cory | 775 | 17.0% | 22.5% | 342 | 80.4% | 9.6% | 9.9% |
| Gonthier | 766 | 7.6% | 13.1% | 337 | 68.2% | 16.3% | 15.4% |
| McLachlin | 771 | 10.1% | 24.6% | 336 | 48.5% | 24.4% | 27.1% |
| Stevenson | 92 | 10.9% | 23.9% | 36 | 58.3% | 25.0% | 16.7% |
| Iacobucci | 742 | 14.0% | 18.9% | 310 | 79.0% | 9.4% | 11.6% |
| Major | 546 | 8.1% | 15.8% | 244 | 68.9% | 10.2% | 20.9% |
| Bastarache | 105 | 13.3% | 21.9% | 42 | 71.4% | 11.9% | 16.7% |
| Bennie | 65 | 6.2% | 15.4% | 29 | 72.4% | 13.8% | 13.8% |
| ALL | 6412 | 14.2% | 24.3% | 2898 | 64.5% | 17.1% | 18.4% |

of how divided the Court might be. For one thing, it depends on the panel size — and in fact, the slight rise in the average number of opinions for the Lamer Court was completely cancelled by a slight rise in panel size. Under both Lamer and Dickson, the members of the Court wrote reasons (decisions, concurrences, or dissents) in almost exactly the same proportion of their total panel appearances, just under one in four, although in the 1990s, slightly more judges signed on to the typical dissent. As was true of the Dickson Court, the major cause of this fragmentation was the Charter cases, which continued to draw larger panels and more opinions per case (both dissents and separate concurrences) and which generally exhibited greater fragmentation than any other type of case. Criminal cases (at least, those that raised no Charter issues) were both the largest element of the caseload and the one on which the Court was the most unified; the less frequent private law cases similarly occasioned little division. It was Charter cases (and to a lesser extent, public law cases) that revealed the fault lines, and these will be explored later.

The numbers in Table 8.1 are slightly complicated by the fact that the Lamer Court was more likely than its predecessors to use multiple-authored decisions. To be sure, this was not unprecedented: for example, *Irwin Toy* (1989)[2] was jointly authored by Dickson, Lamer, and Wilson, and *Sparrow* (1990)[3] by Dickson and La Forest. Nor was this becoming the dominant style of the Court; there were only twenty-two examples under Lamer's chief justiceship.[4] Iacobucci was the most likely to be involved (14 times), followed by Cory (10).

Lamer wrote the most decisions for the Court (174), followed by Sopinka (141) and Cory (132), these three judges accounting for about one-half of the Court's decisions. Almost no one else wrote more than 100 decisions (Iacobucci wrote 104), and nobody else wrote the decision for the Court more frequently than the all-Court average. L'Heureux-Dubé and McLachlin wrote or joined the most separate decisions, although these figures are high enough across the table that it is probably most accurate to indicate them as "frequent" and Cory and Iacobucci as "seldom," with the others clustered in the middle. Both in the frequency of divided panels and in the level of division that existed on those panels, the figures recall the early Laskin Court (Table 6.1), although then there had been a 2–1 balance of dissents over concurrences and now the two were evenly balanced.

## Voting Blocs on the Lamer Court

Two new appointments in the first two years (with Wilson's early resignation and Stevenson's rapid departure) initially appeared to suggest a continuation of the revolving-door Court, but in fact, there were no further changes in personnel until the beginning of Lamer's eighth term. Coming this close to a "natural" Court greatly facilitates the search for the major voting alliances on the Court; I will leave a brief consideration of the last two years (the service of Bastarache and Binnie) for the next chapter. This section will explain why I think Cory's departure was particularly significant, marking the beginning of a personnel-driven shift in style and direction that culminated with the appointment of McLachlin as chief justice.[5]

One way to identify cleavages on the Court is to find the sets of judges who most often combine to deliver the decisions of divided panels. The most successful five-judge coalition for the Lamer Court was clearly the Lamer/Sopinka/Cory/Iacobucci/Major group. This core group in its various combinations (that is, the four-and three-judge groups included within it) explains a total of 47 of the 240 divided court decisions between 1990 and 1997, far more than any other alternative five-judge grouping, and the count goes up significantly higher if we broaden the criteria to include that group plus a single defection. Lamer was clearly the leading spokesperson, having written or cowritten 18 of the group's decisions, and for this reason

I will refer to it as "the Lamer bloc." It is also important, however, to acknowledge that Lamer's leadership was pronounced but not overwhelming. The other members of the bloc also had a voice, and I will unfold some of the nuances of this below.

The single most important factor in understanding the voting dynamics of the Lamer Court is the firmness of this five-judge group, which Patrick Monahan has called the "gang of five." On those occasions when the Court divided, each of these five signed on with each of the others an average of 65 percent of the time; the "weak links" were Major/Lamer and Sopinka/Cory (61%), and the strongest alliance was Cory/Iacobucci (74%). On any nine-judge Court, five is of course the magic number, which cannot be consistently frustrated if it holds together. It is his leadership of this group that allowed Lamer to deliver almost 200 decisions during the decade, and it is their membership within this bloc that allowed Sopinka, Cory, and Iacobucci to deliver 100 or more each. To be sure, it would be a mistake to make the five appear too monolithic — to agree 65 percent of the time means to disagree 35 percent of the time — but more often than not, this was the group that set the course. Collectively, they delivered about two-thirds of the Court's decisions.

Lamer led the Lamer bloc, but not to the extent of eclipsing his colleagues, and the division of labour within the alliance was fairly clear. On defendant's rights issues (Sections 7 through 14 of the Charter), Sopinka's was the most frequent voice and Major his most dependable supporter. The Lamer Court generally laid down a strong statement of defendant's rights under the Charter, and Sopinka's most memorable (and, at the time, most controversial) decision was *Stinchcombe*,[6] on the Crown's duty to disclose its case to the accused's counsel. On equality rights, the Lamer Court generally articulated a more restrained version of s.15 than many litigants and interest groups would have preferred, particularly with regard to the equality rights of women; the string of cases that support this generalization (*McKinney, Dickason, Symes,* and *Thibaudeau*)[7] are discussed in the next chapter, because McLachlin's consistent dissents are a hint about what the next decade might look like. On the issues of gay rights and benefits for same-sex couples, Cory and Iacobucci began (*Mossop* and *Egan & Nesbitt*)[8] by dissenting and ended (*Vriend* and *M v. H*)[9] by leading the Lamer bloc to a broader reading and a firm application of s.15 of the Charter. Lamer's own influence was most pronounced with regard to Aboriginal rights (the *van der Peet* trilogy and *Delgamuukw*),[10] to judicial independence issues (*Lippe, Genereux,* and the *Remuneration Reference*),[11] and to a range of defendant's rights, including the right to counsel (*Bartle* and *Prosper*).[12] It would be too much to think of these as marking out fault lines within the bloc, but they do suggest a partnership of shifting emphases rather than a simple relationship of leader and followers.

The second identifiable group is the one formed by La Forest, L'Heureux-Dubé, Gonthier, and McLachlin; we might think of them as "the outsiders." This group accounted for a total of eighteen decision-delivering combinations of divided courts — quite a surprising total considering that an alternative four-judge group (say, Lamer, Sopinka, Iacobucci, and Major) accounted for only seven. Their leading spokesperson was La Forest, writing or cowriting eleven of their eighteen decisions. Monahan has referred to them as the "gang of four," but this overstates the point. On divided decisions of the Court, the average two-judge agreement rate of the Lamer bloc was 65 percent, but the same figure for the four outsiders was only 45 percent, which means that its members were slightly more likely to disagree among themselves than to agree. The only pair of judges with an agreement rate that exceeded the "low point" of the Lamer bloc was La Forest/Gonthier. The "gang of four" was ultimately not so much a gang in its own right as the fragments left over after the formation of the "gang of five," and this division on the outside simply made it that much easier for the Lamer bloc to prevail. In the most general terms, La Forest (strongly seconded by Gonthier) tended in many areas to take a restrained view of the Charter and to allow more latitude for legislators, a view that was shared by L'Heureux-Dubé and McLachlin in some areas (such as Charter defendant's rights) but not in others (such as Charter equality rights, especially regarding women).

Another way to think of these patterns of agreement, and to spell out the practical implications, is to treat the higher agreement frequencies as pointing to each judge's preferred coalition patterns: when we say that Cory and Iacobucci's 74 percent agreement rate was the highest on the Court, we are also saying that Cory was Iacobucci's favourite coalition partner when the Court divided (and, of course, vice versa). Similarly, Cory's 65 percent agreement rate with Lamer marks him as Cory's second-favourite coalition partner, with Major third (63%) and Sopinka fourth (61%). But the practical face of "favourite partner" is that these are the colleagues (and in this order) that a judge will approach when he or she realizes that a panel is dividing and an important issue hangs in the balance. This search-

## Table 8.2

### Preferred Four- and Five-Judge Coalitions, Based on Actual Agreement Rates Reported Supreme Court of Canada Decisions, 1990–1997[14]

| Judge | Preferred four- [five] judge coalition |
|---|---|
| Lamer | Sopinka, Iacobucci, Cory [Major] |
| La Forest | Gonthier, Iacobucci, Cory [Lamer] |
| L'Heureux-Dubé | Gonthier, La Forest, McLachlin [Cory] |
| Sopinka | Major, Iacobucci, Lamer [Cory] |
| Cory | Iacobucci Lamer, Major [Sopinka] |
| Gonthier | La Forest, Cory, Iacobucci [L'Heureux-Dubé] |
| McLachlin | Gonthier, La Forest, Major [Iacobucci] |
| Iacobucci | Cory, Sopinka, Major [Lamer] |
| Major | Sopinka, Iacobucci, Cory [Lamer] |

ing for coalition partners, for like-minded colleagues who approach major legal issues with a similar set of values and priorities, is an important part of the appellate process, because judges of panel courts do not simply listen to oral arguments and then vote and run. They are engaged in a collegial process of discussion and persuasion, accomplished through conferencing and the circulation of judgments, and this conversation is legitimate — indeed essential — to the process.[13] Table 8.2 diagrams the logic for the members of the Lamer Court, demonstrating both the coherent solidarity of the Lamer bloc and the pivotal role of Cory/Iacobucci.

Two additional elements are necessary to round off the description of the major voting dynamics of the Lamer Court. The first is the "flexible voting" (the term is Edelman and Chen's[15]) of Justice Cory. On the one hand, Cory was a solid member of the Lamer bloc, and his close linkage with Iacobucci (the two had the highest two-judge agreement rate on the Court) further emphasizes his importance to this dominant group. At the same time, however, Cory was the member of the Lamer bloc who was the most likely to defect in such a way as to make him part of an alternative decision-delivery group. Remarkably, the defection of Cory from the Lamer core to the outsiders created a five-judge group that was almost as successful as the core itself. The outsiders alone accounted for eighteen decisions, but the outsiders plus Cory accounted for a total of thirty-nine, almost as many as the core itself. No other defection carries even a quarter of the punch of this one. However, even if Cory's adhesion so dramatically turned the outsiders into "the alternative core," La Forest remained their intellectual leader, writing or cowriting twenty of their thirty-nine decisions. This pivotal position at the centre, and the frequency with which it can be "cashed in," make Cory the most intriguing member of the Lamer Court — and his departure in 1999 was therefore a clear signpost of a potential for a major change in direction.

A second intriguing and significant feature of the Lamer Court was the fact that the two women judges appear to have been isolated at one edge of the Court; L'Heureux-Dubé accounts for the five lowest two-judge agreement scores, McLachlin for the next six. Since one of these scores is the one that links the two women judges, they do not seem to have formed the potential core of a new group. One of the issues debated when women lawyers began to receive their share of positions on the higher courts was whether women judges would "make a difference"[16] or whether they would simply be absorbed into the male-dominated profession. The implication of these cleavages, combined with the fact that Wilson had been one of the most prolific dissenters on the Laskin and Dickson Courts, is that, at least so far, the women members of the Supreme Court are not being absorbed — but the price they are paying for this is that they are being left outside the dominant decision-making coalitions. McLachlin's appointment to the chief justice's chair may, of course, mark an end to this pattern.

## Citation Practices of the Lamer Court

The Dickson Court was very much like the the Laskin Court in the sources from which it drew its judicial authorities, the only difference being a greater use of the decisions of lower Canadian courts. But this observation cannot be generalized to the Lamer Court, as shown in Table 8.3.

Over its six years, the Dickson Court had cited the Judicial Committee about 40 times a year, other English courts about 200 times a year, other Canadian courts about 500 times a year, the courts of other countries about 30 times a year, and itself about 500 times a year. Over its nine years, the Lamer Court cited the Judicial Committee and the other English courts about one-third less than its predecessor did, 25 and 140 times a year respectively. It cited other Canadian courts, American courts, and the courts of other countries almost exactly as often as the Dickson Court had. But it cited itself

## Table 8.3

### Citations to Judicial Authority by the Lamer Court Reported Decisions, 1990–1999

| Source | Number | Frequency | Median Date |
|---|---|---|---|
| Judicial Committee | 233 | 1.4% | 1927 |
| Supreme Court of Canada | 9021 | 55.8% | 1989 |
| Other English Courts | 1293 | 8.0% | 1948 |
| Other Canadian Courts | 4442 | 27.5% | 1985 |
| U.S. Courts | 906 | 5.6% | 1974 |
| Other | 284 | 1.8% | 1978 |

almost exactly twice as often, 1000 times per year compared with just over 500.

English citations, once dominant, became a minor element. References to the Judicial Committee all but vanished and seldom occured outside the context of an appeal dealing directly with the federal–provincial division of powers — important when it comes up, but very infrequent. Nor did Lamer's Court draw very heavily on the other English Courts, such as the House of Lords or the Court of Appeal. Instead, the reliance was overwhelmingly on Canadian authorities: about five citations in every six, two-thirds to the Supreme Court itself. This was no captive court.

The cause of the somewhat higher level of American citations was the Charter, although this is not the complete story.[17] Citations to the USSC increased significantly, and this was disproportionately the product of the Charter cases; however, over the same time period, citations to other American authorities (state courts, especially New York and California, and federal courts, especially the Second Circuit) also increased in absolute terms. The ratio of all American citations to all other citations was the highest (but still not particularly high) for private law cases. When U.S. citations first began to rise, this was due almost entirely to Laskin and, after his departure, to Wilson and La Forest; for Lamer's Court, it was a more pervasive phenomenon. But for every citation to American authorities, there were two citations to English courts (including the Judicial Committee), five to other Canadian courts, and ten to the Supreme Court itself. This was also no new captivity.

Most of the "other" citations were still to Australian and New Zealand cases, although this category became more diverse without becoming proportionately larger. There were some references to the French *cour de cassation,* the European Court of Justice, the European Court of Human Rights, and the International Court of Justice, but not very many of any of these, and all together, they barely surpassed the count for the now-marginalized Judicial Committee of the Privy Council. This makes it ironic that Patrick Glenn should praise the Supreme Court for an approach to the common law that draws on such a wide diversity of sources, including many foreign countries.[18] On the contrary, the Supreme Court was never more focused on Canadian sources than under Lamer, this qualified only by a dwindling use of the English Courts and a limited (and contained rather than growing) use of American citations. Indeed, Glenn's comment about the "extensive" use of "foreign" sources only holds if the term "foreign" includes the English courts — which, for much of our history, it did not.

### The Supreme Court Cites the Supreme Court: Who and What?

But if the big story of the citation patterns of the Supreme Court under Lamer is the dramatic surge in the frequency with which it used its own prior decisions, this raises the further question of what these self-citations looked like, and the answer is given in Table 8.4.

The list continues the general trend of the previous chapters: it is a mixture of current members and past chief justices, with the balance gradually swinging toward the current members. Only McIntyre (who left the Court in 1989) and Beetz (who left in 1988) qualify this generalization, McIntyre because of the influence he continued to have in the area of criminal law[19] and Beetz presumably for the Quebec civil law. The list is intriguing for the near-dead heat between the current and the most recent chief justices at the top of the table, continuing the pattern of chief justice dominance that has marked the Supreme Court for several decades. Between them, Lamer and Dickson accounted for fully one-quarter of all the self-citations (and more than one-eighth of all citations to judicial authority) of the Lamer Court. Had Lamer not kept pace so well, one might be tempted to think of the evolution of Canadian judicial authority over these fifty years as the passing of the mantle from Duff to Dickson.

There was a clear second rank of influence formed by La Forest, Sopinka, and Wilson. Also intriguing is the other end of the table, with Laskin barely clinging to last place only a dozen years or so after his death; Ritchie and Martland were even further back at

## Table 8.4

### Supreme Court of Canada Judges Most Frequently Cited by the Lamer Court
### Reported Cases, Supreme Court of Canada, 1990–1999

| Judge | Number of times cited | Number of times named | "Score" |
|---|---|---|---|
| Dickson[†] | 1168 | 516 | 1684 |
| Lamer[*†] | 1231 | 447 | 1678 |
| La Forest[*] | 809 | 368 | 1177 |
| Sopinka[*] | 619 | 191 | 810 |
| Wilson[*] | 512 | 290 | 802 |
| McIntyre | 456 | 189 | 645 |
| McLachlin[*] | 441 | 188 | 629 |
| Cory[*] | 438 | 168 | 606 |
| L'Heureux-Dubé[*] | 343 | 183 | 526 |
| Iacobucci[*] | 293 | 88 | 381 |
| Beetz | 235 | 110 | 345 |
| Laskin[†] | 223 | 88 | 311 |

* indicates a member of the current Court.
† indicates a past or current chief justice.

fifteenth and seventeenth respectively. The rankings reinforce the basic message of a focus on the Court's own recent jurisprudence, to the relative exclusion of its own older case law.

The reason for the focus on recent case law is simple: the Charter. The cases cited most often by the Lamer Court were all Charter cases, even though Charter cases were not a particularly large fraction of the total caseload. Charter decisions tended to be longer, to create more divisions on the Court, and to use more citations that are drawn from a more constricted range of recent major decisions authored by a small bloc of judges: Dickson, Lamer, and La Forest. To put the point a little differently, only seven of the twenty judges who had sat on the Supreme Court in the previous fifteen years (and of the seventy who had ever sat on the Court) shared in the authorship of the fifteen cases that were cited the most frequently in the 1990s. The apparent democratization of judicial influence I referred to in an earlier chapter was a transitional effect and not an enduring characteristic.

### Citation Practices and Decay Rates

The decay rate for the Lamer Court was 12 percent, giving a half-life of 5.4 years. This was a slight retreat from the pattern of the Dickson

Court, which is to say that the Lamer Court was not replacing older precedents with quite the same rapidity. The reason in both Courts was probably the Charter: the Dickson Court devoted much of its efforts to laying down the first generation of Charter cases, and as the Lamer Court tackled the second generation of cases, it continued to use those first decisions as reference points.

In the previous chapter, I suggested that we have seen an evolution from Duff to Dickson — from the highly regarded last chief justice of the Court of captivity to the highly regarded first chief justice of the Court of the Charter. Of course, it is too early to accept this conclusion; the critical question is whether the Dickson Court's first generation of Charter decisions will provide the same anchor point for precedent and citation as Duff's decisions did for the Supreme Court of the 1950s. Conversely, if the Dickson and Lamer Courts have established a new style focused on current issues and on immediate social context and recent case law, Dickson will soon fade behind Lamer as decisively as Laskin's influence yielded to Dickson. The latter is more likely, although a decade later Dickson's influence has not yet done much fading.

## Expanding the Concept of "Authority": Academic Citations

I suggested earlier that one difference between the Anglo-American systems and the continental European systems is that our judges cite other judges and their judges cite academics. In recent years, however, while still citing other judges, our judges have begun making frequent and extensive use of academic sources as well. At one time, the Supreme Court itself explicitly declared that journals like the *Canadian Bar Review* were "not an authority in this Court,"[20] but practices began to change under Laskin, became more formalized under Dickson,[21] and were routinized under Lamer. The Lamer Court cited academic authorities in roughly half of its decisions, to a total of more than 400 citations per year.[22] These new practices were clearly related to the string of appointments of people who were legal academics as well as (sometimes instead of) legal practitioners.

Books were cited slightly more often than journal articles (the ratio was about four to three), and Canadian sources made up about 60 percent of the total for both books and articles, with the United Kingdom ranking second for books and the United States ranking second for articles. The journal of choice was the *Canadian Bar Review* (Vaughan Black and Nicholas Richter found this to be true for the Dickson court as well[23]), cited at least twice as often as any other source, and the author of choice was Professor Peter Hogg of the Osgoode Hall Law School, primarily for his *Constitutional Law of Canada*.[24]

The shift to academic sources, particularly journal articles, both reflected and reinforced the "new" contextualist style. The selection criteria of academic journals strongly favour topics that are of current relevance, a tone that is analytical and critical, and conclusions that are innovative; and journals' shorter publishing cycle means that new ideas typically emerge first in journals, then in books. It is only a mild exaggeration to suggest that if you are a judge who wishes to support the status quo and slow the pace of change, you should cite the textbooks; but if you want to critique recent precedents and accelerate the evolution of doctrine, you should cite the journal articles. This is perfectly illustrated by *Symes v. Canada*.[25]

The change also reflects the Supreme Court's new definition of its relevant public, which completely changed the style (and the length) of the reasons for judgment. The decisions of the 1950s and the 1960s were clearly directed at trained legal professionals who could decode the technical jargon and fill in the assumed background. The more discursive decisions of the 1980s and the 1990s were directed as well at the academic community and at the educated public.

## Major Decisions of the Lamer Court

It is, of course, early days to be speaking with any certainty about which of the Lamer Court decisions will have the greatest staying power and the most enduring influence. For the Lamer Court, unlike all the others considered in the earlier chapters, there are no data that can be drawn from the citation practices of subsequent Courts to replace contemporary expectations with actual performance. The following three cases, however, will no doubt constitute a significant element of the Lamer legacy.

*McKinney v. University of Guelph*[26] was an early Section 15 case in which university professors and librarians challenged the policy of mandatory retirement, although it also revisited the question of which institutions of our society are "caught" by Charter limitations. It is a lengthy decision — taking up 220 pages (110 in each official language) in the *Supreme Court Reports* — with a seven-judge panel delivering five different reasons for judgment.

La Forest (with Dickson[27] and Gonthier) wrote a plurality judgment for the Court, the outcome supported by five judges but the full

reasons supported by only three. Curiously, the decision began with
the finding that universities were not a "part of government," and
therefore their activities were not covered by the Charter, nor did
their actions constitute "law" in a form that would trigger Charter
scrutiny. Even if they were, the acceptance of a contractual obligation
"might well" constitute a waiver of a Charter right, and "there is no
question" about the power of the universities to negotiate contracts
and collective agreements. Despite these several reasons for saying
that the appellants' claim fails to get off the ground — which a more
traditionally inclined Court would say makes it inappropriate to look
any further — La Forest went on to consider an "even if" scenario
that subjects the universities to scrutiny under s.15. Because it is
"difficult to argue" that mandatory retirement is not discriminatory
on the basis of age, he had "no hesitation in concluding" that it
violated Section 15. But this just triggered a Section 1 test, and he
had no difficulty finding that mandatory retirement is rationally
connected to a valid objective and that its effects are "not so severe
as to outweigh" the pressing and substantial purposes, especially
when it is looked at not in isolation but as part of a total system that
includes a sharply graded salary scale and security of tenure.

Sopinka wrote three pages in concurrence, agreeing with La Forest
on the need to define quite narrowly the government entities whose
actions were limited by Charter rights and agreeing as well that the
"core functions" of universities were nongovernmental. The role of
the Charter is to protect the individual against the coercive power of
the state, but this implies that there must be an element of coercion
involved before the actions of even a governmental institution can
be brought under Charter scrutiny. In more general terms, the Court
should be reluctant to substitute its own judgment on matters such
as mandatory retirement as the product of democratic discussion and
collective bargaining, at the risk of "imposing on the whole country
a regime not forged through the democratic process but by the heavy
hand of the law." This was a classic judicial self-restraint argument,
but not one that described the general mood of the Court. Cory briefly
(in two pages) took rather a different route, agreeing with Wilson's
dissenting argument that universities were government entities for at
least some Charter purposes, although he favoured a more generous
reading of the collective bargaining process; but he agreed with La
Forest that the "reasonable limits" of Section 1 allowed mandatory
retirement to survive Charter scrutiny.

Wilson, in a dissent half again as long as La Forest's decision for the Court, disagreed. She thought that for Charter purposes, the notion of "government" had to be defined broadly, which meant that it overruled the public/private (or common law/statute law) distinction. In the twentieth century, it was not appropriate to think of freedom and the protection of rights only in terms of preventing government action; sometimes what was required in such a case was government action. Nor was the American example determinative, because "Canadians have a somewhat different attitude toward government and its role." Applying three "tests" (control, government function, and public interest) brought universities within "government," but mandatory retirement was a clear violation of s.15, and it could not be saved by s.1 because it was not justifiable as a reasonable limit.

L'Heureux-Dubé reached a similar conclusion by quite a different route. She felt that universities "may perform certain public functions that could attract *Charter* review," but these did not include the hiring and firing of employees. Her conclusion was more roundabout: the Charter invalidated the section of the Ontario Human Rights Act that prohibits discrimination only on the grounds of age that was applied to the 18 to 65 age group. In the absence of this upper limit, the university's policy of mandatory requirement violated the provincial legislation in a way that could not be saved by Section 1. Neither the presumption of the deterioration of ability nor the need for faculty turnover is enough to justify an arbitrary measure that displaces individual evaluation, the more so when the arbitrary measure has a particularly negative effect upon vulnerable groups such as women.

This case demonstrated the second phase of Charter jurisprudence: the general principles had been established, but the "reasonable limits" of Section 1 permitted the upholding of government measures even while specific rights were explored and expanded. At the same time, it began to look forward to the third phase, as the Court's attention turns to the equality rights of Section 15. It was also "modern" for its thorough canvassing of authority; it included seventy-eight judicial citations, mostly Canadian but with a scattering of American and other cases, and almost as many academic citations. The Court continued to divide in complex ways, with some (Wilson and L'Heureux-Dubé — who did not agree on very many things) both wanting to apply the Charter more broadly, even while others (in this case, Sopinka, sounding a bit like Beetz and Le Dain in *Vaillancourt*)[28] wanted a much more restrained approach. In the middle, not even drawing the signatures of a majority of the panel for the full set of reasons, the decision of the Court drew on judicial and academic authorities to explore age discrimination and mandatory retirement before retreating behind the sheltering wall of Section 1's reasonable limits. But what is even more striking is the fact that although a majority of the Court agreed that the Charter did not apply — either because universities were not "government," because their actions lacked the coercive quality of "law," or because of the collective bargaining aspect — they nonetheless explored the matter at length as if none of these things mattered.

*R. v. Stinchcombe*[29] was one of the most prominent and controversial of the Lamer Court's decisions involving the rights of the accused. It involved a lawyer who was charged and convicted of wrongfully appropriating property that he held in trust for a client. The lawyer appealed on the grounds that the Crown had failed in its duty regarding the disclosure of evidence, specifically the tape of one interview and the transcript of a second interview with a person not called as a witness. The trial judge had refused the defence application for access to this information, and the Alberta Court of Appeal upheld the trial judge's decision; the subsequent appeal brought the issue before the Supreme Court, and Sopinka delivered the decision for a unanimous panel of seven.

The background of the case is significant: there was no general statutory requirement in Canada for Crown disclosure in criminal cases, although most jurisdictions had a practice of extensive voluntary disclosure by the Crown of its information relating to a charge. Several reports had recommended enacting comprehensive schemes for Crown disclosure, but there was "considerable resistance" to the idea of making this mandatory, and Parliament declined to pass any such legislation. Sopinka interpreted this as "leaving the development of the law in this area to the courts," although it could also be seen as a reluctance to upset the delicate balance between Crown and defence.

Having acknowledged a "considerable reluctance," Sopinka promptly rejected it, saying, "It is difficult to justify the position which clings to the notion that the Crown has no legal duty to disclose all relevant information. The arguments against the existence of such a duty are groundless while those in favour, are, in my view, overwhelming." The constitutional basis of this new requirement was the right of the accused to be able to make full answer and defence, a common law right which "has acquired new vigour by virtue of its inclusion in s. 7 of the Canadian Charter of Rights and Freedoms" (although one would look in vain for these particular words, because the section in question refers grandly but rather mysteriously to "the principles of fundamental justice"). But this duty did not work both ways; the defence was in a "full adversarial relationship" with the Crown, even if the reverse was not true. The Crown had some discretion — in the timing of disclosure, for example, or in order to protect witnesses or informants — but this was subject to judicial approval. A Law Reform Commission Report was the major springboard for the recommendation, but Sopinka went further: he required, where the Report did not, that "full disclosure" include evidence not used and interviewees not subsequently called as witnesses.

Although this decision was unanimous, its progeny were not, all of them revealing instead the split between the Lamer bloc and the outsiders. *O'Connor*[30] (dealing with the disclosure of material not in the possession of the Crown), *Carosella*[31] (dealing with the disclosure of material that did not belong to, and had never been in the possession of, the Crown), and *La*[32] (dealing with information that could not be disclosed because it had been innocently misplaced) rounded off Sopinka's "disclosure quartet."[33] Many critics regard *Stinchcombe* as conclusive confirmation of Sopinka's sardonic nickname of "The Prisoner's Friend," but the disclosure rule probably cuts both ways; on the one hand, it means more work for the Crown, but on the other, it almost certainly leads to more plea bargains and therefore fewer trials.[34]

The *van der Peet* trilogy is the fullest statement to date of the meaning and scope of "aboriginal right" under the Canadian constitution. Because the full text of the three cases is (by actual count) the same length as this entire book, the comments that follow will focus on *van der Peet*[35] alone as the core case of the trio.

The history of Canadian jurisprudence on Aboriginal rights and Aboriginal title is surprisingly short. *R. v. Calder*[36] (described in an earlier chapter) was the first clear judicial recognition of an Aboriginal right with respect to land that survived European settlement, and *Guerin v. The Queen*[37] extended this principle while clarifying the fiduciary duty on the part of the Crown that it implied. After 1982, the Aboriginal position was made firmer by Section 35 of the Constitution Act 1982, which explicitly "recognized and affirmed" the "existing aboriginal and treaty rights of the aboriginal peoples of Canada." What remained was to spell out what this meant in practice;

the first major statement was *R. v. Sparrow*[38] which both enlarged upon the notion of the Crown's fiduciary duty and laid down the principles that guide the interpretation of s.35. But important issues remained, and they were addressed in *van der Peet*.

Dorothy Marie van der Peet, a Native woman, was charged with selling ten salmon caught under the authority of an Indian food fish licence, although the rules clearly prohibited the sale or barter of fish caught under such a licence. It was argued in her defence that these restrictions infringed her Aboriginal right to sell fish and, accordingly, were invalid because they violated s.35(1) of the Constitution Act 1982. The trial judge held that the Aboriginal right to fish for food and ceremonial purposes did not include the right to sell such fish and found the appellant guilty. The summary appeal judge found an Aboriginal right to sell fish and remanded for a new trial. The Court of Appeal allowed the Crown's appeal and restored the guilty verdict. The subsequent appeal to the Supreme Court raised the issue that the Court had carefully sidestepped in *Sparrow,* namely the extent to which the Aboriginal right to fish included the right to fish for commercial as well as subsistence purposes. The nine-judge panel split 7–2 on this issue (both of the dissenters writing their own reasons), and the decision of the majority was delivered by chief justice Lamer.

The Court said that the practices, customs, and traditions that constitute Aboriginal rights are those that have continuity with the practices, customs, and traditions that existed prior to contact with European society, although these can be established by a general demonstration of continuity and do not require conclusive evidence from precontact times. (The subsequent *Delgamuukw*[39] case "cashed in" this looser approach to evidence by accepting Aboriginal oral traditions even in the absence of the firmer documentary record that courts generally require.) Even the notion of continuity is flexible; a practice existing prior to contact can be resumed after an interruption and will still support an Aboriginal rights claim. But this applies only to those Aboriginal practices that are both distinctive and integral to the Aboriginal society in question. To be distinctive means that the practice cannot relate to an aspect of Aboriginal society that is true of every human society (Lamer's example was "eating to survive") but rather to something that makes that culture different from other cultures, which should not be understood as suggesting that it needs to be unique. To be integral, a practice, custom, or tradition must be of central significance to the Aboriginal society in question, excluding those practices, customs, or traditions that are only incidental or occasional. It is those continuing, integral, and distinctive features that need to be acknowledged and reconciled with the sovereignty of the Crown.

This necessarily raises a historical question: What were the practices of the Aboriginal society in question at the time of European contact? The appellant claimed that the practices, customs, and traditions of the Sto:lo First Nation included as an integral element the exchange of fish for money or other goods. But the trial judge found that prior to contact, exchanges of fish were only "incidental" to fishing for food purposes, that there was no regularized trading system amongst the Sto:lo or between the Sto:lo and their neighbours, and that Sto:lo society had not developed a specialization in the exploitation of the fishery that would support a claim of centrality for the exchange of fish. The trade that developed with the Hudson's Bay Company was quite different from what was typical of Sto:lo culture prior to contact. The Supreme Court found no error in these findings of fact and therefore upheld the Court of Appeal in restoring the conviction. The parallel argument and analysis in *R. v. N.T.C. Smokehouse* concluded that the Sheshaht and Obetchesaht First Nations seldom engaged in the exchange of fish except at potlatches and other ceremonial occasions, and, therefore, that here as well, there was no Aboriginal right to fish that included fishing for commercial purposes. In *Gladstone,* the third case of the trilogy, the decision went the other way: the evidence showed that before contact, the Heiltsuk people regularly sold large quantities of herring spawn to other Indian tribes, not to dispose of surplus food (as in *van der Peet*) or as something incidental to ceremonial purposes (as in *N.T.C. Smokehouse*), and the Supreme Court therefore substituted an acquittal for the lower court conviction. La Forest dissented on this finding, suggesting that the context of the exchange was a desire to share valued resources with less fortunate neighbours and that this was not a reasonable analogue to commercial activity.

(Note that the logical consequence of this approach is that there are a wide range of different "sets" of Aboriginal rights that apply to different Aboriginal communities, depending on their practices at the time of contact. Briefly, this approach seemed to have been abandoned in late 1999 in *Marshall 1,* which on some readings suggested that there is a generic set of Aboriginal rights that belong to all Aboriginal peoples, such that a finding about the Mi'qmaq right to fish for eels had implications for the right of B.C. Natives to cut down trees, but within a few weeks the Court distanced itself from any such notion. One of the implications of this approach is that each Aboriginal rights case opens up a number of difficult historical questions, and the Court has demonstrated in *Marshall 1*[40] that it is no better at this than one would expect from a bench of nine lawyers turned amateur historians.)

In all three cases, McLachlin and L'Heureux-Dubé wrote separate but largely parallel opinions, dissenting in the first two and writing separate concurrences in *Gladstone*. Their primary concern was that the emphasis on integral activities that predate European contact was too narrow and restrictive a reading of the Aboriginal right with regard both to the integral/non-integral dichotomy and the refusal to consider any distinctive activities that might have arisen as a response to European contact. Rather, a "generous, large and liberal" construction should be given to the activities of Aboriginal communities, and the protection of s.35 should extend to all practices, customs, and traditions that are sufficiently connected to the self-identity and self-preservation of organized Aboriginal societies. It is not enough to protect what is left over after features held in common with non-Aboriginal cultures are taken away.

## Most Influential Judges of the Lamer Court

Table 8.5 indicates the number of times that each judge has been cited, and the number of times specifically named, for decisions handed down during the Lamer Court. This table is, of course, not strictly comparable with the parallel tables in earlier chapters for two reasons: first, because the only Court the Lamer Court has been able to "influence" to date is the Lamer Court itself; and second, because the very recency of the Lamer Court's case law means that we can only catch the initial flash with no real idea as to its staying power.

Lamer leads but does not dominate the table. Indeed, prorating the performance of the two members who left the Court in 1997 (one through retirement, the other through sudden death) suggests that La Forest was only slightly behind Lamer and that Sopinka may even have been slightly ahead. There was a solid second rank of the Court in McLachlin and Cory and (somewhat less so) in L'Heureux-Dubé and Iacobucci. The others had not, so far, left much of a mark for their participation in the decisions of the Lamer Court to the summer of 1999, most of them (Wilson, Stevenson, Bastarache, and Binnie) because they had served such a limited time. Gonthier and, espe-

### Table 8.5

### Frequency with which Members of the Lamer Court Are Cited Reported Decisions, 1990–1999

| Judge | Number of times cited | Number of times named | "Score" | Days served (%) |
|-------|----------------------|----------------------|---------|-----------------|
| Lamer* | 617 | 149 | 766 | 3286 (100%) |
| Sopinka | 518 | 164 | 682 | 2703 (82%) |
| La Forest | 395 | 152 | 547 | 2648 (81%) |
| McLachlin | 354 | 135 | 489 | 3286 (100%) |
| Cory | 358 | 83 | 441 | 3286 (100%) |
| L'Heureux-Dubé | 262 | 53 | 315 | 3286 (100%) |
| Iacobucci | 293 | 21 | 314 | 3096 (94%) |
| Gonthier | 151 | 34 | 185 | 3286 (100%) |
| Wilson | 64 | 63 | 127 | 187 (6%) |
| Major | 44 | 0 | 44 | 2420 (74%) |
| Stevenson | 13 | 8 | 21 | 627 (19%) |
| Bastarache | 7 | 0 | 7 | 638 (19%) |
| Binnie | 0 | 0 | 0 | 538 (16%) |

\* indicates the current chief justice.

cially, Major are the exceptions, having had the time but still not having made the impact.

## Conclusion

The major challenge for the Dickson Court was the establishment of the Charter as a significant dimension in Canadian public life and the creation of a first generation of Charter jurisprudence. The major challenge for the Lamer Court was the application of this same progressive methodology to the much more innovative equality rights of Section 15 — something that necessarily moved the Court away from both its traditional expertise in criminal matters and the relative comfort zone of long-standing civil liberties such as free speech. Particularly when connected to an expanded notion of remedies (Lamer's comments in *Schachter*[41] mark a first but not a final exploration), the judicial enforcement of an evolving concept of equality rights promised major controversy and a massive impact on Canadian society. It may have been widely expected that the major impact would come from feminism and the women's movement; in actual fact, the biggest headlines and the greatest resentments were triggered by issues of gay rights and same-sex couples.

Turnover was initially a problem; Lamer came to the chief justiceship with less experience on the bench than almost any of his predecessors, and he headed the most inexperienced Court in this century. Early indications (two early departures from the Court in first two years) to the contrary, however, the revolving door stopped turning and the stability of personnel on the Lamer Court rivalled that of the other "book end" of this enquiry, the Rinfret Court. Only toward the end (of the decade, of the millennium, of the fifty-year period, and of the Lamer chief justiceship itself) did high turnover reemerge as a problem; apart from the departing Lamer himself, Gonthier and McLachlin were already the only survivors from the closing days of the Dickson Court.

As with the Dickson Court, the agenda was dominated by Charter issues, notwithstanding their rather modest share of the docket. However, the Court faced other challenges as well. The *Quebec Secession Reference*[42] brought the Court into the "sovereignty wars" that have preoccupied Canadian public life since the PQ first came to power in 1976; the Court's *per coram* decision was reasonable, measured, and magisterial, although it remains to be seen whether it settled anything or simply gave ammunition to both sides. *Friends of the Oldman River*[43] created an environmental jurisdiction with a role for both levels of government, much to the annoyance of the provinces, which felt that they deserved more of a free hand in resource development; and the *Reference re Remuneration of Provincial Judges*[44] provided an opportunity for chief justice Lamer to develop an expanded notion of judicial independence (grounded not just in the Charter but in Canada's basic constitutional norms) as well as a model procedure for establishing judicial salaries. Rivalling the Charter issues in its long-term significance, the developing concept of Aboriginal rights drew a great deal of attention by the Court, especially (but by no means only) in the *van der Peet* trilogy of 1996.[45]

A string of vacancies, triggered by early retirements and (in one case) by an unexpected death, raised the turnover problem again at the end of the Lamer chief justiceship, suggesting that the period of stable continuity is over and the Court of the beginning of the new millennium will be dominated by recently appointed (and, to some extent, by not-yet-appointed) judges.[46] The Court has not just survived but thrived on the challenge first of patriation, then of the

Charter, and then of equality rights; but as the retiring comments of chief justice Lamer suggest, it is beginning to face a crisis of legitimacy that may yet jeopardize all its achievements.[47] The first half-century of the truly supreme Supreme Court has been slow to develop but impressive in its accomplishments; the second half-century presents new challenges of comparable scale.

# The McLachlin Court: January 2000 "The Outsider"

On January 13, 2000, Madame Justice Beverley McLachlin became the seventeenth chief justice of Canada, the first woman ever to fill the office. The novelty was underlined by the fact that she was sworn in by Adrienne Clarkson, the second woman ever to serve as governor general of Canada, although some commentators thought that it was an error in judgment for Clarkson to use the ceremony to comment on this fact.

The choice was hardly a surprise; McLachlin's name was at the top of every court-watcher's shortlist. Leaving aside the two senior Quebec judges (L'Heureux-Dubé and Gonthier), who are within three years of their retirement, she conforms to the long-standing tradition of seniority as well as to the more recent tradition of French/English alternation. The next most senior member (Iacobucci) was appointed fully three years after McLachlin. We do not need gender politics to explain or to justify McLachlin's accession; had any judge, male or female, with her credentials and experience relative to the rest of the bench been passed over, it would have been highly unusual and very much in need of justification.

What was surprising was the fact that the announcement was made so early. Lamer's resignation would not take effect until January 2000, but two months earlier, the Chrétien government announced that McLachlin would be filling the vacancy. This was unprecedented. Historically, even when the vacancy has been anticipated (when, for example, Dickson indicated that he would step down at the end of the 1989–1990 term rather than waiting the few extra months until he reached retirement age), the new chief justice has not been named until the "old" chief justice has actually retired, and sometimes not until a month or more after. The reason for the early declaration might have been the fact that Lamer announced his January retirement in August, or it might have been because the Chrétien government wanted to avoid the heavy lobbying that has accompanied recent Supreme Court appointments — but it is still unusual. The early announcement had two interesting consequences: first, still-Chief Justice Lamer vanished from the spotlight for the fall sittings (save for ceremonial public sessions celebrating his retirement); and second, McLachlin's appointment was effectively highlighted twice, first when she was named "chief justice elect" and then again when she was formally appointed.

## The McLachlin Record

In one respect, McLachlin's accession to the chief justiceship breaks a pattern that has endured for decades. Dickson was a solid ally of chief justice Laskin (part of the L-S-D Connection that emerged in the early 1970s, with Spence providing the middle letter), although this is not to deny that both on Laskin's Court and on his own, Dickson followed a distinctly independent course on a number of issues. Similarly, Lamer was part of the bloc of judges whose support allowed Dickson to dominate his own Court before Lamer in turn became chief justice, although he too blazed his own trail, shifting away from the other judges who had strongly supported Dickson (La Forest and Wilson) to form quite a different set of alliances.

But McLachlin was clearly and indisputably not part of the Lamer bloc on the Lamer Court. As demonstrated in the previous chapter, the Supreme Court in the 1990s consisted of a strongly coherent "gang of five" (Lamer, Sopinka, Major, Iacobucci, and Cory), which on divided courts, generally prevailed over the more fragmented "gang of four." McLachlin's distance from the doctrinal centre of gravity of the Lamer Court is clearly evidenced by the fact that she signed on with the decision-delivering majority of the Court only 77.6 percent of the time (48.5% of the time when the Court divided) — figures that are well below the all-Court average (84.0% and 64.5%, respectively). Only L'Heureux-Dubé wrote or signed dissents or separate concurrences more often. The Lamer Court laid down a vigorous and controversial body of judicial doctrine in the 1990s, but McLachlin was very much on the fringes looking on rather than at the centre helping to steer.

Of course, the blocs were rather less rigid than the melodramatic terminology of the previous paragraph implies. The voting was not always five–four, and even on those occasions when it was, it was not always a case of the gang of five versus the gang of four. (Even Cory and Iacobucci, at the voting centre of the Court, dissented or separately concurred almost one time in ten.) As well, there were times when the minority group could prevail, by dint either of the composition of a smaller panel or of the defection of a member of the majority group. When this happened, however, the intellectual leader of the alternative group was more often La Forest than McLachlin, who wrote substantially less than the one decision in nine that would represent her fair share of a perfectly balanced Court. And La Forest's leadership was generally directed toward a moderate and restrained reading of the Charter, a generalization that (as we will see) does not at all capture McLachlin's position.

These general observations were true for most of the decade, a time of stable membership when the composition of the Court hardly changed, save for Stevenson's replacement by Major. But in 1997 there were two very important developments: during the summer, La Forest announced his retirement, and in November, Sopinka unexpectedly died of a heart ailment. This double development was profoundly destabilizing. Sopinka had been not just a member of the dominant Lamer bloc but also one of its most articulate spokespersons; only Lamer wrote more decisions for the Court. The gang of five had lost not just the critical fifth vote ensuring that it would usually prevail, but an important part of its intellectual leadership, especially on the set of issues (generally defendants' rights) that Sopinka had marked out as his own. And La Forest had been the leading voice of the four outsiders, most loyally seconded by Gonthier. The tone of the Court was dramatically altered by the two departures. For one thing, the solid five-judge bloc no longer existed; for another, the minority group had lost its predominant voice and would need to find a new one. Much would depend on the votes and the doctrinal alliances formed by the newcomers.

A simple statistical measure demonstrates this critical turning point. Before the beginning of the 1997 fall term, McLachlin wrote the decision of the Court in only 9 percent of her panel appearances; after the beginning of that term, this almost doubled to 16 percent. The flip side of this, of course, is the fact that her dissents and separate concurrences dropped sharply, from almost one-quarter of her panel appearances to just over one-eighth. When she wrote before 1997, it was usually (72.3% of the time) in dissent or concurrence; when she wrote after 1997, it was usually (67.6% of the time) for the Court, despite the fact that the ratio of written reasons to panel appearances did not change. Conversely, before the 1997 personnel changes Lamer had written the decision for the Court fully one time in every three panel appearances, but this fell by almost one-half (to 17.7%) during the final thirty months of his chief justiceship. The late Lamer Court was a Court in transition, and the dynamics of this change were making McLachlin an increasingly major player on the Court. In the last quarter of the decade, but not earlier, she was beginning to lead the Court — at least some of the time and at least on some issues. The important question, of course, is on what issues and in what direction this leadership was operating.

## Where Will She Try to Lead the Court?

Within three weeks of the announcement that she would become the next chief justice, and even before Lamer stepped down, McLachlin led the Court in two dramatic decisions that appeared to signal a dramatic turnaround in the style and direction of the Court. The first of these cases was *Marshall 2*[1] in which the Court formally decided not to reconsider its recent decision on Aboriginal rights on the east coast but in the process managed to restate its position rather significantly; the second was *Mills v. R.*[2] in which the Court upheld a variant of a "rape shield" law that was somewhat different from the Court's own earlier hints about the preferred parliamentary action. On closer investigation, the change in direction represented by these two particular cases is largely illusory, although the change in style is nonetheless significant, the more so if it signals an enduring new strategy for the new chief justice.

Trying to predict the future performance of a Supreme Court justice must appear both presumptuous and mildly insulting. I would suggest that it is neither and that it is perfectly legitimate — and very much a compliment rather than an insult — to suggest that we can extrapolate from a judge's past performance to describe what she will do in the future. This is because principled consistency is something judges value very highly, a critical component of judicial reputation and self-image.[3] This is not to say that their ideas cannot develop over time or that they can never be persuaded to change their mind, but it is still true that judges are more discomfited than most of us to have it pointed out that what they are saying on a subject today is quite different from what they said a few years ago. Looking at the general pattern of McLachlin's position on the major cases of the Lamer Court is therefore a useful indicator not just of where she would have led the Court had she held the centre chair and the leadership role through the 1990s, but of the directions in which she would like to lead the Court today. At the same time, the principle of *stare decisis* ("let decided matters stand") means that the new chief justice will not simply revisit the earlier decisions to "get it right" now that she has the votes. The interplay between these two principles — between personal consistency and institutional consistency — will be a critical dimension of her leadership.

There have been several big issues for the Supreme Court over the last decade. I will consider some of the most important.

## Legal or Defendant Rights

The Charter lays down in very general terms a string of legal rights (Sections 7 through 14), and it is the Court's duty gradually to refine and clarify these principles as they are applied in specific circumstances at specific times. But this involves striking a balance between the rights of the accused on the one hand and the protection of the public on the other, with obvious problems if the balance is lost in either direction. The situation is aggravated by the fact that many of the cases involving legal rights also involve unsavory or even shocking details, particularly problematic at a time when a concern with law and order issues has been gaining momentum among the general public.

McLachlin, at first glance, seems to have been part and parcel of Supreme Court jurisprudence in this area. Her most high profile decision of the 1990s was *Seaboyer*,[4] which found the rape shield law (a strict legislated ban on defence questioning about the victim's sexual history) to be an unconstitutional violation of the defendant's right to a fair trial. Roundly condemned by women's organizations across the country, this particular decision illustrates the way that a concern for the rights of the defendant has often seemed to involve a disregard for the rights of the victim.

Over the longer run, however, McLachlin has in fact been much more restrained on this front than the majority of the Court, and she dissented vigorously on a long string of the Lamer Court's most controversial cases. In *Carosella*,[5] Sopinka declared that rape crisis centres must be prepared to present their records when they counsel rape victims; McLachlin dissented. In *Heywood*,[6] Cory found that the Criminal Code section barring convicted sex offenders from schoolyards and playgrounds was unconstitutionally vague; McLachlin dissented. In *Stillman*,[7] Cory enunciated strict rules on the acceptability of evidence; McLachlin dissented. In *Feeney*,[8] when a majority reversed a murder conviction because the arresting policeman had pushed open an unlocked door, McLachlin again dissented.

One of the first decisions handed down by the Supreme Court after McLachlin's designation as chief justice elect was *Mills*. This was a sexual assault case, and the point at issue was the constraints that recent Criminal Code amendments had put around the right of the defendant to investigate and to pursue questions relating to the records of the victim's counseling sessions with a rape crisis center. At first glance, it seemed that the odds very much favoured the defendant: for one thing, the statutory criteria directing the trial judge's handling of this matter differed from those that the Lamer-led majority had endorsed in an earlier decision, and McLachlin's *Seaboyer* decision suggested that on this issue (even if not on a wider range of criminal issues), she would go along. In fact, McLachlin delivered a decision (over Lamer's lonely dissent) that upheld the statute.

A dramatic turnaround? The beginning of a new era for the Court? I think not. The critical dimension, it seems to me, is that the Court has never wavered on the basic issue that has guided its deliberations on this issue from *Seaboyer* on: the principle that the decision on the admissibility of evidence, the critical balancing between the accused's right to a fair trial and the victim's right to privacy and self-respect, must be left to judicial discretion and must not be decided in advance by the flat legislative ban that was struck down in *Seaboyer*. The debate within the Court, and the contributions to the evolving argument that Parliament had made by amending the Criminal Code, concerns only the details and not the basic point. McLachlin may be less willing than Lamer to drop heavy hints about legislative draftsmanship, and this difference in style is important, but there is no fundamental turnaround here — at most "five steps forward and one step back."

Based on her track record, McLachlin will try to lead the Court to a somewhat more restrained position on defendant's rights, not so much repudiating the recent jurisprudence as declining to push it further. This may be less exciting than the dramatic new era that the media has been proclaiming, but it should be reassuring for those who like to think that we have (to steal the American phrase) a "government of laws" and that it takes more than a single new appointment, even of someone so important as a chief justice, to accomplish a significant change in the law that leaves ten years of high court decisions in the dust.

## Aboriginal Rights

From *Sparrow*[9] in 1991 to *Marshall 1* and *2* in 1999, the Supreme Court in the 1990s has created (on the basis of very little Supreme Court or Judicial Committee precedent) a jurisprudence of Aboriginal rights. Sometimes it has imposed solutions, and sometimes it has redefined the issues in ways that send the matter back for renegotiation in a more political arena, but there is no doubt that the new realities of Aboriginal politics in Canada have the Supreme Court's fingerprints all over them.

The most publicly controversial of this string of decisions was *Marshall,* handed down on September 17, 1999. Binnie wrote the majority decision (over a dissent authored by McLachlin and signed by Gonthier), finding in the historical record evidence of a long-standing but long-ignored Aboriginal right to "truck and barter" on the Atlantic coast. Although the immediate case dealt with a Mi'qmaq man catching eels out of season, the decision was couched in more sweeping terms, to such an extent that it was invoked not just for hunting and fishing but for natural resources as well, and not just on the east coast but right across the country. Meanwhile, Aboriginal fishing boats jumped the gun on the lucrative lobster-fishing season, and their non-Aboriginal neighbors protested in ways that spilled over into sporadic violence. Relations between the Aboriginal community and its fellow citizens have probably been set back by at least a decade.

No sooner had McLachlin been designated as the next chief justice than the Court was reconsidering the issue, responding to an application by a non-Aboriginal fishing association for a rehearing of the matter. Strictly speaking, the unanimous Court (in a *per coram* decision signed by all the members of the panel) refused the rehearing and upheld its earlier decision, but it did so for reasons that were almost as long as the original decision. More significantly, the new reasons reflected the earlier dissent as much as they did the earlier decision, finding on the basis of a closer reading of the historical record that the Aboriginal right was far more narrowly defined in scope and in geography. While refusing to reconsider, the Court nonetheless reconsidered; while insisting they were not changing their mind, they nonetheless changed their mind. It was one of the more curious episodes in the Supreme Court's recent history — and hardly one of its proudest moments.

But does the McLachlin-led reconsideration, combined with the McLachlin dissent before she became chief justice elect, add up to a new era in the Supreme Court's handling of Aboriginal issues? I think not. The most important decisions of the 1990s dealing with Aboriginal rights were the *van der Peet* trilogy[10] and the *Delgamuukw*[11] case. McLachlin wrote her own reasons for judgment in all four of these cases (one dissent and three separate concurrences), but on none was she staking out a more moderate position than the majority. In *Delgamuukw*, she fully agreed that Aboriginal oral histories have to be given considerable evidentiary value, contrary to the prior practice of Canadian and other courts. And in the trilogy, she criticized the majority for its "frozen rights" approach to Aboriginal rights, which would ground all such claims in the historical practices of the Aboriginal community at the time of European contact. *Marshall 1*, with McLachlin in stern dissent while the majority upheld an Aboriginal claim, is not at all typical of her stance in this area and suggests to me that this case and its sequel must simply be taken at face value; this was a case in which the Supreme Court majority made a mistake (spoiling Binnie's first major decision for the Court in the process), and McLachlin saw the mistake earlier than most of her colleagues. My expectation is that the McLachlin Supreme Court will continue the doctrinal evolution of Aboriginal rights begun under the Lamer Court (*Marshall* cases aside), and here as well there will be no retreat, no repudiation of the earlier doctrine, little more than a softening of the rhetoric.

## Equality Rights

A third high-profile area for Supreme Court decisions in the 1990s was equality rights under Section 15 of the Charter. Two general sets of cases predominated. The first involved gay and lesbian rights (including those of same-sex couples), and on this issue McLachlin was ahead of the Court, adopting early the position that the entire Court adopted in the end. In *Mossop*,[12] a case involving federal public service regulations that granted leave to attend the funeral of a partner's parent to members of heterosexual partnerships but not to same-sex couples, Lamer for the Court delivered an ambiguous judgment[13] that upheld the regulation; McLachlin dissented. In *Egan v. Canada*,[14] La Forest wrote the decision for a Court that split 5–4, conceding that federal policy denying marital retirement benefits to same-sex couples was a *prima facie* violation of the equality rights but upholding the regulation as a "reasonable limit" under Section 1 of the Charter; McLachlin wrote a dissent, paralleling the jointly-authored dissent of Cory and Iacobucci. Three years later, when the

Court ruled in *Vriend*[15] that Alberta's Individual Rights Protection Act violated equality rights by not including sexual orientation among the prohibited grounds for discrimination, McLachlin signed on to Cory and Iacobucci's jointly authored decision, and she did so again in *M v. H*[16] when the Court struck down Ontario legislation that defined "spouse" as "a member of the opposite sex." This makes the evolution of gay rights in Canada an interesting story, with a three-judge minority that included McLachlin finally carrying a unanimous decision, although it seems more plausible to acknowledge that the leading role belonged to Cory.

The second set of equality rights cases involved women's rights, and the results here were much more modest, placing McLachlin consistently offside from a majority that did not fragment or change directions over the decade. A trilogy of important cases makes the point. In *Symes*[17] (the so-called "nanny case"), the Supreme Court ruled that it was not a violation of the equality rights of women that the Income Tax Act did not allow for the full deduction of child care expenses from a mother's income; McLachlin dissented. In *Thibaudeau*,[18] it was argued before the Court that it violated equality rights that maintenance and support payments after divorce were taxed as income in the hands of the ex-wife, rather than paid out of the ex-husband's after-tax income; a majority of the Supreme Court rejected this argument, but McLachlin in dissent endorsed it. In *Dickason*,[19] it was argued that it was a violation of equality rights for women academics to be subject to the same compulsory retirement age as male academics, given that the career trajectory of women was so different as to leave them well behind their male colleagues at such an age; the Supreme Court, again over McLachlin's dissent, rejected this argument as well. The odd one out from this pattern is *Miron v. Trudel*[20] in 1995, in which McLachlin wrote the decision for the majority of the Court, finding that it was a violation of equality rights for common-law wives to be treated differently from those who were formally married.

On cases involving women's rights, then, McLachlin consistently supported the claims to such an extent as frequently to leave her offside from the majority and in dissent. The Lamer Court's track record was strong on expanding the equality rights of gays and same-sex couples but more restrained on women's rights; the McLachlin Court is unlikely to beat a retreat on gay rights and same-sex couples, but likely to strike a stronger line on women's rights. Much of the journalistic commentary on McLachlin assumes that she will steer the Court toward a somewhat more restrained and less interventionist role on Charter rights generally and equality rights in particular, but I would be most surprised if this were the case, especially on women's equality rights.

## Will She Succeed?

Chief justices do not necessarily get their way all the time or even most of the time. Both Dickson and Lamer stood very tall on their own Courts, as did Laskin (at least in the closing years of his chief justiceship), and this makes it easy to assume that a considerable degree of strong leadership is a normal feature of the modern Court. But we should avoid generalizing too quickly; as I have argued in earlier chapters, Kerwin led the Rinfret Court as well as his own, and Martland was arguably the dominant figure under a string of chief justiceships, including at least half of Laskin's — the centre chair is an advantage but not a guarantee. Arguably, it is always better to be chief justice than not to be chief justice, because the chief justice makes the decisions about panel sizes and panel assignments, and, when in the majority, she makes the decision about who will draft the judgment. Without suggesting that there is anything devious about the use of these opportunities and without denying that there is a price to pay if that use is too clumsy or too heavy-handed, these choices can, in aggregate, be highly significant. But ultimately, McLachlin herself has just one vote on a panel, and it is the behaviour of the other members that determines whether that vote puts her in dissent, in separate concurrence, or in (and often writing) a majority decision.

One circumstance that is very much to the chief justice's advantage is the fact that the Court is once again undergoing a massive turnover in personnel. When she was sworn in, the Court included Louis LeBel, who had just joined the Court; Arbour, who had served for four months; and Bastarache and Binnie, who had been members for about two years. L'Heureux-Dubé and Gonthier will reach compulsory retirement within three years. When they are replaced, the years of service of the average member of the Court will fall to about five years for only the third time in the Court's history.[21] To be sure, all judges come to the Court with a considerable degree of experience, professionalism, and intelligence, but there is still normally a transition period (typically, I would suggest, of two years or more) before new judges are "up to speed" with their senior colleagues, and during that transition period, seniority carries more weight than usual. For the first several years of her chief justiceship, McLachlin will be presiding over one of the most junior and inexperienced Courts in its history, and this means that she will enjoy more leverage from the centre chair than is normally the case.

One circumstance not to McLachlin's advantage is the fact that she is not the only one enjoying the benefit of a considerable seniority on a very junior Court. The same will be true of Iacobucci and Major, who have the further distinction of being the two surviving members of the Lamer-led gang of five that dominated the Supreme Court for most of the 1990s, with Iacobucci have written by far the larger number of decisions for that Court of the two (104 to Major's 44). This does not necessarily make them a solid bloc that leaves McLachlin on her own; Major's closest connection was to Sopinka and Iacobucci's was to Cory, so they represent the wings rather than the core of the Lamer bloc. But there is clearly a possibility (though hardly a certainty) of principled division between Iacobucci and McLachlin, in which case everything will hinge on which way the new appointments (including those that have not yet been made) choose to go. And since Iacobucci has a dozen years to go before his own retirement (six less than McLachlin), any such division will shadow the next decade. But, depending to some extent on what major issues are brought before the Court, it is also possible that the division will be episodic rather than central; on issues such as gay rights and same-sex couples, for example, the Cory/Iacobucci wing of the former Lamer bloc took much the same position as McLachlin.

The chances are that the combination of high public profile, very junior colleagues, and a degree of luck in the early issues will allow McLachlin to extend the twenty-plus-year pattern of chief justice domination of the Court. One further factor may tilt the balance in her favour. To an unprecedented extent, McLachlin (as both "chief justice elect" and then as chief justice) has made herself available to the media. The week in which the initial announcement was made in November 1999, she gave lengthy interviews to the major print media and then appeared on the major television networks as well, speaking more casually and often more candidly than we have ever seen a chief justice do before. When the formal ceremony took place in January 2000, she conducted a second "media tour," and she has followed it up by suggesting that the Court is necessarily engaged in a dialogue with the people and with government and that decisions must be to some extent guided by this dialogue. This is quite a different style from that of the man she replaced, Chief Justice Antonio Lamer.

The net effect of all this is to make the chief justice more than ever the visible spokesperson for and public access point to the Supreme Court. Especially if media availability becomes a regular feature of the McLachlin chief justiceship rather than a one-time transitional effect, she has an added point of leverage over her colleagues: when the Court divides, she will (but they will not) be on the national news for the next few days, putting the "spin" on the outcome. This is no small thing in terms of shifting the hard-to-define balance between the "first" and the "equal" in the usual description of the chief justice as "first among equals."

# The Supreme Court in the New Millennium

This book would be incomplete without at least a guess about what lies ahead. The Supreme Court is finally the institution that some people in 1875 thought it would be, that more people in 1949 hoped it would become, and that still more people in 1982 dreamed it might one day develop into with the entrenchment of the Charter. It is a Canadian court developing a Canadian jurisprudence in a way that is both visible and relevant to an increasingly large segment of the Canadian public. This is a very significant accomplishment. But it was achieved only gradually, and it has to be renewed over and over again as its mandate expands and expectations grow.

## The Future of the Court and the Future of the Charter

My own feeling is that the Court is now entering a third phase of Charter interpretation. The first phase "succeeded in building a foundation for broad judicial review" that involved a very "broad scope" for its review powers.[1] *Hunter v. Southam*[2] established the principle of purposive interpretation, and *Big M*[3] said that the Court had to look at both the purpose and the effects of legislation. In *Operation Dismantle*,[4] the Court explicitly rejected any self-limiting Canadian equivalent to the American "political questions" doctrine, which simply means that the Court "may decline to rule because it decides that a case raises a political question that should be resolved by the other political branches."[5] But (with the massive exception of *Morgentaler*[6]) the Court generally delivered powerful rhetoric linked to modest outcomes — more bark than bite. Much of the substance of this first phase of Charter rulings involved "Legal Rights" (Sections 7 through 14 of the Charter). This was a logical starting place, because many of these were constitutionalized versions of parts of the Criminal Code in the first place, because the courts have acknowledged experience and expertise in the criminal law, and because these cases involved the Court's criticizing public officials and police officers rather than challenging Parliament.

In the second phase (which roughly coincided with the early Lamer Court), the Court was generally somewhat more restrained. A major thrust involved solidifying the general test for the "reasonable limits" clause of Section 1 of the Charter — the general outline, of course, was in *Oakes* but those general phrases could have been taken in several different directions.[7] To oversimplify, the style was to give a broad interpretation to the Charter right but to uphold the statute as constituting a reasonable limit. *Irwin Toy*[8] established that freedom of expression included "commercial speech" (advertising), a position that the USSC had taken 200 years to work up to, but Quebec's Consumer Protection Act was upheld anyway. In the *Prostitution Reference,*[9] the Court agreed that soliciting for the purposes of prostitution was constitutionally protected speech but found that the limit was justified. With regard to pornography, that traditional battleground of civil liberties, *Butler*[10] conceded the free speech issues but upheld the relevant Criminal Code sections. And in *Egan,*[11] a badly divided Court found that the pension laws discriminated against same-sex couples but that this limitation was justified by the importance of the traditional family. All took the same general form: vigorously stated rights behind an increasingly solid wall of reasonable limits.

The equality rights section (Section 15) has provided the focus for the third phase. This began in 1997, with *Eldridge*[12] (the B.C. medicare system violated equality rights by not providing interpreters for the deaf), *Vriend*[13] (Alberta violated the equality rights of gays by not including them on the list of protected categories), and *M v. H*[14] (Ontario's legislation on family rights and duties violated the rights of same-sex couples). These cases represented a new, aggressive thrust, a willingness to tackle hot issues in ways that challenge political orthodoxies, and they also broke new ground with regard to remedies, reading words into statutes that legislatures had deliberately omitted.

This shift is partly a matter of having new people on the Court. It is ironic that *Eldridge* marks the shift, given that the decision was written by La Forest, who was generally more deferential to legislatures than were his colleagues. But La Forest has retired, and neither of the new members appointed seems to be picking up his mantle. More fundamentally, the fast/slow/fast pattern — that is to say, a period of relative restraint between two periods of strong rhetoric and intervetion — represents an intelligent use of potentially controversial power, a good use of the strategic-planning potential of an organized and conferencing Court.

## A Building Backlash?

It would be easy to make a case for the idea that the Supreme Court has been "riding a bubble" with its controversial decisions — and bubbles can always burst. Some people suggest that if the Court overreaches itself, if it pushes too far too fast in a direction that public opinion and elected officials are unwilling to accept, then the widespread support it now enjoys will evaporate. The Court, after all, has neither a bureaucracy to follow up on its decisions nor a police force to ensure that its decrees are observed. Its decisions matter because people — elected officials, police, public servants, ordinary citizens — think they ought to matter; and they would matter less if fewer people accepted this importance as self-evident and axiomatic.

It would even be easy, at the moment, to sketch the scenario that would lure the Supreme Court into overreaching. At the time of writing, a British Columbia trial judge has ruled, and a divided British Columbia Court of Appeal has agreed, that Charter rights are violated by those sections of the Criminal Code that make it a crime to possess "kiddie porn." The Supreme Court may very well go along — the B.C. Court of Appeal is reversed less often than most. True, the Supreme Court has already looked at pornography in the light of the Charter, in *Butler*[15] in 1992, and upheld the law as a reasonable limit. But this precedent did not stop the B.C. courts, and a lot of water has flowed under the Charter bridge in the last seven years.

Suppose the "kiddie porn" case comes before the Supreme Court. Suppose they decide that the lower courts were right to find this part of the statute unconstitutional. Suppose they do this in the face of polls showing that Canadian public opinion opposes this by massive margins. Could this be the Charter straw that breaks the back of public support? Could we then expect moves to tame the Court by invoking the notwithstanding clause, amending the Charter, or opening up the appointments process?

I believe the answer is "almost certainly not." This is the Court that tackled the abortion issue, the most divisive issue in Western industrialized societies in the late twentieth century, and came away without a scratch; it was the Mulroney government that took the flak, from some people for trying to pass an amended abortion law tailored to meet the Supreme Court's standards and from others for failing to do so. This is the Court that took on Alberta's Ralph Klein over gay rights. This is the Court that has found the marriage laws of most provinces unconstitutional. These have all been pretty big waves — this is a boat that does not swamp easily.

One reason that the Court will not suffer any consequences is that the lower court decisions have already paved the way — we are, so to speak, "outraged out" and becoming reconciled to an idea that was unthinkable six months ago. The national government has no interest in confronting the Court; they will amend the Criminal Code to see if more careful drafting can regain part of the lost territory, and in two or three years, we will find out if they have succeeded.

But the reasons go deeper: the simple fact is that in the modern world courts have real advantages when it comes to taking a leadership role. James L. Gibson, Gregory A. Caldeira, and Vanessa A. Baird[16] looked at the level of public support for national high courts in the United States and seventeen European countries. Although they did not include Canada in their survey, their findings are clearly relevant. For one thing, they found that "generally, to be aware of a court is to be supportive of it" because of "the legitimizing symbols that all courts so assiduously promulgate."[17] This has two important implications: first, the controversy that draws the national headlines is more likely to build support than to erode it; and second, support for the Court is higher among better informed citizens, who also tend to be more politically active.

Another significant finding was that there is a "very strong" relationship between "the age of the court and the level of satisfaction with inputs."[18] Many of the countries surveyed, such as those in Eastern and Southern Europe, already demonstrate significant and growing support even for very new national courts, but support for the more long-established institutions (Germany, France, England, and the United States) is even higher. The cutoff point Gibson, Caldeira, and Baird used to distinguish between the "younger" and the "more established" institutions was thirty years, which puts our Supreme Court well over on the "extremely established" side of the continuum. And the additional factor that drives up the correlation between age and satisfaction is what the authors call "salience," which simply means the degree to which the court has made decisions of interest to ordinary people. On this criterion as well, the Supreme Court of Canada scores well.

Finally, Gibson, Caldeira, and Baird found that "courts garner legitimacy from pleasing decisions but lose little or nothing from displeasing decisions," because they can transfer the responsibility for unpopular decisions to the wording of the constitution or to the technical requirements of legal professionalism. For this reason, courts are less likely than more overtly political institutions to suffer from "negativity bias, the common tendency for negative policy outputs to be more readily noticed than positive outputs."[19] There is a sort of "ratchet effect" on support for national high courts, with support levels going up when some group sees a decision of which they approve, but not going down (or at least not going down as much) when they see a decision of which they disapprove.

More specifically, courts are not majoritarian institutions. They are neither organized to identify, nor motivated to respond to, the positions that may be preferred by strong public opinion. Each case is, at least formally and procedurally, complete unto itself. Political parties must put together platforms designed to appeal to an optimal mix of potential voters, but courts hand down a string of formally distinct decisions — people are aware of the bricks rather than the wall. This means that

> courts may be able to build legitimacy by developing support among a succession of minorities. To the extent that a national high court appeals to and satisfies only a single constituency, it is unlikely to acquire legitimacy. But if different areas of policy-making please different constituents, then legitimacy is attainable through the cumulation of satisfied minorities.[20]

This "cumulation" explains the capacity of the Supreme Court to withstand public outcry over a single decision, even when that outcry seems unusually strong. To put it bluntly, if the people it satisfies feel a considerable gratitude and the people it annoys have short memories, any visible and powerful institution is bound over time to build up an impressive level of support.

One must be careful not to push the argument too far. It is possible for a court to establish salience, visibility, and support over a period to time and then to dissipate that support through a spectacularly bad decision. The iconic example is always *Dred Scott*,[21] when the USSC tried to "fix" the race question by ruling that the constitution precluded Negroes from ever being citizens; miscalculations of this magnitude are rare but not impossible. But note the high threshold:

to lose (for a generation) the credibility that it had built up over half a century, the USSC had to get the slavery issue "wrong" just when the disagreement was building toward a bloody civil war. Controversies of a lesser nature can be weathered more easily. When the USSC handed down its school desegregation decision in *Brown v. Board of Education*,[22] many white Southerners thought it was a spectacularly bad decision, but their annoyance was directed at an individual ("Impeach Earl Warren") rather than at the institution itself. This is how legitimacy works.

## The Global Expansion of Judicial Power

The study by Gibson, Caldeira, and Baird discussed in the previous section implicitly makes another very important point, and that is the worldwide ubiquity of courts and judges that are heavily involved in the process of resolving disputes or answering questions with at least one eye (and sometimes both) firmly fixed on the policy implications of their decisions. As Martin Shapiro and Alec Stone put it, "a political jurisprudence of rights is today endemic and occasionally epidemic."[23] At one time, one approached discussions of judicial power and judicial policy-making as if they were something unique to the United States, or at least something invented in the United States with tentative imitation elsewhere. This is no longer appropriate. To consider only a few examples:

- Even in the absence of an entrenched bill of rights, the High Court of Australia has been establishing a rights-oriented jurisprudence grounded in the very general wording of the preamble to the constitution.[24]

- As a result of apparently minor amendments in the mid-1970s, the French Constitutional Council has become very active and France's legislative process has been "judicialized."[25] The council's treatment of constitutional issues "invites comparison to the United States Supreme Court" by virtue of its "surprisingly expansive approach."[26]

- The German federal constitutional court "has profoundly changed the perception of law and politics as being two separate arenas of decision making."[27]

- Within the European Community, the European Court of Justice has been much more effective than was anticipated, not just by playing "a leader role in the development of European integration,"[28] but also by serving as a mechanism whereby judicial review and entrenched rights have been introduced to national courts that lacked an indigenous tradition of such practices.[29]

Contemporary democratic practice is not just about elections and legislatures and appropriate mechanisms for political accountability; it is also about courts and judges and constitutions and rights, as well as a mode of political discourse and activity that works as much through the judicial branch as through the more overtly and traditionally political branches.[30] C. Neal Tate and Torbjorn Vallinder suggest that "the judicialization of politics may be or may become one of the most significant trends in late-twentieth and early-twenty-first-century government."[31]

## Courts and Democracy in the Late Twentieth Century

It is often argued that there is something undemocratic about powerful courts exercising judicial review, and at least on the face of it, this is a powerful argument. Judges are not elected, and therefore if they do something that the majority of the citizens do not like, they cannot be "de-elected." Worse, the legal profession as a whole and the judges as an elite subprofession within it constitute a fortress of technical expertise at the core of the modern democratic polity. Even the appearance of a Court — professionals and officials wearing special costumes, a "bar" that laypeople are not permitted to cross, the use of honorific titles, people bowing as they enter and leave the courtroom — stands at variance with the levelling egalitarianism of democracy. In Alberta or Ontario, you can turn a conversation to politics just by asking people what they think about "Ralph" or "Mike." But when a regional magazine (*Alberta Report*) ran a cover story on the chief justice under the title "Tony the Fixer,"[32] the legal profession stuttered in outrage and the letters of protest flowed; and when Lamer resigned in 1999, nine years ahead of his compulsory retirement, he warned against "judge-bashing" and worried that the institution would be severely damaged by it.[33]

But democracy is not just about majoritarianism; it is also about individual and minority rights, about limits to what even a large and determined majority can do. Therefore, there is a sense in which a strong and independent judiciary *is* democratic — not because the Courts are overtly democratic in their organization or their selection or their process (they are not), but because they are the mechanism that serves this "other face" of democracy. In recent decades, democratic politics have been transformed by what we often call the politics of identity[34] as distinct from the more "old-fashioned" politics of interest. Similarly, there is a burgeoning literature on "new social movements" that supplements (it is a bit much to say "replaces") the more traditional literature on "interest groups," the difference being that the new social movements are more directed toward a value-based transformation of society than to a more materially-defined self-interest. There is a new emphasis on individual rights protected by judicial officials who have a reasonable degree of independence.

But this is the crux: a reasonable degree of independence is not a total independence, but any mechanism of accountability is necessarily a limit on independence. Independence and accountability are opposites, the two poles between which a balance must be struck; you cannot increase accountability without reducing independence, and vice versa. The challenge is to find the balance, to find the way of making judicial independence fully congruent with majority rule, so that we protect the judges who are making the decisions that involve principled but unpopular applications of the law but not the judges who make decisions based on their own biases and prejudices. But finding the balance is quite a different project from getting the judges back under legislative and/or executive control. It is a difficult challenge, and I am not about to make any focused recommendation about how to resolve it.[35] But I will insist that the balance is important; popularly elected and politically accountable legislatures may no longer be the only important face of democracy at the turn of the millennium, but executive-appointed and politically unaccountable Courts are not the only face either.

## Powerful Courts in a Democratic Country: What Is the Problem?

If the Court has an Achilles' heel, it lies in the fact that "purposive interpretation" with a strong emphasis on contextualism and policy implications sometimes looks as if "the Court is holding legislation valid or invalid on the basis of standards which it is making up as it goes along."[36] It is no longer the case that the "anchor point" for a major Supreme Court decision is a constitutional phrase rigidly interpreted according to mechanical rules or a statement of judicial doctrine laid down several decades ago (by the Supreme Court or the Judicial Committee or the English House of Lords) and it is no longer the case that the judges who are working out from this anchor point pride themselves on not being creative or original. Instead, the major reference point is now a case that is only a few years old; it may already have been seriously modified once or twice by subsequent decisions, and part of the point of the current decision is to move on to a new anchor point for the immediate future (although one that will itself soon be transcended).

The most obvious example is the four-year evolution from *Egan* (which found pension rules a reasonable limit on the rights of same-sex couples) to *M v. H*[37] (which found the whole edifice of family law invalid because it limited the rights of same-sex couples). Why did the Court turn around so abruptly? Essentially, of the five judges in the *Egan*[38] majority, two (La Forest and Sopinka) had left the Court and two (Lamer and Major) changed their minds, leaving Gonthier high and dry on the beach; meanwhile, the *Egan* dissent written by Cory and Iacobucci had now become the *M v. H* decision — written by Cory and Iacobucci and supported by the two new people with Lamer, Major, McLachlin, and L'Heureux-Dubé (the latter two having also dissented in *Egan*). It was less that the two situations were massively different (indeed, La Forest's rhetoric on the family probably fits better with *M v. H*) than that the personnel had changed and the Court's centre of gravity had changed with it.

Given such a rapid evolution of doctrine, legislators must feel that they are shooting at hidden targets without knowing if the targets have been moved since the last time the lights were on. Even if you approve of the Court's ruling in any individual case, this mutability might make you a little nervous. If you disapprove, it tends to make you angry.

It seems to me that we must recognize that the Courts do not have a monopoly on the interpretation of the Charter. They are not infallible (although they are, by definition, authoritative) when they hand down their judgments on these subjects — to use the appropriate Roman Catholic term, they are not speaking *ex cathedra*. Under the pre-Laskin style of decision-making, the Court's main function was the mechanical application of formal rules to the extraction of meaning from legal texts, guided by the past decisions of their own but, also and particularly, of the English courts. If this had unfortunate practical consequences, the fault lay not with the people who interpreted the words but with the people who had drafted them. This was a narrow technical task, and the professionals could rightly demand that we acknowledge and defer to their proficiency. But applying to the very general terms of the Charter a purposive analysis guided by concern for the context and for policy consequences is a horse of a different colour. It means that the Courts deserve a lower level of deference — which is not to say that they deserve no deference at all.

What we need is a mechanism that will allow other actors into the debate, even when the Court has spoken or is speaking or is about to speak, without marginalizing the Court's very strong (and often determinative) input. It really is too bad that the notwithstanding clause did not work out.

The notwithstanding clause, Section 33 of the Charter, was intended to provide just such a mechanism. The idea was that if the Courts interpreted the Charter in a way that had objectionable policy consequences, then the legislature could repass the legislation "notwithstanding" the Charter (as interpreted by the Court). After each election, if the legislature was still so minded, it could extend this effect. This would allow the Courts to determine the meaning of the Charter but from time to time, through a ponderous procedure that invited public scrutiny and political accountability, the politicians could have their way. Ironically, it was argued that this would encourage the judges to be a little more daring, because if the consequences were politically or administratively impractical, the damage could be contained. Whatever the theoretical merits of such a device — and the academic debate continues — it clearly has not worked that way, and it has become something of a constitutional dead letter. In the meantime, we have an institution whose new and evolving powers have outgrown its traditional constraints.

## Powerful Courts in a Federal Country: What Is the Problem?

A second Achilles' heel lies in the fact that the Supreme Court is a purely national institution within a federal system. Its members are appointed by the government of Canada as an exercise of pure executive fiat; there is no ratification process, no way of blocking an objectionable appointment, not even a leverage point from which to negotiate compromise or future concessions. The provincial premiers find out about the new Supreme Court appointments at the same time and in the same way that you do — they hear it on the news. And this is for a Court which rules on the federal/provincial division of powers directly, as well as indirectly when the Charter is applied to bring an outlying province into line. I see no reason to suggest that prime ministers in general have shown any tendency to stack the Court, but the point is that a prime minister could do so at any time, without formal constraint or hindrance.

André Bzdera has argued that there are structural implications in the very existence of a national high court, which reveal themselves only gradually but are nonetheless extremely significant. (Glaciers move slowly, too, but they can still add up to ice ages.) He suggests that the political impact of a national court of final appeal is "centralist in the area of federalism disputes (division of powers between the two levels of government) and nationalist in the area of social and political values (charter of rights, general legal principles)."[39] The point is not that such courts act in a blatant way in every single case, but that they tend to do so most of the time, and the incremental shift is relentless.

There are, Bzdera suggests, several factors accounting for this tendency. Typically, the national government "is responsible for the existence of the court, its administration, its budget, its internal procedures, and most notably for the selection of its judges."[40] But even where there are ratification processes for appointments to the highest court (and Canada lacks even these), the process is still dominated by the national government, and the ratification is often by other national institutions, such as the U.S. Senate. Members of national supreme courts reside in the national capital, surrounded by other national actors and institutions and officials, and they themselves are members of a national institution. Why not national standards? Why not a gentle guiding hand from the centre to coax divergent regional minorities to join the consensus? And what body better than a court to transmit the messages without having them drowned out by partisan political animosities?

Bzdera is not implying that prime ministers make deals with Supreme Court justices before their appointments, consult with them before important decisions, or anything of the sort. There is no need for anything so clumsy, particularly when the current practice is so heavily weighed toward the elevation of judges from the lower courts. It you appoint politicians or lawyers, you can sometimes be surprised by what they turn into once they enjoy the independence of the bench; the classical example is Eisenhower's appointment of Governor Earl Warren to the USSC. But if you elevate an appeal court judge, especially one with reasonably extensive service, you have a voting record and dozens of written opinions on which to base your assessment of probable future performance. Given that consistency is such a critical element of the judicial self-image,[41] this is an even more reliable indicator for judges than it would be for many other professions.

As agents of a process of creeping centralization, says Bzdera, the judges of a national supreme court have many advantages. They are respected professionals, overtly neutral, autonomous actors protected from influence or coercion by the principle of judicial independence; in recent years, fewer and fewer of them have any overt connection to political office or the political process. Their actions are connected to values such as constitutionalism and the rule of law, wrapped in legitimacy, and linked to compellingly attractive national symbols, such that it is difficult and politically risky to oppose them. Disagreements are (usually) cloaked in technical language and conducted with exquisite politeness; whenever judges disagree, it is "with great respect," and when they disagree particularly vociferously, it is "with the greatest of respect." As Bzdera writes, "Ideally, federal high courts are not even perceived to be political institutions, as was the case until very recently in the Australian and Canadian legal communities and is still largely the case within European academic circles."[42] National governments can genuinely *be* (not just *pretend* to be) surprised or even embarrassed by their winnings. The problem is the glacial pace of this incrementalism; the centralization can be so gradual as to be almost imperceptible, and, by the same token, it can be so slow as to frustrate any single government.

Bzdera illustrates his point by looking at the federal high courts of seven democratic federations (the United States, Switzerland, Canada, Australia, Germany, Austria, and Belgium) and of two other similar structures (European Community and Italy), suggesting that the experience of all nine supports his thesis. And although Bzdera only briefly alludes to it, the Judicial Committee makes his point from the other side: it functioned in practice (in Beth's phrase) as a "Super-Supreme Court"[43] exercising judicial review and policing the division of powers, but it was widely criticized by contemporaries for not showing sufficient solicitude of national powers and prerogatives, a charge none would lay at the door of the post-Laskin Supreme Court or the twentieth-century USSC.

To Bzdera's rather grim determinism, I can only suggest the following: It may well be true that national high courts inevitably favour a gradual "creeping centralization" so that in the end, all federal systems become centralist. But if the run is long enough and the creeping is slow enough, they may still be a good deal. This is the other half of the challenge I suggested above: if one problem is the need to find a way of permitting a dialogue between courts and politicians on rights and constitutional interpretation, an equally important second problem is the need to find a way of involving both national and provincial governmental structures in both the appointment process and the dialogue.

## Final Thoughts

In the meantime, the judiciary, spearheaded by a powerful and confident (if internally divided and sometimes bickering) Supreme Court will continue to use the Charter to cut a swath through broad societal expectations and practices. In doing so, it will frequently collide with politicians, who will sometimes complain but always step aside, and it will enjoy — for the general run of its decisions but not necessarily for each and every individual decision — a wide degree of broad support. And it is acting legitimately when it does so because it represents the "other face" of democracy — if "people power" is one side, the other side is a concern for individual identity and individual rights.

This is the great accomplishment of the men and women who served on the Supreme Court of Canada over the first fifty years since the end of appeals to the Judicial Committee of the Privy Council: that they have created a Court that is willing to tackle this difficult and challenging responsibility. It will not always get it right, and every once in a while even it will have to admit it "got it wrong"[44] and take a second whack at something, and every one of us will from time to time fulminate against some particular decision we find wrongheaded. But it is not going to go away, nor should we want it to, because its power and its opportunity is grounded deep in the late-twentieth-century evolution of democratic practice.

# Notes

## Chapter 1

1. More correctly, it *almost* makes sense to ask such a question, because even if we accept that the chief justice exercises power in any real sense (and a decade ago such an assertion was still very controversial), it is not the same kind of power, nor is it exercised in the same way, under the same circumstances, subject to the same constraints, as the power of the prime minister.

2. There is, of course, no fixed number for a national high court; if nine seems natural to us, it is only because both our Court and the U.S. Supreme Court (USSC) have been at that size for as long as most of us have been paying attention. But the Supreme Court of Canada started at six and grew to seven and then to nine, the USSC started as a seven-judge court, and the Australian High Court started at three and for a while had five judges before reaching its current size of seven. To complicate things further, the Supreme Court of Canada for several decades occasionally had provincial superior court judges sit for limited periods as ad hoc members of the Court, a procedure that was abandoned after 1949.

## Chapter 2

1. Ian Bushnell, *The Captive Court: A Study of the Supreme Court of Canada* (Montreal and Kingston: McGill-Queen's University Press, 1992).

2. *Johnston v. St Andrew's Church* (1877) 1 S.C.R. 235, which was, quite literally, about whether Mr. Johnston had the right to occupy a particular pew in a Presbyterian church in Montreal.

3. Loren P. Beth, "The Judicial Committee: Its Development, Organisation and Procedure," *Public Law* 3 (1975), 219.

4. Beth, "The Judicial Committee."

5. James G. Snell and Frederick Vaughan. *The Supreme Court of Canada: History of the Institution*, (Toronto: Osgoode Society and University of Toronto Press, 1985).

6. Quoted in Beth, "The Judicial Committee."

7. Swinfen, *Imperial Control of Colonial Legislation, 1813–1865* [1970]; quoted in Loren P. Beth, "The Judicial Committee of the Privy Council and the Development of Judicial Review," *American Journal of Comparative Law* 24 (1976), 32.

8. Beth, "The Judicial Committee of the Privy Council and the Development of Judicial Review," 22.

9. Beth, "The Judicial Committee of the Privy Council and the Development of Judicial Review," 33: "historians are all but unanimous."

10. Beth, "The Judicial Committee," 225.

11. Snell and Vaughan report a reversal rate of about 20% up to 1913 and the unavailability of information after that date; Snell and Vaughan, *The Supreme Court of Canada*.

12. Snell and Vaughan, *The Supreme Court of Canada*.

13. Although in terms of K.C. Wheare's famous "check list" of federalism, it was still deficient in enough respects to draw the label of "quasi federal." See K.C. Wheare, *Federal Government*, 4th ed. (London: Oxford University Press, 1963).

14. Alan C. Cairns, "The Judicial Committee and Its Critics," *Canadian Journal of Political Science* 4 (1971).

15. Frederick Vaughan, "Critics of the Judicial Committee of the Privy Council: The New Orthodoxy and an Alternative Explanation," *Canadian Journal of Political Science* 19 (1986).

16. For example, *Severn v. The Queen* (1878) 2 S.C.R. 70, which rather extravagantly finds the notion of a provincial power to require a license for the selling of important spirits to be a doctrine "pregnant with evil."

17. Bushnell, *The Captive Court*.

18. See F.R. Scott, "Some Privy Counsel," *Canadian Bar Review* 28 (1950).

19. [1926] A.C. 482.

20. The main issue was less the ending of appeals from the Supreme Court itself than the cutting off of the option, exercised more frequently, of taking a *per saltum* appeal directly from a provincial court of appeal to the Judicial Committee.

21. [1960] A.C. 18. For a description of the occasion, see Morrow, "The Last Case," *Alberta Law Review* 16 (1978) 1.

## Chapter 3

1. See Snell and Vaughan, *The Supreme Court of Canada*.

2. Although it should be noted that (for example) Ian Bushnell is rather skeptical about Duff's reputation as "Canada's greatest jurist" and his own judgment is more negative: "The simple conclusion with respect to Duff is that this uncreative judge epitomized the 'sterile years' of the court's history" (Bushnell, *The Captive Court*, 266).

3. Snell and Vaughan, *The Supreme Court of Canada*.

4. Peter Russell lists Kerwin's pre–Supreme Court experience as including service as a provincial chief justice, but this is not correct (Peter Russell, *The Judiciary in Canada: The Third Branch of Government* [Toronto and Montreal: McGraw-Hill Ryerson, 1987]).

5. Bushnell, *The Captive Court*, 251.

6. Snell and Vaughan suggest that Robert Taschereau was related to not two but to four previous Supreme Court justices, but they do not name the other two (*The Supreme Court of Canada*).

7. E. Marshall Pollock, "Mr. Justice Rand: A Triumph of Principle," *Canadian Bar Review* 53 (1975), 521.

8. Snell and Vaughan, *The Supreme Court of Canada*, 151.

9. Snell and Vaughan, *The Supreme Court of Canada*, 154.

10. Although technically, 1900 is the last year of the nineteenth century and not the first year of the twentieth, in which case this distinction belongs to Ronald Martland.

11. This is par for the course; of the first fifty judges appointed to the Supreme Court of Canada, just over half had prior judicial experience, although most of them had served on the bench for five years or more before elevation to the highest court. See George Adams and Paul J. Cavalluzzo, "The Supreme Court of Canada: A Biographical Study," *Osgoode Hall Law Journal* 7 (1969).

12. This includes several dozen cases reported in the *Dominion Law Reports* but not in the *Supreme Court Reports*.

13. Snell and Vaughan, *The Supreme Court of Canada*.

14. These are, of course, overlapping rather than mutual exclusive categories, and the same case will sometimes be counted as falling within more than one category.

15. Lawrence M. Friedman, *American Law: An Introduction,* 2nd ed. (New York: W.W. Norton, 1998).

16. Burton M. Atkins, "Interventions and Power in Judicial Hierarchies: Appellate Courts in England and the United States," *Law and Society Review* 24 (1990).

17. For present purposes, a decision is coded as *seriatim* only if there were plural decisions badly dividing the Court *and* if none of the reasons for judgment contributing to the successful outcome explicitly supported another.

18. *Winner v. S.M.T.* [1951] S.C.R. 887

19. Bora Laskin, "The Supreme Court of Canada: A Final Court of and for Canadians," *Canadian Bar Review,* 29 (1951), 1047.

20. For a contemporary discussion of the issue, see Edward McWhinney, "Judicial Concurrences and Dissents: A Comparative View of Opinion-Writing in Final Appellate Tribunals," *Canadian Bar Review* 31 (1953).

21. Michael Wells, "French and American Judicial Opinions," *Yale Journal of International Law* 19 (1994), 93: "French opinions contain no dissents or concurring opinions, and the author of the decision remains anonymous."

22. Svein Eng, "Precedent in Norway," in Neil MacCormick and Robert S. Summers (eds.), *Interpreting Precedent: A Comparative Study* (Ashgate/Dartmouth: Aldershot & Brookfield USA, 1997), 192: "The final decision of the Supreme Court consists of the opinion of each judge; that is, each and every judge has *a right and a duty* to voice his own opinion."

23. See, e.g., Mirjan Damaska, *The Faces of Justice and State Authority: A Comparative Approach to the Legal Process* (New Haven, CT: Yale University Press, 1986), and Goutal, "Characteristics of Judicial Style in France, Britain and the U.S.," *American Journal of Comparative Law* 24 (1976). For a similar point in a more explicitly Canadian context, see Claire L'Heureux-Dubé, "By Reason of Authority or by Authority of Reason," *University of British Columbia Law Review* 27 (1993).

24. Laskin, "The Supreme Court of Canada," 1046.

25. Laskin, "The Supreme Court of Canada," 1075.

26. Laskin, "The Supreme Court of Canada," 1046.

27. Gilbert Kennedy, "Case Comment: *Brewer v. McCauley,*" *Canadian Bar Review* 33 (1955), 340. Surprisingly, his main target in this particular attack was Mr. Justice Rand, who is more commonly depicted as the articulator of an alternative and more promising approach.

28. H. Patrick Glenn, "The Common Law in Canada," *Canadian Bar Review* 74 (1995), 262.

29. Glenn, "The Common Law in Canada," 263.

30. For a recent example, in *Smith v. Jones* (S.C.C. File No. 26500; decision delivered March 25, 1999), Peter Cory said, "The House of Lords recently considered this issue in *R. v. Derby Magistrates' Court* [1995] 4 All E.R. 526.... With great respect, I prefer the reasoning of Martin J.A. [in *R. v. Dunbar and Logan* (1982), 68 C.C.C. (2d) 13 (Ont. C.A.)]."

31. William M. Landes, Lawrence Lessig, and Michael E. Solimine, "Judicial Influence: A Citation Analysis of Federal Courts of Appeals Judges," *Journal of Legal Studies* 27 (1998), 272.

32. David Klein and Darby Morrisroe, "The Prestige and Influence of Individual Judges on the U.S. Courts of Appeals," *Journal of Legal Studies* 28 (1999), 376.

33. Bushnell, *The Captive Court.*

34. Snell and Vaughan, *The Supreme Court of Canada,* 130.

35. See, e.g., G. LeDain, "Sir Lyman Duff and the Constitution," *Osgoode Hall Law Journal* 12 (1974) and W. Kenneth Campbell, "The Right Honourable Sir Lyman Poore Duff: The Man as I Knew Him," *Osgoode Hall Law Journal* 12 (1974).

36. For a fuller explanation of the logic and methodology used to suggest merit rankings and the "superCourt," see Peter McCormick, "The Supreme Court Cites the Supreme Court: Follow-Up Citation on the Supreme Court of Canada, 1989–1993," *Osgoode Hall Law Journal* 33 (1995).

37. Claire L'Heureux-Dubé, "The Length and Plurality of Supreme Court of Canada Decisions," *Alberta Law Review* 28 (1990), 587.

38. [1953] 2 S.C.R. 299

39. Snell and Vaughan, *The Supreme Court of Canada,* 208.

40. [1954] S.C.R. 127

41. *R. v. Furtney* [1991] 3 S.C.R. 89

42. Frederick Schauer, "Precedent," *Stanford Law Review* 39 (1987), 573.

43. [1952] S.C.R. 292

## Chapter 4

1. Bushnell, *The Captive Court,* 317.

2. Snell and Vaughan, *The Supreme Court of Canada,* 201.

3. W. Kenneth Campbell, "Mr. Justice Emmett Matthew Hall," *Osgoode Hall Law Journal* 15 (1977).

4. Frederick Vaughan, "Emmett M. Hall: A Profile of the Judicial Temperament," *Osgoode Hall Law Journal* 15 (1977).

5. Frederick Vaughan, "Emmett Matthew Hall: The Activist as Judge," *Osgoode Hall Law Journal* 10 (1972).

6. L'Heureux-Dubé, "The Length and Plurality of Supreme Court of Canada Decisions."

7. Snell and Vaughan, *The Supreme Court of Canada,* 213.

8. *Re Proprietary Articles Trades Assn. [P.A.T.A.]* [1931] A.C. 310 and *Lymburn v. Mayland* [1932] A.C. 318

9. Frederick Schauer, "Precedent," *Stanford Law Review* 39 (1987), 571; emphasis in original.

10. Ethan Katsh, *The Electronic Media and the Transformation of Law* (New York and Oxford: Oxford University Press, 1989), 46.

11. Twenty or thirty years ago it was controversial to suggest that judges "make" law in the sense of consciously modifying legal principles to fit evolving circumstances, but today most judges would concede that they do so at least some of the time; see McCormick & Greene, *Judges and Judging* (Toronto: James Lorimer & Co., 1990).

12. [1959] S.C.R. 121

13. This is, to put it mildly, not a good statement of the Supreme Court's current position on this particular issue; for further discussion, see the closer look at *CUPE v. N.B. Liquor Corp.* in Chapter 7.

14. [1960] S.C.R. 804

15. *Provincial Secretary of Prince Edward Island v. Egan* [1941] S.C.R. 396

16. Albert S. Abel and John I. Laskin, *Laskin's Canadian Constitutional Law* (Toronto: Carswell, 1975), 43.

17. [1960] S.C.R. 871

18. The English case cited was *Reg. v. Bishop of Oxford* [1879], 4 Q.B.D. 245, which in turn cited the 1693 decision in *R. v. Barlow.*

19. *Director of Public Prosecutions v. Beard* [1920] A.C. 479

20. [1994] 3 S.C.R. 63

21. [1978] 1 S.C.R. 29

22. Dale Gibson "— And One Step Backward: The Supreme Court and Constitutional Law in the Sixties," *The Canadian Bar Review* 53 (1975), 622. Gibson is, of course, writing of the entire decade, but the Kerwin Court straddles the two decades, and the factors he mentions (including the departures of Rand, Kellock, and Locke) divide the early Kerwin Court from the later Kerwin Court just as surely as they divide the two decades.

23. Gibson, "— And One Step Backward," 639.

24. *Re Industrial Relations and Disputes Investigation Act* [1955] S.C.R. 529

25. *Reference Re Farm Products Marketing Act* 1957 S.C.R. 198

26. *Switzman v. Elbling* [1957] S.C.R. 285

# Chapter 5

1. Bushnell, *The Captive Court,* 353, refers to "the neutral seniority principle."

2. Snell and Vaughan, *The Supreme Court of Canada.*

3. U.S. Chief Justice Wilson H. Rehnquist has already served as long in that position as the longest serving Canadian chief justice — the 13.7 years of

Sir William Johnson Ritchie, the second chief justice — but six U.S. chief justices served even longer terms.

4. Bushnell, *The Captive Court*, 353.

5. Bushnell, *The Captive Court*, 338.

6. Snell and Vaughan, *The Supreme Court of Canada*, 216.

7. Bushnell, *The Captive Court*, 343.

8. Bushnell, *The Captive Court*, 374.

9. There were also about a dozen three-judge panels, which is surprising because from the Court's very beginning the minimum size of a panel was five — even in the nineteenth century when there were only six judges on the court.

10. Snell and Vaughan, *The Supreme Court of Canada*, 216.

11. Gregory A. Caldeira and Christopher J.W. Zorn, "Of Time and Consensual Norms in the Supreme Court," *American Journal of Political Science* 42 (1998).

12. David Solomon, "Controlling the High Court's Agenda," *Western Australian Law Review* (1993).

13. Snell and Vaughan report "an alliance and compatibility between Pigeon and Laskin" on the basis of "a review of the reported judgments" (*The Supreme Court of Canada*, 228), but my own count shows no such convergence. On divided panels, Laskin and Pigeon agreed only 21.8% of the time, compared with 19.6% for Laskin and Martland.

14. Gibson, "— And One Step Backward," 633.

15. Gibson, "— And One Step Backward," 633.

16. Paul Weiler, *In the Last Resort: A Critical Study of The Supreme Court of Canada* (Toronto: Carswell-Methuen, 1974), 227.

17. For example, see *Diggon-Hibben Ltd. v. The King* [1949] S.C.R. 712 and the way in which it is referred to in the later decision of *Woods Manufacturing v. The King* [1951] S.C.R. 504.

18. *Woods Manufacturing Co. Ltd. v. The King* [1951] S.C.R. 504; quotation on 515.

19. "Private litigants were discouraged from presenting evidence of legislative facts by the Court's demonstrated hostility to such material in *Saumur* ..." (Katherine E. Swinton, *The Supreme Court and Canadian Federalism: The Laskin–Dickson Years* [Toronto: Carswell, 1990], 78).

20. Gibson, "— And One Step Backward," 622.

21. Gibson, "— And One Step Backward," 639.

22. Frederick Shaver, "Formalism," *Yale Law Journal* 97 (1988) 509.

23. Weiler, *In the Last Resort*, 117. For a further discussion of the "thereness" of rules, see Judith N. Shklar, *Legalism: Law, Morals and Political Trials* (London, England and Cambridge, Mass.: Harvard University Press, 1986), especially Part I.

24. Louis-Philippe Pigeon, "The Meaning of Provincial Autonomy," *Canadian Bar Review* 29 (1951) 1126.

25. See William E. Conklin, *Images of a Constitution* (Toronto: University of Toronto Press, 1989), 176.

26. *Manulife Bank of Canada v. Conlin* [1996] 3 S.C.R. 415, para. 35.

27. Lord Denning, it turns out, was cited by the Taschereau/Cartwright/Fauteux Court fifty times and explicitly named thirty-five of those times, for a "reputation score" of eighty-five that would put him just above Ritchie and just below Anglin.

28. The three cases in the "family law trio" are *Pelech v. Pelech* [1987] 1 S.C.R. 801, *Richardson v. Richardson* [1987] 1 S.C.R. 857, and *Caron v. Caron* [1987] 1 S.C.R. 892; the label has been widely used, for example, in a number of articles in academic journals, and was applied to the three cases by L'Heureux-Dubé in *G.(L.) v. B.(G.)* [1995] 3 S.C.R. 370. The "trio" is, of course, a little dated, and at time of writing the leading case in family law is probably *Moge v. Moge* [1992] 3 S.C.R. 813.

29. The three cases in the "damages trilogy" are *Andrews v. Grand & Toy Alberta Ltd.* [1978] 2 S.C.R. 229, *Thornton v. Board of School Trustees of School District No. 57 (Prince George)* [1978] 2 S.C.R. 267, and *Arnold v. Teno* [1978] 2 S.C.R. 287); the label is used by both Sopinka and L'Heureux-Dubé in *Ter Neuzen v. Korn* [1995] 3 S.C.R. 674.

30. The four cases in the "bankruptcy quartet" are *Deputy Minister of Revenue v. Rainville* [1980] 1 S.C.R. 35, *Deloitte Haskins and Sells Ltd. v. Workers' Compensation Board* [1985] 1 S.C.R. 785, *Federal Business Development Bank v. Quebec (Commission de la santé et de la sécurité du travail)* [1988] 1 S.C.R. 1061, and *British Columbia v. Henfrey Samson Belair Ltd.* [1989] 2 S.C.R. 24. They are repeatedly referred to under this label by (for example) both Charles Gonthier and Frank Iacobucci in *Husky Oil Operations Ltd. v. Minister of National Revenue* [1995] 3 S.C.R. 453.

31. The three cases in the "administrative tribunal Charter trilogy" are *Douglas/Kwantlen Faculty Assn. v. Douglas College* [1990] 3 S.C.R. 570, *Cuddy Chicks Ltd. v. Ontario (Labour Relations Board)* [1991] 2 S.C.R. 5, *Tétreault-Gadoury v. Canada (Employment and Immigration Commission)* [1991] 2 S.C.R. 22. They are so identified in *Mooring v. Canada* [1996] 1 S.C.R. 77, most explicitly by John Major.

32. [1970] S.C.R. 282

33. The accepted term for this group of people has cycled through "Aboriginal"and "Native" to "First Nations"; I appreciate the concerns that have led to this terminological evolution, but "Indian" is the term that is used in the Canadian constitution (s.91[24] of what is now called the Constitution Act 1867) and in the decision itself; for simplicity's sake, I will use it in this immediate discussion.

34. The fact that there were no Indian reserves in the Territories was, all the judges agreed, completely irrelevant.

35. Nineteen-seventy was the first year in which the *Supreme Court Reports* appeared in the current format, each page including a column in each of the two official languages; more precisely, then, Ritchie's reasons take up eleven pages of text, each page being half in English and half in French.

36. [1963] S.C.R. 651

37. [1953] 347 US 483

38. [1973] S.C.R. 313

39. [1971] S.C.R. 272

40. [1995] 2 S.C.R. 206

41. Gibson, "— And One Step Backward," 626–27.
42. Gibson, "— And One Step Backward," 629.

# Chapter 6

1. Among the most notable were the dissent in *Di Iorio v. Warden of Montreal Jail* [1977] 2 S.C.R. 152 regarding federal jurisdiction in prosecutions and policing, the dissent in *Murdoch v. Murdoch* [1975] 1 S.C.R. 423 regarding the disposition of marital property upon divorce, and the dissent in *A-G Canada v. Lavell* [1974] S.C.R. 1349 regarding the role of the Bill of Rights.

2. These include the dissents in *Four B Manufacturing Ltd. v. United Garment Workers of America* [1980] 1 S.C.R. 1031 and *Montcalm Construction v. Minimum Wage Commission* [1979] 1 S.C.R. 754, regarding the application of "enclave theory" to federal jurisdiction over "lands reserved to Indians" and aeronautics, respectively.

3. This observation remains appropriate despite its apparent inconsistency with the frequency and the vigour of Laskin's own dissents.

4. *Re Resolution to Amend the Constitution* [1981] 1 S.C.R. 753

5. Dickson saw only one fewer in a much shorter chief justiceship; these two comprise the "revolving door" period for the Supreme Court. It should be conceded that Duff (chief justice, 1933–44) saw seven new faces at a time when the Court had only seven members.

6. Bushnell, *The Captive Court,* 404.

7. Snell and Vaughan, *The Supreme Court of Canada,* 225.

8. Snell and Vaughan, *The Supreme Court of Canada,* 234.

9. *The Supreme Court Act* requires that at least three members of the Court be from the bar of the province of Quebec; the parallel representation of Ontario and the practices involving appointments from other provinces are purely conventional.

10. Snell and Vaughan, *The Supreme Court of Canada,* 235.

11. Snell and Vaughan, *The Supreme Court of Canada,* 236.

12. Snell and Vaughan, *The Supreme Court of Canada,* 236.

13. See Peter Hogg, *Constitutional Law of Canada* (Toronto: Carswell, 1997).

14. See Peter McCormick, "The Supervisory Role of the Supreme Court of Canada," *Supreme Court Law Review* (2nd ser.) (1992).

15. Hogg, *Constitutional Law of Canada,* 221.

16. See Russell, *The Judiciary in Canada.*

17. See Peter McCormick, "Assessing Leadership on the Supreme Court of Canada: Towards a Typology of Chief Justice Leadership," *Supreme Court Law Review* (2nd ser.) 4 (1993).

18. See, e.g., Stacia L. Haynie, "Leadership and Consensus on the U.S. Supreme Court," *The Journal of Politics* 54 (1992); Thomas G. Walker, Lee J. Epstein, and William J. Dixon, "On the Mysterious Demise of Consensual Norms in the United States Supreme Court," *The Journal of Politics* 50 (1988); but c.f. Caldeira and Zorn, "Of Time and Consensual Norms in the Supreme Court."

19. It is generally agreed that in the United States, chief justices John Marshall, Morrison Waite, Melville Fuller, William Taft, and Charles Evans Hughes had considerable success in achieving consensus; Harlan Fiske Stone, Fred Vinson, Earl Warren, Warren Burger, and William Rehnquist had little or none. See Caldeira and Zorn, "Of Time and Consensual Norms in the Supreme Court."

20. Haynie, "Leadership and Consensus," 1158.

21. So much for the theory that the criminal appeal success rate is pushed down by a large number of appeals by right that are briefly and routinely dismissed by the minimum panel!

22. Although it is surprising how seldom all three signed on to a single dissent; the more frequent pattern was for two of them to sign on to a dissent and for the third to write his own separate dissent.

23. It is not very often that one can pinpoint change in this way, but it is always tempting to try; for a more extended treatment in the U.S. context, see David M. Levitan, "The Effect of the Appointment of a Supreme Court Justice," *University of Toledo Law Review* 28 (1996).

24. [1975] 1 S.C.R. 423

25. *Reference Re Anti-Inflation Act* 1976 2 S.C.R. 373

26. Bushnell, *The Captive Court,* 414.

27. Bushnell, *The Captive Court,* 494.

28. For a more focused examination of the dynamics of the Laskin Court, see Peter McCormick, "Follow the Leader: Judicial Leadership and the Laskin Court, 1973–1984," *Queen's Law Journal* 24 (1998).

29. *Construction Montcalm Inc. v. Minimum Wage Commission* [1979] 1 S.C.R. 754

30. *Four B Manufacturing v. United Garment Workers* [1980] 1 S.C.R. 511

31. *Reference Re Resolution to amend the Constitution* [1981] 1 S.C.R. 753

32. Paul H. Edelman and Jim Chen, "The Most Dangerous Justice: The Supreme Court at the Bar of Mathematics," *Southern California Law Review* 79 (1996); for a critique, see Lynn A. Baker, "Interdisciplinary Due Diligence: The Case for Common Sense in the Search for the Swing Justice," *Southern California Law Review* 70 (1996); for a response, see Edelman and Chen, "'Duel' Diligence: Second Thoughts About the Supreme Court as the Sultans of Swing," *Southern California Law Review* 70 (1996). I have tried to apply a modified version of the same methodology to the Canadian Supreme Court in Peter McCormick, "The Most Dangerous Justice: Penetrating the Voting Patterns of the Lamer Court 1990–7," *Dalhousie Law Journal* (forthcoming).

33. It has been demonstrated for the USSC that gaining the necessary signatures for a majority decision is a process as much of negotiation, compromise, and accommodation as of doctrinal purity and rigidity backed by inflexible logical reasoning. See Paul J. Wahlbeck, James F. Spriggs II, and Forrest Maltzman, "Marshalling the Court: Bargaining and Accommodation on the United States Supreme Court," *American Journal of Political Science* 42 (1998).

34. Bushnell, *The Captive Court,* 494.

35. In the case of the American citations, it was Laskin himself who accounted for almost all of the increase; see Peter McCormick, "The Supreme Court of Canada and American Citations 1949–1994: A Statistical Overview," *Supreme Court Law Review* (2nd Ser.) 8 (1997).

36. [1979] 2 S.C.R. 227

37. Although readers may recall that this is essentially the position that Cartwright took in *Roncarelli v. Duplessis,* as discussed in Chapter 5.

38. [1984] 2 S.C.R. 145

39. [1975] 1 S.C.R. 729

40. Bushnell, *The Captive Court.*

41. Shaver, "Formalism," *Yale Law Journal* 97 (1988) 509.

42. *Doré v. Attorney-General of Canada* [1975] 1 S.C.R. 756

43. Bushnell, *The Captive Court.*

44. See Peter McCormick, "Assessing Leadership on the Supreme Court of Canada: Towards a Typology of Chief Justice Performance," *Supreme Court Law Review* (2nd ser.) 4 (1993).

45. *Reference Re Anti-Inflation Act* 1976 2 S.C.R. 373

46. [1983] 2 S.C.R. 284

47. *Reference Re Resolution to amend the Constitution* [1981] 1 S.C.R. 753

## Chapter 7

1. On the other hand, Bushnell reports rumours that Beetz had been offered the chief justiceship over Dickson but had declined for health reasons. See Bushnell, *Captive Court.*

2. I can still recall the feeling of anticipation when it seemed that a case arising from Calgary's "hooker bylaw" would give Laskin the opportunity to make the first Charter decision, but in the event, this case was decided on classical "division of powers" grounds. See *Westendorp v. The Queen* [1983] 1 S.C.R. 46.

3. [1978] 1 S.C.R. 152

4. [1983] 2 S.C.R. 284

5. At least, this is my reading of the cryptic and otherwise inexplicable separate concurrence jointly penned by Beetz and Lamer in *R. v. Wetmore* [1983] 2 S.C.R. 284, in which the "we feel bound" opening sentence seems to be saying "and you should, too."

6. Bushnell, *The Captive Court.*

7. Bushnell, *The Captive Court,* 489.

8. Bertha Wilson, "Decision-Making in the Supreme Court," *University of Toronto Law Journal* 36 (1986).

9. Regarding panels, see Andrew Heard, "The Charter in the Supreme Court of Canada: The Importance of Which Judges Hear an Appeal," *Canadian Journal of Political Science* 24 (1991); regarding the assignment of decision writing, see Peter McCormick, "Career Patterns and the Delivery of Reasons for Judgment in the Supreme Court of Canada," *Supreme Court Law Review* (2nd ser.) 5 (1994).

10. Of course, every Charter case must be a criminal case, a public law case, or a private law case before it can raise the Charter issue. I concede this lack of logical parallellism, but I shall simply treat the Charter category as if it were of the same sort as the others.

11. To be sure, the Dickson Court did not invent this device; I can identify nine postwar, pre-Laskin reported examples and fifteen under Laskin (none before December 1979); the Lamer Court delivered twenty *per coram* decisions in nine years.

12. See, e.g., McCormick, "The Supervisory Role of the Supreme Court."

13. The most important would be *Protestant School Boards* [1984] 2 S.C.R. 66, the *Manitoba Language Reference* [1985] 1 S.C.R. 721, *Chaussures Brown* [1988] 2 S.C.R. 713, and *Daigle v. Tremblay* [1989] 2 S.C.R. 530 — three "hot" language cases and one case bearing on the abortion issue. Similarly, for the Laskin Court, the most significant examples are the two *Blaikie* decisions, [1979] 2 S.C.R. 1016 and [1981] 1 S.C.R. 312, and *Forest* [1979] 2 S.C.R. 1032, which is the first Manitoba language decision; and the major example for Lamer is the *Quebec Secession Reference* [1998] 2 S.C.R. 217.

14. Carol Gilligan, *In a Different Voice: Psychological Theory and Women's Development* (New Haven, Conn.: Harvard University Press, 1982).

15. Wilson, "Decision-Making in the Supreme Court," 227.

16. See, for example, Robert Harvie and Hamar Foster, "Ties that Bind?: The Supreme Court of Canada, American Jurisprudence, and the Revision of Canadian Criminal Law Under the *Charter*," *Osgoode Hall Law Journal* 28 (1990); and Harvie and Foster, "Different Drummers, Different Drums: The Supreme Court of Canada, American Jurisprudence and the Continuing Revision of Criminal Law Under the *Charter*," *Ottawa Law Revue* 24 (1992). Both articles generally conclude that although the Supreme Court of Canada now cites American sources more often, the Court is very much plotting its own course and is often deliberately indifferent to the subtleties of the American case law.

17. A coincidence of dates makes this argument even stronger. It was in 1978 that the Supreme Court, per Laskin, declined to follow a Judicial Committee precedent in *Re Agricultural Marketing Act* [1978] 2 S.C.R. 1198. That same year, even before the formal end of appeals, the High Court of Australia said that it was not bound by Privy Council decisions in *Viro v. The Queen* [1978] 141 C.L.R. 88. See Solomon, "Controlling the High Court's Agenda."

18. [1984] 2 S.C.R. 145

19. Robert J. Sharpe and Katherine Swinton, *The Charter of Rights and Freedoms* (Toronto: Irwin Law, 1998), 37.

20. [1986] 1 S.C.R. 103

21. [1985] 1 S.C.R. 295

22. [1986] 2 S.C.R. 713

23. [1985] 1 S.C.R. 613

24. [1985] 2 S.C.R. 486

25. [1987] 1 S.C.R. 265

26. L'Heureux-Dubé, in *R. v. Burlingham* [1995] 2 S.C.R. 206

27. [1986] 1 S.C.R. 863
28. [1987] 2 S.C.R. 636
29. *R. v. Morgentaler* [1988] 1 S.C.R. 30
30. [1988] 1 S.C.R. 401
31. [1989] 2 S.C.R. 225
32. [1989] 1 S.C.R. 641
33. [1984] 2 S.C.R. 335
34. [1985] 2 S.C.R. 673

## Chapter 8

1. [1998] 2 S.C.R. 217
2. [1989] 1 S.C.R. 927
3. [1990] 1 S.C.R. 1075
4. There was also a comparable number of jointly authored dissents and separate concurrences.
5. For the more extended discussion of which this section is essentially the conclusion, see Peter McCormick, "Birds of a Feather: Alliances and Influences on the Lamer Court 1991–7," *Osgoode Hall Law Journal* 36 (1998).
6. [1991] 3 S.C.R. 326
7. [1990] 3 S.C.R. 229, [1992] 2 S.C.R. 1103, [1993] 4 S.C.R. 695, and [1995] 2 S.C.R. 627
8. [1993] 1 S.C.R. 554 and [1995] 2 S.C.R. 513
9. [1998] 1 S.C.R. 493 and [1999] 2 S.C.R. 3
10. [1996] 2 S.C.R. 507 and [1997] 3 S.C.R. 1010
11. [1991] 2 S.C.R. 914, [1992] 1 S.C.R. 259, and [1997] 3 S.C.R. 3
12. [1994] 3 S.C.R. 173 and [1994] 3 S.C.R. 236
13. See, e.g., Lewis A. Kornhauser and Lawrence G. Sager "Unpacking the Court," *Yale Law Journal* 96 (1986–87).
14. Adapted from McCormick, "Birds of a Feather: Alliances and Influences on the Lamer Court 1991–7," *Osgoode Hall Law Journal* 36 (1998).
15. Paul H. Edelman and Jim Chen, "The Most Dangerous Justice: The Supreme Court at the Bar of Mathematics," *Southern California Law Review* 79 (1996) 63.
16. Bertha Wilson, "Will Women Judges Really Make a Difference?" *Osgoode Hall Law Journal* 28 (1990).
17. See Ian Bushnell, "The Use of American Cases," *University of New Brunswick Law Journal* 35 (1986) and Gerard V. La Forest, "The Use of American Precedents in Canadian Courts," *Maine Law Review* 46 (1994).
18. Glenn, "The Common Law in Canada."
19. See, e.g., Michael J. Bryant, "Criminal Fault as per the Lamer Court and the Ghost of William McIntyre," *Osgoode Hall Law Journal* 33 (1995).
20. See Gordon Bale, "W.R. Lederman and the Citation of Legal Periodicals by the Supreme Court of Canada," *Queen's Law Journal* 19 (1994).

21. Vaughan Black & Nicholas Richter, "Did She Mention My Name? Citation of Academic Authority by the Supreme Court of Canada 1985–1990," *Dalhousie Law Journal* 16 (1993).

22. See Peter McCormick, "Do Judges Read Books, Too? Academic Citations by the Supreme Court of Canada 1991–7," *Supreme Court Law Review* (2nd Ser.) 9 (1998).

23. Vaughan Black and Nicholas Richter, "Did She Mention My Name?: Citation of Academic Authority by the Supreme Court of Canada 1985–1990," *Dalhousie Law Review* 16 (1993).

24. Peter Hogg, *Constitutional Law of Canada* (Toronto: Carswell).

25. [1993] 4 S.C.R. 695

26. [1990] 3 S.C.R. 229

27. This demonstrates the problem of a "clean" cutoff point between chief justiceships; but because the oral arguments occurred in the last month of the Dickson Court and Dickson did not write any reasons for judgment, it seems more reasonable to attribute the decision to the Lamer Court.

28. [1987] 2 S.C.R. 636

29. *R. v. Stinchcombe* [1991] 3 S.C.R. 326

30. *R. v. O'Connor* [1995] 4 S.C.R. 411; see also the "companion case" of *A.(L.L.) v. B.(A.)* [1995] 4 S.C.R. 536, decided at the same time.

31. *R. v. Carosella* [1997] 1 S.C.R. 80

32. *R. v. La* [1997] 2 S.C.R. 680

33. *O'Connor* was complicated by the fact that the case raised several different issues and the Court split different ways on each issue; but regarding disclosure, Sopinka and Lamer jointly wrote the majority opinion, supported by Cory, Iacobucci, and Major.

34. See, e.g., Michael Mandel, *The Charter of Rights and the Legalization of Politics in Canada,* revised ed. (Toronto: Thompson, 1994).

35. [1996] 2 S.C.R. 507

36. [1973] S.C.R. 313

37. [1984] 2 S.C.R. 335

38. [1990] 1 S.C.R. 1075

39. [1997] 3 S.C.R. 1010

40. Not yet reported — File No 26014, 17 September 1999.

41. *Schachter v. Canada* [1992] 2 S.C.R. 679

42. [1998] 2 S.C.R. 217

43. [1992] 1 S.C.R. 3

44 [1997] 3 S.C.R. 3

45. Including *R. v. van der Peet* [1996] 2 S.C.R. 507, *R. v. N.T.C. Smokehouses* [1996] 2 S.C.R. 672, *R. v. Gladstone* [1996] 2 S.C.R. 723.

46. On average, the judges appointed to the Supreme Court have served terms of just over thirteen years; but of the appointments made since 1960, only two (Spence and Dickson) have served terms as long as fifteen years and only two others (Laskin and Beetz) have exceeded this long-term average.

## Chapter 9

1. Not yet reported — File No. 26014, 17 November 1999.
2. Not yet reported — File No. 26358, 25 November 1999.
3. See Reed C. Lawlor, "Personal Stare Decisis," *Southern California Law Review* 41 (1968).
4. [1991] 2 S.C.R. 577
5. [1997] 1 S.C.R. 80
6. [1994] 3 S.C.R. 761
7. [1997] 1 S.C.R. 607
8. [1997] 2 S.C.R. 13
9. [1990] 1 S.C.R. 1075
10. *R. v. van der Peet* [1996] 2 S.C.R. 507; *R. v. N.T.C. Smokehouse* [1996] 2 S.C.R. 672; *R. v. Gladstone* [1996] 2 S.C.R. 723.
11. [1997] 3 S.C.R. 1010
12. [1993] 1 S.C.R. 555
13. This decision was ambiguous in the sense that Lamer suggested that the case might have gone differently had it been a Charter case — which was simultaneously a loss for same-sex couples in the immediate case and a heavy hint that they should come back again with a differently worded question.
14. [1995] 2 S.C.R. 513
15. [1998] 1 S.C.R. 493
16. [1999] 2 S.C.R. 3
17. [1993] 4 S.C.R. 695
18. [1995] 2 S.C.R. 627
19. [1992] 2 S.C.R. 1103
20. [1995] 2 S.C.R. 418
21. The others were the Lamer Court (1990), at 3.7 years, and the Fitzpatrick Court (1906), at 3.9 years.

## Chapter 10

1. Christopher P. Manfredi, "Adjudication, Policy-Making and the Supreme Court of Canada: Lessons from the Experience of the United States," *Canadian Journal of Political Science* 22 (1989), 321.
2. [1984] 2 S.C.R. 145
3. [1985] 1 S.C.R. 295
4. [1985] 1 S.C.R. 441
5. David M. O'Brien, *Storm Center: The Supreme Court in American Politics* (New York: W.W. Norton, 1993), 220.
6. [1988] 1 S.C.R. 30
7. See, e.g., Leon E. Trakman, William Cole-Hamilton, and Sean Gatien, "*R. v. Oakes* 1986–1997: Back to the Drawing Board," *Osgoode Hall Law Journal* 36 (1998).
8. [1989] 1 S.C.R. 927

9. *Reference Re ss. 193 and 195.1(1)(c) of the Criminal Code* [1990] 1 S.C.R. 1123
10. [1992] 1 S.C.R. 452
11. [1995] 2 S.C.R. 513
12. [1997] 3 S.C.R. 624
13. [1998] 1 S.C.R. 493
14. [1999] 2 S.C.R. 3
15. *R. v. Butler* [1992] 1 S.C.R. 452
16. James L. Gibson, Gregory A. Caldeira, and Vanessa A. Baird, "On the Legitimacy of National High Courts," *American Political Science Review* 92 (1998).
17. Gibson, Caldeira, and Baird, "On the Legitimacy of National High Court," 356.
18. Gibson, Caldeira, and Baird, "On the Legitimacy of National High Court," 355.
19. Gibson, Caldeira, and Baird, "On the Legitimacy of National High Court," 354.
20. Gibson, Caldeira, and Baird, "On the Legitimacy of National High Courts," 356.
21. *Dred Scott v. Sandford* [1857] 60 U.S. 393
22. *Brown v. Board of Education* [1954] 347 U.S. 483
23. Martin Shapiro and Alec Stone, "The New Constitutional Politics of Europe," *Comparative Political Studies* 26 (1994), 409.
24. See, e.g., Jeremy Kirk, "Constitutional Implications from Representative Democracy," *Federal Law Review* 23 (1995); Geoffrey Kennett, "Individual Rights, The High Court and the Constitution," *Melbourne University Law Review* 19 (1994); H.P. Lee, "The Australian High Court and Implied Fundamental Guarantees," *Public Law* (1993) 606; Peter Bailey, "'Righting' the Constitution without a Bill of Rights," *Federal Law Review* 23 (1995).
25. See Alec Stone, *The Birth of Judicial Politics in France* (New York: Oxford University Press, 1992).
26. Doris Marie Provine, "Courts in the Political Process in France," in Herbert Jacob et al., *Courts, Law and Politics in Comparative Perspective* (New Haven and London: Yale University Press, 1996), 192.
27. Erhard Blankenburg, "Political Regimes and the Law in Germany," in Jacob et al., *Courts, Law and Politics,* 309.
28. Renaud Dehousse, *The European Court of Justice: The Politics of Judicial Integration* (New York: St. Martin's Press, 1998), 177; c.f., J.H.H. Weiler, "A Quiet Revolution: The European Court of Justice and Its Interlocutors," *Comparative Political Studies* 26 (1994).
29. See, e.g., Karen J. Alter, "The European Court's Political Power," *West European Politics* 19 (1996); Jason Coppel and Aidan O'Neill, "The European Court of Justice: Taking Rights Seriously?" *Common Market Law Review* 29 (1992); J.H.H. Weiler and Nicolas J.S. Lockhart "'Taking Rights Seriously' Seriously: The European Court and Its Fundamental Rights Jurisprudence — Part I" *Common Market Law Review* 32 (1995) and "Part

II" *Common Market Law Review* 32 (1995); John R. Stack, "Judicial Policy-Making and the Evolving Protection of Human Rights: The European Court of Justice in Comparative Perspective," *West European Politics* 15 (1992).

30. The term that is used in the literature for this phenomenon is "legal mobilization." See, e.g., Susan Lawrence, "Justice, Democracy, Litigation and Political Participation," *Social Science Quarterly* 72 (1991), and Frances Kahn Zemans, "Legal Mobilization: The Neglected Role of Law in the Political System," *American Political Science Review* 77 (1983).

31. C. Neal Tate and Torbjorn Vallinder, *The Global Expansion of Judicial Power* (New York: New York University Press, 1995), 5.

32. The story itself was entitled "Benevolent Monarch," *Alberta Report* 25(40) (1998), 20.

33. "Lamer's departure a loss of a fine legal craftsman," *Globe and Mail,* August 23, 1999, A3.

34. See, e.g., Manuel Castells, *The Power of Identity* (Vol. II of *The Information Age*) (Oxford: Blackwell, 1997).

35. Indeed, I am more inclined to expand upon the logical and practical difficulties that are involved. See, e.g., Peter McCormick, "Twelve Paradoxes of Judicial Discipline," *Constitutional Forum* 9 (1998).

36. Weiler, *In the Last Resort*, 173.

37. [1999] 2 S.C.R. 3

38. [1995] 2 S.C.R. 513

39. André Bzdera, "Comparative Analysis of Federal High Courts: A Political Theory of Judicial Review," *Canadian Journal of Political Science* 26 (1993), 27.

40. Bzdera, "Comparative Analysis of Federal High Courts," 27.

41. See Lawlor, "Personal Stare Decisis."

42. Bzdera, "Comparative Analysis of Federal High Courts," 27.

43. Beth, "The Judicial Committee of the Privy Council and the Development of Judicial Review," 22.

44. Of course, Courts will hardly ever say "we got it wrong" in so many words; what they tend to say is "we have no idea how we could have been so badly misunderstood." This is what the Court said in *Morin* ([1992] 1 S.C.R. 771), its second crack at "trial within a reasonable time," about the confusion resulting from its first attempt to lay down guidelines on the subject in *Askov* ([1990] 2 S.C.R. 1199). For an excellent discussion of this particular episode, see Carl Baar, "Criminal Court Delay and the *Charter,*" *Canadian Bar Review* 72 (1993).

# Sources

Abel, Albert S. and Laskin, John I. *Laskin's Canadian Constitutional Law.* Toronto: Carswell, 1975.

Adams, George and Cavalluzzo, Paul J. "The Supreme Court of Canada: A Biographical Study." *Osgoode Hall Law Journal* 7 (1969) 61.

Alter, Karen J. "The European Court's Political Power." *West European Politics* 19 (1996) 458.

Atkins, Burton M. "Interventions and Power in Judicial Hierarchies: Appellate Courts in England and the United States." *Law and Society Review* 24 (1990).

Baar, Carl. "Criminal Court Delay and the Charter." *Canadian Bar Review* 72 (1993) 305.

Bailey, Peter. "'Righting' the Constitution Without a Bill of Rights." *Federal Law Review* 23 (1995) 1.

Baker, Lynn A. "Interdisciplinary Due Diligence: The Case for Common Sense in the Search for the Swing Justice." *Southern California Law Review* 70 (1996).

Bale, Gordon. "W.R. Lederman and the Citation of Legal Periodicals by the Supreme Court of Canada." *Queen's Law Journal* 19 (1994) 36.

Beth, Loren P. "The Judicial Committee: Its Development, Organisation and Procedure." *Public Law* 3 (1975) 219.

———. "The Judicial Committee of the Privy Council and the Development of Judicial Review." *American Journal of Comparative Law* 24 (1976).

Black, Vaughan and Richter, Nicholas. "Did She Mention My Name?: Citation of Academic Authority by the Supreme Court of Canada 1985-1990." *Dalhousie Law Journal* 16 (1993) 377.

Blankenburg, Erhard. "Political Regimes and the Law in Germany" in *Courts, Law and Politics.* New Haven: Yale University Press, 1996.

Bryant, Michael J. "Criminal Fault as Per the Lamer Court and the Ghost of William McIntyre." *Osgoode Hall Law Journal* 33 (1995) 79.

Bushnell, Ian. "The Use of American Cases." *University of New Brunswick Law Journal* 35 (1986) 157.

———. *The Captive Court: A Study of the Supreme Court of Canada.* Montreal & Kingston: McGill-Queen's University Press, 1992.

Bzdera, Andre. "Comparative Analysis of Federal High Courts: A Political Theory of Judicial Review." *Canadian Journal of Political Science* 26 (1993) 3.

Cairns, Alan C. "The Judicial Committee and Its Critics." *Canadian Journal of Political Science* 4 (1971).

Caldeira, Gregory A. and Zorn, Christopher J.W. "Of Time and Consensual Norms in the Supreme Court." *American Journal of Political Science* 42 (1998) 874.

Campbell, W. Kenneth. "The Right Honourable Sir Lyman Poore Duff: The Man as I Knew Him." *Osgoode Hall Law Journal* 12 (1974) 243.

———. "Mr. Justice Emmett Matthew Hall." *Osgoode Hall Law Journal*. 15 (1977) 300.

Castells, Manuel. *The Power of Identity. The Information Age*, Vol 2. Oxford: Blackwell, 1997.

Conklin, William E. *Images of a Constitution*. Toronto: University of Toronto Press, 1989.

Coppel, Jason and O'Neill, Aidan. "The European Court of Justice: Taking Rights Seriously?" *Common Market Law Review* 29 (1992) 669.

Damaska, Mirjan. *The Faces of Justice and State Authority: A Comparative Approach to the Legal Process*. New Haven: Yale University Press, 1986.

Dehousse, Renaud. *The European Court of Justice: The Politics of Judicial Integration*. New York: St. Martin's Press, 1998.

Edelman, Paul H. and Chen, Jim. "The Most Dangerous Justice: The Supreme Court at the Bar of Mathematics." *Southern California Law Review* 70 (1996) 63.

———. "'Duel' Diligence: Second Thoughts About the Supreme Court as the Sultans of Swing." *Southern California Law Review* 70 (1996) 219.

Friedman, Lawrence M. *American Law: An Introduction*. New York: W.W. Norton, 1998.

Gibson, Dale. "– And One Step Backward: The Supreme Court and Constitutional Law in the Sixties." *The Canadian Bar Review* 53 (1975).

Gibson, James L., Caldeira, Gregory A., and Baird, Vanessa A. "On the Legitimacy of National High Courts." *American Political Science Review* 92 (1998) 343.

Gilligan, Carol. *In a Different Voice: Psychological Theory and Women's Development*. Cambridge, MA: Harvard University Press, 1982.

Glenn, H. Patrick. "The Common Law in Canada." *Canadian Bar Review* 74 (1995) 261.

Goutal, Jean-Louis. "Characteristics of Judicial Style in France, Britain and the U.S." *American Journal of Comparative Law* 24 (1976).

Harvie, Robert & Foster, Hamar. "Ties That Bind?: The Supreme Court of Canada, American Jurisprudence, and the Revision of Canadian Criminal Law Under the Charter." *Osgoode Hall Law Journal* 28 (1990) 729.

———. "Different Drummers, Different Drums: The Supreme Court of Canada, American Jurisprudence and the Continuing Revision of Criminal Law Under the Charter." *Ottawa Law Review* 24 (1992) 41.

Haynie, Stacia L. "Leadership and Consensus on the U.S. Supreme Court." *The Journal of Politics* 54 (1992) 1158.

Heard, Andrew. "The Charter in the Supreme Court of Canada: The Importance of Which Judges Hear an Appeal." *Canadian Journal of Political Science* 24 (1991) 289.

Hogg, Andrew. *Constitutional Law of Canada*. Toronto: Carswell, 1997.

Jacob, Herbert et al. *Courts, Law and Politics in Comparative Perspective*. New Haven: Yale University Press, 1996.

Katsh, Ethan. *The Electronic Media and the Transformation of Law.* Oxford: Oxford University Press, 1989.

Kennedy, Gilbert. "Case Comment: *Brewer v McCauley.*" *Canadian Bar Review* 33 (1955) 340.

Kennett, Geoffrey. "Individual Rights, The High Court and the Constitution." *Melbourne University Law Review* 19 (1994) 581.

Kirk, Jeremy. "Constitutional Implications from Representative Democracy." *Federal Law Review* 23 (1995) 37.

Klein, David and Morrisroe, Darby. "The Prestige and Influence of Individual Judges on the U.S. Courts of Appeals." *Journal of Legal Studies* 28 (1999) 371.

Kornhauser, Lewis A. and Sager, Lawrence G. "Unpacking the Court." *Yale Law Journal* 96 (1986-7).

L'Heureux-Dubé, Claire. "The Length and Plurality of Supreme Court of Canada Decisions." *Alberta Law Review* 28 (1990).

———. "By Reason of Authority or by Authority of Reason." *University of British Columbia Law Review* 27 (1993).

La Forest, Gerard V. "The Use of American Precedents in Canadian Courts." *Maine Law Review* 46 (1994).

Laskin, Bora. "The Supreme Court of Canada: A Final Court of and for Canadians." *Canadian Bar Review* 29 (1951) 1038.

Landes, William M., Lessig, Lawrence, and Solimine, Michael E. "Judicial Influence: A Citation Analysis of Federal Courts of Appeals Judges." *Journal of Legal Studies* 27 (1998).

Lawlor, Reed C. "Personal Stare Decisis." *Southern California Law Review* 41 (1968).

Lawrence, Susan. "Justice, Democracy, Litigation and Political Participation." *Social Science Quarterly* 72 (1991).

LeDain, G. "Sir Lyman Duff and the Constitution." *Osgoode Hall Law Journal* 12 (1974) 261.

Lee, H.P. "The Australian High Court and Implied Fundamental Guarantees." *Public Law* (1993) 606.

Levitan, David M. "The Effect of the Appointment of a Supreme Court Justice." *University of Toledo Law Review* 28 (1996) 37.

MacCormick, Neil, and Summers, Robert S., eds. *Interpreting Precedent: A Comparative Study.* Ashgate: Aldershot: 1997.

McCormick, Peter. "The Supervisory Role of the Supreme Court of Canada." *Supreme Court Law Review* (2nd series) 3 (1992).

———. "Assessing Leadership on the Supreme Court of Canada: Towards a Typology of Chief Justice Leadership." *Supreme Court Law Review* (2nd series) 4 (1993) 409.

———. "Career Patterns and the Delivery of Reasons for Judgment in the Supreme Court of Canada." *Supreme Court Law Review* (2nd series) 5 (1994).

———. "The Supreme Court Cites the Supreme Court: Follow-up Citation on the Supreme Court of Canada, 1989-1993." *Osgoode Hall Law Journal* 33 (1995).

————. "The Supreme Court of Canada and American Citations 1949-1994: A Statistical Overview." *Supreme Court Law Review* (2nd Series) 8 (1997).

————. "Birds of a Feather: Alliances and Influences on the Lamer Court 1991-7." *Osgoode Hall Law Journal* 36 (1998).

————. "Follow the Leader: Judicial Leadership and the Laskin Court, 1973-1984." *Queen's Law Journal* 24 (1998).

————. "Do Judges Read Books, Too?: Academic Citations by the Supreme Court of Canada 1991-7." *Supreme Court Law Review* (2nd Series) 9 (1998).

————. "Twelve Paradoxes of Judicial Discipline." *Constitutional Forum* (1998).

————. "The Most Dangerous Justice: Penetrating the Voting Patterns of the Lamer Court 1990-7." *Dalhousie Law Journal* 22 (1999).

McCormick, Peter and Greene, Ian. *Judges and Judging: Inside the Canadian Judicial System*. Toronto: James Lorimer & Company, 1990.

McWhinney, Edward. "Judicial Concurrences and Dissents: A Comparative View of Opinion-writing in Final Appellate Tribunals." *Canadian Bar Review* 31 (1953) 594.

Mandel, Michael. *The Charter of Rights and the Legalization of Politics in Canada*. Toronto: Thompson Educational, 1994.

Manfredi, Christopher P. "Adjudication, Policy-Making and the Supreme Court of Canada: Lessons from the Experience of the United States." *Canadian Journal of Political Science* 22 (1989) 313.

Morrow, W.L. "The Last Case." *Alberta Law Review* 16 (1978) 1.

Pigeon, Louis-Philippe. "The Meaning of Provincial Autonomy." *Canadian Bar Review* 29 (1951) 1126.

Pollock, E. Marshall. "Mr. Justice Rand: A Triumph of Principle." *Canadian Bar Review* 53 (1975) 519.

Russell, Peter. *The Judiciary in Canada: The Third Branch of Government*. Toronto: McGraw-Hill Ryerson, 1987.

Schauer, Frederick. "Precedent." *Stanford Law Review* 39 (1987) 573.

Scott, F.R. "Some Privy Counsel." *Canadian Bar Review* 28 (1950).

Shapiro, Martin and Stone, Alec. "The New Constitutional Politics of Europe." *Comparative Political Studies* 26 (1994) 397.

Shklar, Judith N. *Legalism: Law, Morals and Political Trials*. Cambridge, MA: Harvard University Press, 1986.

Sharpe, Robert J. and Swinton, Katherine. *The Charter of Rights and Freedoms*. Toronto: Irwin Law, 1998.

Snell, James G. and Vaughan, Frederick. *The Supreme Court of Canada: History of the Institution*. Toronto: Osgoode Society and University of Toronto Press, 1985.

Solomon, David. "Controlling the High Court's Agenda." *Western Australian Law Review* 23 (1993) 33.

Stack, John R. "Judicial Policy-Making and the Evolving Protection of Human Rights: The European Court of Justice in Comparative Perspective." *West European Politics* 15 (1992).

Stone, Alec. *The Birth of Judicial Politics in France.* New York: Oxford University Press, 1992.

Swinton, Katherine E. *The Supreme Court and Canadian Federalism: The Laskin-Dickson Years.* Toronto: Carswell, 1990.

Tate, C. Neal and Vallinder, Torbjorn. *The Global Expansion of Judicial Power.* New York: New York University Press, 1995.

Trakman, Leon E., Cole-Hamilton, William, and Gatien, Sean. "*R. v Oakes* 1986-1997: Back to the Drawing Board." *Osgoode Hall Law Journal* 36 (1998) 83.

Vaughan, Frederick. "Emmett Matthew Hall: The Activist as Judge." *Osgoode Hall Law Journal* 10 (1972) 411.

———. "Emmett M. Hall: A Profile of the Judicial Temperament." *Osgoode Hall Law Journal* 15 (1977) 308.

———. "Critics of the Judicial Committee of the Privy Council: The New Orthodoxy and an Alternative Explanation." *Canadian Journal of Political Science* 19 (1986).

Wahlbeck, Paul J., Spriggs II, James F., and Maltzman, Forrest. "Marshalling the Court: Bargaining and Accommodation on the United States Supreme Court." *American Journal of Political Science* 42 (1998) 294.

Walker, Thomas G., Epstein, Lee J., and Dixon, William J. "On the Mysterious Demise of Consensual Norms in the United States Supreme Court." *The Journal of Politics* 50 (1988).

Weiler, Paul. *In the Last Resort: A Critical Study of The Supreme Court of Canada.* Toronto: Carswell-Methuen, 1974.

Weiler, J.H.H. "A Quiet Revolution: The European Court of Justice and Its Interlocutors." *Comparative Political Studies* 26 (1994) 510.

Weiler, J.H.H. and Lockhart, Nicolas J.S. "'Taking Rights Seriously' Seriously: The European Court and Its Fundamental Rights Jurisprudence — Part I." *Common Market Law Review* 32 (1995) 51.

Wells, Michael. "French and American Judicial Opinions." *Yale Journal of International Law* 19 (1994) 81.

Wheare, K.C. *Federal Government,* 4th ed. London: Oxford University Press, 1963.

Wilson, Bertha. "Decision-making in the Supreme Court." *University of Toronto Law Journal* 36 (1986) 227.

———. "Will Women Judges Really Make a Difference?" *Osgoode Hall Law Journal* 28 (1990).

Zemans, Frances Kahn. "Legal Mobilization: The Neglected Role of Law in the Political System." *American Political Science Review* 77 (1983).

# Index